CollegeBoard
connect to college success™

College Success

What It Means and How to Make It Happen

Michael S. McPherson and
Morton Owen Schapiro, Editors

CollegeBoard
connect to college success™

College Success

What It Means and How to Make It Happen

Michael S. McPherson and
Morton Owen Schapiro, Editors

The College Board: Connecting Students to College Success

The College Board is a not-for-profit membership association whose mission is to connect students to college success and opportunity. Founded in 1900, the association is composed of more than 5,400 schools, colleges, universities, and other educational organizations. Each year, the College Board serves seven million students and their parents, 23,000 high schools, and 3,500 colleges through major programs and services in college admissions, guidance, assessment, financial aid, enrollment, and teaching and learning. Among its best-known programs are the SAT®, the PSAT/NMSQT®, and the Advanced Placement Program® (AP®). The College Board is committed to the principles of excellence and equity, and that commitment is embodied in all of its programs, services, activities, and concerns.

In all of its book publishing activities the College Board endeavors to present the works of authors who are well qualified to write with authority on the subject at hand and to present accurate and timely information. However, the opinions, interpretations, and conclusions of the authors are their own and do not necessarily represent those of the College Board; nothing contained herein should be assumed to represent an official position of the College Board or any of its members.

Copies of this book are available from your local bookseller or may be ordered from College Board Publications, 45 Columbus Ave., New York, NY 10023. The price is $18.95.

Editorial inquiries concerning this book should be directed to The College Board, 45 Columbus Avenue, New York, New York 10023-6992.

Library of Congress Cataloging-in-Publication Data

College success : what it means and how to make it happen / Michael S. McPherson and Morton Owen Schapiro, editors. — 1st ed.
    p. cm.
Includes bibliographical references and index.
ISBN-13: 978-0-87447-830-3
ISBN-10: 0-87447-830-8
1. College students—United States—Economic conditions. 2. Minority college students—United States. 3. Educational attainment—United States. I. McPherson, Michael S. II. Schapiro, Morton Owen.

LC208.8.C66 2006
378.1'98—dc22
            2008004198

Printed in the United States of America.
Distributed by Macmillan.

This volume is dedicated to the memory of Marge McPherson, a great teacher both inside and outside the classroom.

College Success:
What It Means and How to Make It Happen
Michael S. McPherson and Morton Owen Schapiro, Editors

CONTENTS

SECTION IV: College Success—Student and Faculty Perspectives

SECTION V: Looking Beyond Material Success

Introduction

Michael S. McPherson and Morton Owen Schapiro

Much of the focus in American higher education over the past six decades has understandably been on matters of access. How can we make sure that as many talented young men and women as possible enroll at one of our colleges or universities? The success of such early initiatives as the G.I. Bill and later the creation of a network of community colleges, along with a range of federal and state-based financial aid programs, have put us in the enviable position of having one of the world's highest college enrollment rates. Roughly two out of three high school graduates currently enroll at one of America's approximately 4,000 not-for-profit colleges or universities within a year of leaving high school.

Unfortunately, this overall success obscures a number of persistent inequities. There are huge differences in college completion rates of high school graduates both by income background and by race, and little progress has been made in narrowing those gaps. Moreover, this reinforces earlier differences in the degree of high school success. In order for our educational system to truly be a force towards equalization rather than stratification, four issues must be resolved: (1) students of color and/or from low-income backgrounds are less likely to develop their talents and become college ready; (2) too many who do nonetheless fail to pursue a postsecondary education; (3) many of those who continue into higher education enroll either at community colleges or at less selective four-year colleges or universities that are relatively underfunded; and (4) they not surprisingly meet with disappointing levels of college success once they are there.

The current volume takes up where its companion, *College Access: Opportunity or Privilege?* left off. Our earlier work examined in some detail the impediments to college enrollment, while concentrating on such questions as how financial aid contributes to college affordability, what is the impact of race-sensitive and income-sensitive admissions, and how institutions, states, and the federal government can better identify and support students who could thrive in higher education. This book moves to the next step, examining what happens to those men and women who make it into one of our colleges or universities. In doing so, this work not only explores all four of the issues enumerated above but also examines what higher education success means in the context of the extraordinary heterogeneity in American higher education. For some students, success can be measured through the accumulation of human capital that can lead to financial success regardless of whether or not a degree is earned. For instance, for many older students attending community colleges, an associate degree is neither the aim nor the prerequisite for determining college success; these students' aim instead is to select certain courses to strengthen specific job-related skills. Other students think of enrollment at a two-year institution as a first step on the road to a bachelor's degree. For them, even with the completion of an associate degree, anything less than a four-year degree means failure. Among those who enroll immediately at a four-year school, success may be measured in terms of graduation within a reasonable period of time, in terms of ultimate financial gain, or in terms of harder-to-measure outcomes such as enhanced citizenship.

The multiple outcomes of college are perhaps best enumerated in Howard Bowen's classic book, *Investment in Learning*. Although economists tend to define college success in rather narrow monetary terms, Bowen laid out an impressive range of outcomes, including moral, emotional, and aesthetic development.

So the aim of this book, to define success in higher education, isn't an easy one. The ambitious goal to also come up with ways to enhance college success makes our task even harder. Still, the chapters that follow provide a reasonably comprehensive look at American higher education today. Essays examine success from the eyes of a student, from the perspective of a faculty member, from the standpoint of the institution, and from the view of foundations and the federal and state government. There are many actors in this play, and we try to give each a voice.

The book begins by examining the transition between high school and college, with a focus on the financial and informational barriers that inhibit progression to higher education. Melissa Roderick and Jenny Nagaoka discuss their work on the transition to college among Chicago Public School (CPS) students, using both quantitative and qualitative methods.

The authors report that 83 percent of CPS seniors say they want to get a bachelor's degree or higher. Most end up disappointed. Only 34 percent of CPS graduates enroll within a year at a four-year college, and only 45 percent of them manage to earn a bachelor's degree within six years. So over 80 percent have the goal of attaining a four-year degree; 15 percent actually get one. Even more discouraging, after restricting the sample to minority (Hispanic and African American) males, that number plummets to 8 percent.

Using data mainly from the National Student Clearinghouse, Roderick and Nagaoka analyze the factors underlying these depressing findings. In particular, they focus on why it is that CPS graduates disproportionately attend a small number of colleges, schools that, with few exceptions, are either nonselective or only somewhat selective. Are these students actively deciding to attend schools that are relatively resource-poor, or is it low levels of academic preparation, along with informational and financial barriers, that restrict their choice set? And, finally, does it matter in terms of college outcomes?

First of all, CPS graduates, and particularly Hispanics and African Americans, perform very poorly on average on standardized tests. That fact is perhaps better known than the data on high school GPAs. Thirty-five percent of CPS graduates graduate with a GPA below a 2.0. With a high school dropout rate that is well above the national level, those who graduate are the success stories, even with a third of them graduating with below a C average. Regardless of their educational aspirations, many CPS graduates are unqualified to enroll at a four-year postsecondary institution, and many of those who do enroll are not ready for a selective one. Looking specifically at African American men, fully half of those who graduate high school leave with less than a C average. No wonder their college success is so limited.

Going beyond the numbers, the authors search for cultural and other explanations of why, for example, even after controlling for high school grades, test scores, and curriculum, Latinos enroll in college in unexpectedly small numbers. It turns out that cost matters, with sticker price and financial aid being major issues. Many qualified students take themselves out of the process early, not even identifying a four-year school to which to apply or failing to complete a financial aid application. Students say they want to go, and even expect to go, but do not do what is necessary to make that happen.

Even among those who persist, the news isn't all good. Of the CPS graduates who are eligible to attend a selective four-year institution, only 22 percent end up at one. Overall, the authors estimate that 23 percent end up at a college that is far below their match, and another 33 percent end up slightly below their match, while 23 percent don't go to college at all. Does it matter where they go?

Examining the CPS graduating classes of 1998 and 1999 and calculating six-year college graduation rates, Roderick and Nagaoka find a graduation rate of only 45 percent, compared with 64 percent nationally. This number is held down by the dismal graduation rates of CPS students leaving high school with very low GPAs. But even after controlling for qualifications, the college you attend appears to have a powerful impact on your chances of graduating. While 72 percent of CPS graduates who enroll at the University of Illinois at Urbana-Champaign graduate, graduation rates at some of the unselective colleges are below 20 percent. Even controlling for the different student characteristics (test scores, GPA, honors courses, and the like), the chances of graduating in a reasonable amount of time from certain open-enrollment colleges is extremely low.

In sum, CPS students who graduate with a very low high school GPA aren't likely to succeed in college, regardless of where they attend. But for those who are college ready, where they attend matters greatly.

This suggests that getting talented inner-city students into flagship public universities has a significant impact on their chances for college success. That is the focus of the second chapter, coauthored by the two editors of this book, along with Francie Streich. This study is part of a larger project that examines college access and success in the context of elite public research universities. The data sample consists of first-time, full-time students who matriculated in the fall of 1999 at one of 18 public flagship universities throughout the country. The focus is on how tuition discounts are allocated based on need versus merit.

Moving beyond standard institutional designations of need-based and merit-based financial aid, this study examines statistically the relationship between aid and measures of both need and merit. The analysis focuses specifically on the influence of family income and SAT® scores by estimating financial aid receipt as a function of family income, SAT score, race, gender, and institution of attendance. Results show that an additional $1,000 in income, all else equal, is associated with a $32 decrease in total grant aid (an amount that is averaged over all students, including those who are not receiving any financial aid). On the other hand, a 100-point increase in a student's SAT score is associated with $314 in additional grant aid. Gender matters as well, with females, all else equal, receiving $265 more in aid than their male counterparts. Race also plays a role, with all race/ethnicity categories having a positive marginal effect on grant dollars relative to their white counterparts, led by an additional $2,579 in grant aid for African American students versus otherwise similar white students.

An income-quartile-specific analysis produces some interesting results. While family income plays a role in the allocation of financial aid in each income quartile, the largest impact is for incomes in the $29,000 to $52,000 range. On the other hand, SAT scores matter most for higher-income students. Race matters across income quartiles, with the data suggesting that colleges recruit minority students by offering them more generous grant aid than their white counterparts.

In the final phase of the study, the sample is divided by the selectivity tier of the university attended. Although family income and SAT are significant determinants of aid at all selectivity levels, there is an understandable but striking difference in the impact of SAT scores on tuition discounts in the different tiers. While a 100-point increase in SAT scores for a student attending a highly selective public university earns that student only $102 in grants, that student would earn more than four times as much at a much less selective public flagship.

We conclude that colleges and universities, state and federal governments, and private sources are indeed directing money to needy and academically deserving students, while being conscious of aiding students of color across family incomes and SAT levels. Based on the Roderick and Nagaoka study highlighting the importance of enrolling talented low-income students of color in the "right" schools, this appears to be good public policy.

The next chapter sets forth the role that external organizations—namely, foundations—might play in enhancing success in college. William Trent reviews the lessons based on the experience of the Gates Millennium Scholars (GMS) program. The aim of the GMS program is to increase the representation of low-income, high-ability minority students at both the undergraduate and graduate levels. Launched in 2000 with support for freshmen, continuing undergraduates, and graduate students, the GMS program has in subsequent years awarded fellowships to freshmen. These are last-dollar scholarships that replace the self-help components (work and loans) of a typical financial aid package.

This report analyzes the college success of GMS recipients and reinforces findings discussed elsewhere in this volume. For instance, working hard in high school (taking challenging courses, etc.) pays off in terms of college outcomes, while enhanced financial support leads to greater persistence in college as GMS recipients become more engaged academically and socially.

For the Gates Foundation, reducing or eliminating work and loans means increasing the focus on classroom and community activities. It makes school more of a priority, and GMS scholars are not surprisingly more likely than nonscholars to be academically engaged, to have higher college GPAs, to spend more time studying, and to find a faculty mentor. In addition, they are more likely than their counterparts to attend a four-year college and a private one versus a public one. This GMS study reinforces the Roderick and Nagaoka findings about students failing to enroll in schools for which they are qualified. It appears that the quality of the financial aid package influences both access to college and the choice of college, as GMS aid increases the likelihood of attending more selective colleges and universities. Reducing worries about cost produces a range of positive outcomes.

But are we so sure that students succeed best by attending more prestigious institutions? Do they learn more when they are surrounded by talented peers? Does that pay off in labor market earnings? Why don't students prepare more effectively for success in college? What exactly do we know about college success and why don't we know more? That is the topic of our next group of chapters.

James Rosenbaum and Lisbeth Goble return to an issue Roderick and Nagaoka grappled with: Who is to blame for the dismal graduation rates at some colleges,

colleges disproportionately attended by low-income students and by students of color? Rosenbaum and Goble point to the poor articulation between high schools and colleges. While students expect to take college classes immediately, many end up in remedial classes and receive no college credits for their efforts. They often have little idea how long their degree will take (full-time students take on average around three and a half years to complete a "two year" associate degree). In total, the community college experience is far from the stepping stone that many students expect it to be.

Rosenbaum and Goble see a need to create a clear set of incentives for high school success. Low-achieving high school graduates may make it into college, but precious few ever achieve a college degree. Even ambitious high school students may fail to put in the effort to adequately prepare for college success. The solution? High schools must create incentives for students to achieve success. High school students need clear information about what colleges expect, they need feedback about whether they are on track for college, and they need to understand that different colleges and programs demand very different types of preparation.

Finally, Rosenbaum and Goble ask what colleges can do to enhance student success. By studying private for-profit two-year colleges ("occupational colleges"), they focus in particular on what community colleges can do to improve learning and raise graduation rates. First, these private schools are more adept at dealing with college costs, devising ways for low-income students to pay their higher tuitions. Providing help with financial aid applications is key—with Pell grants and state grants reducing or eliminating the difference in tuition between public and private two-year schools. Second, the best of the private two-year colleges do a good job of steering students into courses that are at the proper level of difficulty and are necessary for the stated degree choice, and then making sure those courses are offered at predictable and convenient times. Finally, they realize that the success of these students depends on the availability of proper counseling, and the best of these colleges allocate their expenditures accordingly.

Sarah Turner also tries to define success in college, but concentrates more on the four-year segment instead of the two-year. She begins by pointing out a disturbing fact—that although college enrollment has increased over the past few decades, college completion rates have fallen. Fifty-one percent of the high school cohort of 1972 ended up with a bachelor's degree, while only 45 percent of the high school cohort of 1992 did the same. Why, with the large increase in the economic return to college completion, haven't college graduation rates risen?

Keeping with the theme of the preceding chapters, Turner points out that aggregate graduation rates obscure great differences across educational segments. At the elite public universities examined in the McPherson, Schapiro, and Streich chapter, graduation rates have risen and time-to-degree has decreased. On the other hand, Turner cites the work of Roderick and her coauthors that show that timely graduation from nonselective colleges and universities is, at best, unlikely.

There are multiple explanations for differences in graduation rates. Student characteristics affect the likelihood for remediation and for overall college success. But Turner argues that the decline in college graduation rates over time is not explained by any deterioration in college readiness. What about changes in institutional resources? Have expenditures per student fallen over time, leading to larger classes and the deceased availability of required classes? It is evident that this has been the case. An important downside to increasing college enrollment is that, in the absence of concomitant increases in revenues, colleges and universities are unable to provide the same level of educational excellence.

Finally, to what degree have credit constraints contributed to disappointing college completion rates? The combination of rising tuition and stagnant real income for families in the bottom half of the American income distribution might have exacted a steep price in terms of college enrollment and completion. Unfortunately, for a variety of empirical reasons, it is not easy to tease out the role that financial factors have been playing.

The chapter by Jeffrey Smith reviews the reasons why quantitative analyses of educational outcomes, no matter how sophisticated, typically leave questions less than fully answered. In a word, it is heterogeneity that wreaks havoc on empirical studies—American higher education encompasses an amazingly diverse group of students, of colleges, and of programs. As mentioned in earlier chapters, students bring to college very different levels of academic preparation, and they attend community colleges, private two-year institutions, relatively unselective public comprehensive universities, and public flagship research universities, as well as private colleges and universities both in the nonprofit and proprietary sectors. The "system" of higher education in this country contains a range of options, and educates a range of students, that is unheard of elsewhere in the world.

Smith argues that this degree of heterogeneity greatly complicates any notion of evaluating college success. Does attendance at a community college without earning an associate degree yield economic returns? Does attending a more selective college or university lead to higher income than attending a less prestigious school? Do private colleges and universities raise future income enough to justify the difference in price? Do certain majors—business and engineering, for instance—lead to larger economic returns than majoring, for example, in philosophy or history? Is it always best (in an economic sense) for a student to attend the most selective college possible, or would it be better to go to a school where the average test scores are more in line with that of the student?

It is often difficult for the general public to understand why it is so hard to answer these questions empirically. Certainly it is unusual to find natural experiments in which students are randomly allocated to different kinds of schools and different kinds of programs. Wouldn't it be nice, Smith suggests, if some selective colleges randomly selected a portion of their students and then studied their academic and labor market outcomes versus those of students selected in the normal fashion? It sure would, but our experience as college presidents of highly selective colleges suggests that would lead to some really lively board meetings and alumni functions.

Smith concludes by focusing on perhaps the best known of the empirical studies: the calculation of the economic return associated with attending college. Of course, looking at the average income for those with say a bachelor's degree versus the income of somebody who stopped at high school tells us little about what the person who stopped at high school would be earning if he or she continued on. Simply put, that person didn't randomly stop at high school. He or she might have a range of characteristics that would have led to limited success in college, and therefore limited economic returns. What if a new federal financial aid program were created to encourage high school students from low-income backgrounds to progress to college? Would the economic return to such a program justify its creation? If the reason why these students stopped at high school was financial, or informational, perhaps such a program would be justified. But if these students made their decision because they knew that they were lacking the academic background and interest to succeed in college, it could be a different story.

Finally, Smith provides recommendations for data collection and research that might allow us to better understand how to promote college success in light of the staggering differences that characterize American higher education.

The next two chapters consider college success in the context of a range of institutional types. David Breneman summarizes the discussion among presidents of a community college (Ann Wynia of North Hennepin Community College), a comprehensive public university (Wilson Bradshaw of Metropolitan State University), a highly selective private research university (Henry Bienen of Northwestern University), and a specialty (engineering) private college (Richard Miller of Franklin W. Olin College of Engineering). That is followed by an essay from the president of an elite liberal arts college, Diane Chapman Walsh of Wellesley College.

Previous chapters have made the point that college success can only be evaluated in light of the expectations of different students and the missions of different colleges. That is made abundantly clear in this section of the book.

After providing a useful overview of the general subject, Breneman contrasts the comments of the various presidents. For Northwestern's Bienen, graduation rates are a poor indicator of college success, with the expectation being that the vast majority of enrollees will end up receiving degrees. Bienen points to success after college as an indicator of having had a meaningful college experience. Again, he discusses a great empirical difficulty in looking at a range of survey results—what is the value-added of a particular institutional experience? Can Northwestern rightly claim the credit for the success of one of its graduates, or might that student have done just as well had he or she attended the University of Illinois, a liberal arts college, or maybe even had stopped at high school? The value-added question is now very much under discussion at the federal level (other authors weigh in on this below), and Bienen is skeptical that government efforts will lead to anything of substance.

It is a different world for Bradshaw at Metropolitan State in St. Paul, Minnesota. Almost two-thirds of its students are part-time, and the average age is 32. His students enter college with a wide range of talents and expectations, and a single outcome measure tells little about college success. The graduation rate, for example, is a poor measure even for those who seek a bachelor's degree, given that many students transfer and complete their academic work elsewhere. Moreover, any evaluation of institutional success should take into consideration the income background of its students, so as to reduce the incentive that schools would have to limit enrollment only to those well-prepared, more affluent students who are likely to graduate. If government efforts to promote excellence were to lead nonselective institutions to reduce their commitment to broad access, it would be a public policy nightmare.

Olin's Miller faces a different set of challenges. This start-up (founded in 1997) charges no tuition and seeks to enroll students who have the potential to become leaders after a rigorous engineering education that bridges science and technology, enterprise, and the workings of our society. While it is too early to assess institutional success, Olin is eager to evaluate the creativity and entrepreneurial fervor of its graduates, among other outcomes.

Wynia, from North Hennepin Community College in Brooklyn Park, Minnesota, educates a student body more reminiscent of Metropolitan State than of Northwestern or Olin. She divides her students into three groups when asked to consider the success of her institution. For students "ready-to-go," it is whether or not they meet their specific, pre-formed goals, whether the goal be the acquisition of business skills, or for high school students, college credits. For the "at-risk-unsure" group, it is whether they can take advantage of what might be a second chance to acquire learning skills. Finally, a small percentage of North Hennepin's students (about 10 percent) are "university ready." For them success means getting an associate degree and progressing to a four-year institution.

Breneman concludes by pointing out that four experienced presidents define college success using measures that reflect the nature and type of students they enroll. External parties who wish to impose simple metrics for determining college success should take heed, even though Breneman ends by lamenting that our inability to back up our educational claims reduces the credibility of the higher education industry. This lament is shared by a number of economists and other higher education observers, including the two editors of this book.

Diana Walsh's essay describes the broad sweep of her career and was written at the end of a very successful 14 years as Wellesley president. After a brilliant, and deeply personal, description of her educational life, she distills four general lessons dealing with college success. First, we need a commitment to intellectual integrity—to be not only consumers of knowledge but also preservers and protectors of critical thinking. Second, the various disciplines and their world views should be approached from a critical stance, resisting their power to seduce adherents into giving up their independent judgment. Third, the heart, soul and spirit need not be sacrificed in the pursuit of objective reasoning, as science and spirit can productively coexist. Fourth, as an educational leader, one needs curiosity, receptivity, and a respect for the marginalized, plus a healthy dose of humility, to truly prosper.

Walsh goes on to express her worry that we allow our students to graduate from college thinking that all belief systems are of equal value, that (borrowing from Harvard's Derek Bok) we enroll relativists and graduate them in the same condition four years later. College success for Walsh means that our graduates know their hearts and their minds, that they have compassion for others and, most important, that they develop a love of learning. How to do this? Here Walsh shares the worries articulated by others that naïve government interference is destined to fail. But at the same time, echoing Breneman, she argues that we in the academy should not be blind to our vulnerabilities and to the opportunities that exist to evaluate our successes and failures in a meaningful way. We need feedback in order to continually improve the education we offer.

The chapter by Richard Light examines several of the kinds of student-centered inquiry that Walsh suggests are worth trying. Light draws on his decades of experience at the forefront of college assessment in covering three core ideas: What do we mean by college success? What data could be brought to bear to enhance college success? What examples are there of campus initiatives that have fostered success?

In terms of defining college success, Light discusses the acquisition of knowledge and skills and presents five principal findings based on extensive interviews and experiments. First, interactive relationships revolving around academic work enhance learning. It is often assumed that study groups pay off intellectually, and Light has some evidence to back up this claim. Second, distributing student papers in advance of the class meeting leads to greater student effort and to better writing. This leads to the third finding: writing is a key to student success. Students report that improving their writing is an important goal in college, and the evidence suggests that the relationship between the amount of writing a student does and the student's reported engagement with the course is stronger than any other relationship between student success and other course characteristics (class size, required course versus elective, etc.). Fourth, for a given amount of writing, more frequent, shorter papers appear to be much more effective than a small number of longer papers, presumably because the feedback provided to the student helps him or her learn throughout the semester and make midcourse corrections. Finally, undergraduates are clear about which of their courses they appreciate most—those with quick and detailed feedback and those that focus on revisions to papers they write.

While Light is the first to admit that many of his findings are based on the rarified world of Harvard, he encourages all campuses to do the kind of surveying and experimentation that he has done. Treat your students seriously by asking them what works in their college experiences. Respect them, as you expect them to respect you.

Susan Engel follows Light in asking one of the most important questions one can ask—What is good college teaching? With all the empirical studies of college outcomes out there, it is surprisingly rare to focus on what exactly leads to classroom success. As Engel points out, higher education analyses are much more likely to focus on such matters as admissions and finance than on teaching and learning.

She discusses three dilemmas with which many college teachers struggle. First, there is the critical question of what to cover and what not to cover. The urge to cover all the material, she argues, confuses covering with learning. Many professors think that covering material in a lively and engaging way means that students will "get it." But rather than tell students what you know, a professor is better off helping students develop their own knowledge. And acquiring facts means little without a sense of how these facts relate to the larger world. Second, students learn more when they act upon the material to be learned. Designing experiments and applying theory to the real world are but two ways to have students share in the intellectual work. There is nothing like a powerful seminar discussion to enhance student learning. Engel describes the craft of teaching in some detail—prod here, inform there, challenge now, reinforce an idea, guide and build. Be comfortable with giving up some control, and, as Light pointed out, respect the minds and aspirations of the students. Finally, always seek to understand your audience. Are they looking to pursue your subject in graduate school or are they generalists seeking a liberal education? Are they sitting on the sideline or are they actively engaged in learning? In sum, good teaching is essential to college success and should be encouraged and nurtured. Without it, we fail our students in fundamental ways.

The concluding chapter reminds us that the outcomes of higher education go far beyond the monetary gains on which economists tend to focus. Thomas Dee assesses the contribution that colleges make to civic engagement. Dee reminds us that belief in the social benefits of educational investments played a major role in motivating the expansion of the federal role in educational funding. While numerous studies confirm that more educated people are more civically engaged, Dee presents new evidence that takes into consideration the selection effects discussed above that restrict the usefulness of simple empirical studies. The results indicate that college attendance increases all six forms of civic participation examined—registering to vote, actually voting in a presidential election, voting in any election, or volunteering in a youth organization, in a civic or community organization, or in a political campaign, Moreover, a second empirical analysis based on a different data set shows that college attendance not only increases voter participation, it also leads to increased civic knowledge, as more educated citizens are more likely to read a newspaper and to be able to name their governor and congressional representative. The question with all of these empirical studies is whether the findings are causal. Dee points out, for example, children raised in families that stress civic responsibility are probably more likely to attend college. But this analysis suggests that college attendance is strongly correlated with a range of civic engagement measures and that at least some of them are in fact causally related.

Are there things that colleges can do to enhance future civic engagement of their students? Community service in college seems to have long-run consequences, but again students who self-select into volunteer programs are likely to be predisposed to high levels of post-graduate civic engagement. Careful empirical testing suggests that volunteering in college does in fact lead to greater civic participation in adulthood, although, says Dee, these results should be interpreted cautiously.

That admonition might be usefully applied more broadly to the various topics discussed in this volume. As we pointed out earlier, to define college success is an ambitious undertaking. To come up with ways to promote it is more ambitious still. In these chapters, the authors resist the notion of defining success in a simple way. The essays instead remind us, perhaps above all, about the remarkable variety in American higher education, which is made up of colleges that differ more in size, in governance, in resources, and in purposes than do those of any other country. The clientele of these institutions differ too in remarkable ways: in age and life circumstance, in background and preparation, in intensity of attendance and, again, in purposes. Almost any generalization one is tempted to make about "success" in such a bewilderingly various universe of education seems almost certain to be wrong.

And yet we are reluctant to end this introductory essay with some tired homily on the lines of "different strokes for different folks." In fact, reflecting on the rich analysis and evidence these essays offer leads us to hazard three points that we think have bearing both on understanding success in American higher education and on making wise policy toward producing more success.

First, whatever else higher education is about, it is always about changing people—moving them from Point A to Point B. Starting points differ enormously and so do destinations. But the ultimate aim of any educational encounter is "transformation"—it is to produce some kind of desired change in the student, whether that be to strengthen her earning power or civic engagement or love of learning. The implication, clearly, is that, in thinking about effectiveness and in measuring how successful colleges' efforts are, we simply have to think in "value added" terms. It is ultimately of no credit to a college that it attracts bright, engaging students to its classes. No matter how terrific those students are upon arrival, if they are not different in ways that matter upon departure, the college experience has been a failure. The values being added don't align along a single scale—one college may make students into better musicians, another into better engineers but, even though measuring such changes is very difficult, it is upon these, and not on conventional measures of prestige or class size that our attention ultimately has to rest.

The second point follows directly from the first, at least in a society where students are as varied in interests and backgrounds as the United States. This is the point that the worth or quality of a college as an educational institution should be understood to depend primarily on how well it "moves students along." Prestige hierarchies and national ratings systems are for the most part highly inadequate for this purpose. This is a very hard point to hold onto in the American context. Indeed, the high priority that private and now increasingly public universities now place on raising their average SAT scores almost seems to suggest that their main priority is not to do better at teaching the students they have, but rather to teach different and "better" students. We should strive in this country to develop educational policies that focus colleges' energies on doing a great job in improving the lives of the students they have, and we should find ways to value and to reward excellence without confusing it with prestige.

Our final generalization concerns the goals of higher education relative to which success is judged. It's neither surprising nor disturbing that young people (or older adults) who come from constrained circumstances see the primary role of higher education as job preparation and understand success in terms of employment outcomes. And it is plausible enough to think that students from wealthier backgrounds can distance themselves further from near-term financial pressures and attend better to the aspects of higher education that promote "higher" purposes than putting dinner on the table—purposes like improved citizenship or more refined aesthetic experiences. But it is important not to accept such a generalization too readily or too completely. The fact is that the fraction of students, even at the most prestigious colleges, who report that making a lot of money was a key factor in their college decision is very high. (In the American Freshman Survey published by the Higher Education Research Institute at UCLA, more than two-thirds of both men and women reported in 2005 that their principal goal in attending college was to make more money.) The popularity of investment banking or private equity as career goals among students at leading East Coast private universities suggests more similarity of goals than might be apparent. On the other hand, it seems quite plausible that the educational experiences low-income students encounter may very well wind up increasing their civic competence or love of literature, even if such improvement was not their major goal. Indeed, there is little evidence that the type of college one went to, or the intended major one chose, has a measurable differential impact on civic or aesthetic development. Thus, while the goal of preparing to make money may be more salient (and more justifiable) to low-income and first-generation students than to their more affluent colleagues, it is our view that policymakers and institutional leaders throughout higher education should aim at a broad range of educational goals for all their students, seeking to enrich their lives as well as thicken their wallets.

These at any rate are observations that occurred to us in reviewing the wide-ranging papers for this volume. You may, and we hope you will, arrive at different observations and judgments as you explore this complex subject.

Section I:
From High School to College—Raising Expectations and Lowering Financial Burdens

Increasing College Access and Graduation Among Chicago Public High School Graduates

Melissa Roderick and Jenny Nagaoka

Closing the aspiration–attainment gap is one of the most vexing problems in education today. Over the past 20 years, there have been dramatic increases in the proportion of students who aspire to complete a four-year college degree. While there has been an increase in the number of students who enroll in college, there have been few changes in the proportion of students who complete a college degree. Moreover, minority students continue to lag in both four-year college enrollment and degree completion rates.

How do we understand why African American and Latino students who aspire to complete a four-year college degree seldom attain this aspiration? Over the past several years, the policy discussion has coalesced around two central explanations: (1) Low academic preparation that undermines minority and low-income students' access to and performance in college, and (2) the declining real value of financial aid combined with rising college costs. National reports call for investments in high school reform in order to increase students' academic preparation, as well as policies that address the rising costs of college attendance.[1]

Often missing from the current debate, however, is discussion of whether first-generation college students who attain the same level of academic qualifications for college as their more advantaged counterparts will have the same probability of enrolling in and graduating from college. One recent Congressional Report

1. Clifford Adelman, *Answers in the Tool Box: Academic Intensity, Attendance Patterns, and Bachelor's Degree Attainment* (Washington, DC: U.S. Department of Education, Office of Educational Research and Improvement, 1999); Education Commission of the States, *Advanced Placement Courses and Examinations—State-level Policies* (Denver, CO: 2000); National Research Council, *Learning and Understanding: Improving Advanced Study of Mathematics and Science in American High Schools* (Washington, DC: Center for Education, Division of Behavioral and Social Sciences and Education, 2002); American Diploma Project, *Ready or Not: Creating a High School Diploma that Counts* (Washington, DC: 2004); Kristin Klopfenstein, "The Advanced Placement Expansion of the 1990s: How Did Traditionally Underserved Students Fare?" *Education Policy Analysis Archives, 12*, No. 68 (December 2004): 1–14; American Diploma Project, *Rising to the Challenge: Are High School Graduates Prepared for College and Work?* (Washington, DC: 2005); Center for Best Practices, *Getting it Done: Ten Steps to a State Action Agenda* (Washington, DC: National Governors Association, 2005); Center for Best Practices, *A Profile of State Action to Improve America's High Schools* (Washington, DC: National Governors Association, 2005); Clifford Adelman, *The Toolbox Revisited: Paths to Degree Completion from High School Through College* (Washington, DC: U.S. Department of Education, 2006).

calculated the "diploma loss" associated with financial barriers to enrolling in college by assuming that if low-income students had equivalent academic qualifications and financial support, they would enroll in and graduate from college at the same rate as their middle- and high-income peers.[2] Implicit in this policy argument is the assumption that the only barriers to enrolling in college that minority, low-income, and first-generation college students face are academic qualifications and financial resources. Specifically, it assumes these students have equivalent access to the guidance, information, and support they need to effectively navigate both the college application process and the subsequent college experience. While it is clear that a high level of preparation is important for college access and success, there is evidence that it is not enough. For example, Andrea Venezia and colleagues found that few minority students and their families fully understand the requirements of college application and admission.[3] Similarly, others have found that low-income students lack critical information about the steps they must take to effectively participate in college and financial aid applications, often conducting quite limited college searches.[4]

Also implicit in this policy argument is that college choice does not matter— essentially, that students with similar qualifications and net college costs will face the same likelihood of college degree attainment regardless of what college they attend. However, poor academic qualifications, lack of financial resources, and lack of information and guidance have implications beyond constrained college searches and lower enrollment rates; students who face these barriers are also more likely to enroll in institutions that do not afford them a high probability of attaining a college degree. There is a prevailing belief that institutional differences in college graduation rates are driven by differences in the academic and socioeconomic characteristics of their student bodies, not differences in the quality of the institutions themselves. Yet, there is evidence that low-income and urban minority students often enroll in colleges that

2. Advisory Committee on Student Financial Assistance, *Mortgaging Our Future: How Financial Barriers to College Undercut America's Global Competitiveness* (Washington, DC: 2006).

3. Andrea Venezia, Michael Kirst, and Anthony Antonio, *Betraying the College Dream: How Disconnected K–12 and Postsecondary Education Systems Undermine Student Aspirations* (Stanford, CA: Bridge Project, Stanford Institute for Higher Education Research, 2003).

4. Stephen B. Plank and Will J. Jordan, "Effects of Information, Guidance, and Actions on Postsecondary Destinations: A Study of Talent Loss," *American Educational Research Journal* 38, No. 4 (2001): 947–979; Patricia M. McDonough, *Choosing Colleges: How Social Class and Schools Structure Opportunity* (Albany: State University of New York, 1997); Christopher Avery and Thomas K. Kane, "Student Perception of College Opportunities: The Boston COACH Program," in *College Choices: The Economics of Where to Go, When to Go, and How to Pay for It*, edited by Caroline M. Hoxby (Chicago: University of Chicago Press, 2004).

provide significantly lower probabilities of completing a degree (e.g., two-year and less selective four-year colleges), and that these lower probabilities of degree completion cannot be solely attributed to the characteristics of students who enroll.[5] The recent U.S. Department of Education report on higher education, *A Test of Leadership: Charting the Future of U.S. Higher Education*, raised the controversial issue of whether higher education institutions should pay attention to the quality of education that they provide and be held accountable for their students' performance.[6]

How important is expanding this debate? In this chapter, we use data from a multiyear research project at the Consortium on Chicago School Research (CCSR) to take a close look at the college preparation, application, enrollment, and graduation rates of Chicago Public Schools (CPS) graduates. The first section of this paper examines the extent to which academic qualifications shape access to four-year colleges—particularly selective and very selective four-year colleges—among CPS graduates of 2002 and 2003.[7] We then extend our analysis to examine the impact of academic qualifications on the six-year college graduation rates of two earlier cohorts (CPS graduates from 1998 and 1999). Data from Chicago suggest that the current policy focus on increasing qualifications is warranted; low qualifications pose a significant barrier to college enrollment and degree attainment for CPS graduates, particularly Latino, African American, and male graduates.

In the remainder of this paper, we use a new postsecondary tracking system to examine whether CPS students who aspire to attain four-year college degrees take the necessary steps to apply to and enroll in four-year colleges. This analysis is preliminary, but it suggests that CPS students, even those who are qualified to attend four-year colleges, often do not plan to immediately enroll in four-year colleges, do not apply to four-year colleges, or do not enroll in

---

5. James C. Hearn, "Academic and Nonacademic Influences on the College Destinations of 1980 High School Graduates," *Sociology of Education, 64* (1991): 158–171; Sarah E. Turner, "Going to College and Finishing College: Explaining Different Educational Outcomes," in *College Choices: The Economics of Where to Go, When to Go, and How to Pay for It*, edited by Caroline M. Hoxby (Chicago: University of Chicago Press, 2004); Sigal Alon and Marta Tienda, "Assessing the 'Mismatch' Hypothesis: Differences in College Graduation Rates By Institutional Selectivity," *Sociology of Education, 78* (2005): 294–315; Thomas G. Mortenson, "Institutional Graduation Rates by Family Income, Student SAT Scores and Institutional Selectivity: 1994 Freshman Cohort," Postsecondary Education Opportunity 180, http://www.postsecondary.org (2007); chapter in this volume.

6. The Secretary of Education's Commission on the Future of Higher Education, *A Test of Leadership: Charting the Future of U.S. Higher Education* (Washington, DC: U.S. Department of Education, 2006).

7. Melissa Roderick, Jenny Nagaoka, and Elaine Allensworth, *From High School to the Future: A First Look at Chicago Public School Graduates' College Enrollment, College Preparation, and Graduation from Four-Year Colleges* (Chicago: Consortium on Chicago School Research, 2006).

four-year colleges, or else they enroll in colleges that are less selective than they are qualified to attend. Finally, using our earlier analysis of the college graduation rates of prior cohorts, we demonstrate the importance of college choice for low-income minority students. We argue that supporting students in the college application and enrollment process, as well as paying attention to the wide variation in college outcomes across colleges of differing selectivity, should be an important part of the policy discussion. Research suggests that if we are to address the central barrier to college access—raising qualifications— there must be an equivalent attempt to ensure that students aspire to attend the colleges that demand those qualifications, and that they receive the concrete supports they need to translate their qualifications into college enrollment and degree completion.

The Aspirations–Attainment Gap

In the last two decades of the twentieth century, a dramatic transformation occurred in high schools: students' aspirations changed, reflecting a new economic reality. Nationally, the percentage of tenth-graders who stated that they hoped to obtain a bachelor's degree or higher nearly doubled, from 41 percent in 1980 to nearly 80 percent in 2002 (see Figure 1). These rising aspirations were shared across racial/ethnic groups, with the largest increase occurring among low-income students. Similar trends emerged in urban school systems. In Chicago, over 80 percent of seniors hoped to earn a bachelor's degree or higher, and an additional 14 percent aspired to attain a two-year or vocational degree.[8]

The central policy problem is that rising aspirations have not translated into concomitant increases in college enrollment and graduation rates. While increasing numbers of minority and low-income high school graduates are making the transition to college, their enrollment rates continue to lag behind those of middle- and higher-income students.[9] Even among students who plan to attend a four-year college, minority students are much more likely to attend a

8. Unpublished tabulations. CCSR conducts biennial surveys of all CPS high school students and teachers. The results are based on the responses of 8,033 seniors in 2005.

9. Estimates from the October Current Population Survey show that from 1980 to 2002 the percentage of recent high school graduates who were enrolled in college increased from 51 percent to 63 percent and among low-income students from 32.2 percent to 51 percent. The college enrollment of white high school graduates increased more than African American and, particularly, Latino graduates. In 2002, 66.4 percent of white, 57 percent of African American, and 54 percent of Latino recent high school graduates were enrolled in college (National Center for Education Statistics, *The Condition of Education*, Supplemental Table 20–1 (Washington, DC: U.S. Department of Education, 2005)).

Figure 1. Percentage of U.S. 10th graders who expect to attain a bachelor's degree or higher in 1980, 1990, 2002

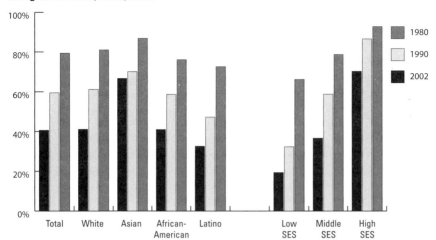

Source: U.S. Department of Education. National Center for Education Statistics (2004) *The Condition of Education 2004* (NCES 2004-077) Washington, D.C.: U.S. Government Printing Office. Supplemental Table 15-1. A student socioeconomic status was determined using parents' and students' report of their parent's educational attainment, occupation, and family income.

two-year college or none at all.[10] Moreover, minority and first-generation college students who do enroll in four-year colleges are much more likely to be placed in remedial courses that do not count for college credit.[11] Most importantly, few of these students ever attain four-year college degrees. From 1990 to 2004, the percentage of African American young adults aged 25–29 who had graduated from high school and attended some college increased by 16 percentage points, so that by 2004 over half of African American young adults had attended some college. But only 17 percent of them had graduated from college, an increase of just 4 percentage points since 1990. During this same time period, Latino students have shown little progress in either college enrollment or completion rates. In 2004, less than one third of Latino young adults had attended some college and only 11 percent had obtained a bachelor's degree or higher, a rate only slightly higher than it was about 15 years earlier.

---

10. National Center for Education Statistics, *Access to Postsecondary Education for the 1992 High School Graduates*, NCES 98–105, by Lutz Berkner and Lisa Chavez, C. Dennis Carroll (project officer) (Washington, DC: U.S. Department of Education, 1997).

11. Of students in NELS:88, who represent 1992 high school graduates, less than 40 percent of Latino and African American twelfth-graders were able to enroll in college without taking remedial course work, compared with fully 64 percent of whites and 62 percent of Asian students (National Center for Education Statistics, *Bridging the Gap: Academic Preparation and Postsecondary Success of First-Generation Students*, NCES 2001-153, by Edward C. Warburton, Rosio Bugarin, and Anne-Marie Nunez (Washington, DC: U.S. Department of Education, 2001)).

We see the same patterns in CPS. Data from the National Student Clearinghouse (NSC; see Table 1) reveals that only 34 percent of CPS graduates from 2002 and 2003 enrolled in a four-year college within the year following high school graduation. While these students have not yet had time to complete college, we can estimate the proportion of students who will attain college degrees within six years using earlier data. Our analysis of the college completion rates of two previous CPS cohorts (graduates from 1998 and 1999) reveals that only 45 percent of CPS graduates who enrolled in a four-year college during the year following high school graduation attained a four-year college degree within six years.[12] Based on this earlier data, we expect that only 15 percent of those who had graduated from high school in 2002 or 2003 will obtain a four-year college degree within six years of high school graduation.[13] This dismal statistic stands in stark contrast to the over 80 percent of seniors who aspire to attain a four-year college degree. African American and Latino graduates, particularly males, are even less likely to attain a four-year college degree; we expect that only 8 percent of minority males will attain a four-year college degree within six years of high school graduation. These may be underestimates of the proportion of CPS graduates who will eventually graduate from a four-year college. Certainly, some students will delay enrollment, some who enter two-year colleges will eventually earn four-year degrees, and some will take more than six years to graduate. Notwithstanding, only a limited number of CPS graduates will ever attain a four-year degree, despite their high aspirations.

What can account for these trends? The first place to start is high school preparation. There is a growing body of research linking students' high school performance and course work to postsecondary access and college performance. Perhaps the most well-known work in this area is Clifford Adelman's (1999)

12. One may argue that these statistics underestimate the proportion of CPS students who may complete four-year degrees, because we do not include students who started at two-year colleges. We were not able to estimate the progress of these students because the City Colleges of Chicago, which the majority of Chicago students who enroll in two-year institutions attend, did not join the NSC until 2000. However, national data suggest that few students (less than 6 percent) who enter two-year colleges complete bachelor's degrees within six years.

13. In an analysis of the Beginning Postsecondary Students Longitudinal Studies, Laura Horn and Rachel Berger (National Center for Education Statistics, *College Persistence on the Rise? Changes in 5-Year Degree Completion and Postsecondary Persistence Rates Between 1994 and 2000*, NCES 2005-156, by Laura Horn and Rachel Berger (Washington, DC: U.S. Department of Education, 2004)) compared five-year degree completion and postsecondary persistence rates for the entering classes of 1989–1990 and 1995–1996. They report that there has been little change in five-year completion rates over this period, particularly in four-year colleges, although they found a significant rise in five-year persistence rates— the percentage of students who were still enrolled after five years. This positive trend may indeed result in an increase in bachelor's degree completion in the most recent cohorts.

Table 1. A simulation of four-year degree attainment among Chicago Public School Graduates: Aspirations of Chicago seniors, four-year college enrollment within the year after high school graduation, and projected graduation rates for four-year colleges

	Total	African-American		White/other ethnic		Latino		Asian	
		Male	Female	Male	Female	Male	Female	Male	Female
Percentage of 2005 graduates who aspire to a four-year degree or higher	83%	87%	86%	87%	87%	76%	77%	94%	95%
Percentage of 2002 and 2003 graduates who enrolled in a four-year college within a year of graduation	34%	31%	38%	42%	46%	22%	27%	55%	65%
Percentage of 1998 and 1999 graduates who enrolled in a four-year college and graduated within six years	45%	28%	39%	58%	64%	36%	50%	67%	68%
Estimated four-year degree attainment rate of all graduates from the 2002 and 2003 cohort	15%	9%	15%	24%	29%	8%	14%	37%	44%

Note: Aspirations are based on CPS graduates who stated on the 2005 CCSR survey that they hoped to attain a four-year degree or higher. Estimates of the four-year degree attainment are derived from the proportion of graduates in 2002-2003 who entered a four-year college (see Table 3) and the proportion of CPS graduates from two earlier cohorts (1988 and 1989) who graduated from a four-year college within six years (see Table 4). The estimates are not sensitive to increases in either rate; they would vary by only 1 percentage point if the proportion of students enrolling in four-year colleges increased by 5 percent or if the graduation rates increased by 5 percent.

Answers in the Tool Box, which draws on transcript data from the U.S. Department of Education's longitudinal high school studies to examine the link between high school preparation and college performance. Adelman found that students' high school GPAs, their achievement test scores, and the rigor of their course work are strongly related to their likelihood of college graduation. Other studies have similarly documented a strong association between students' high school grades and college entrance exams and their likelihood of being placed in remedial courses in college and their college performance.[14] We also know

---

14. ACT, Inc., *Crisis at the Core: Preparing All Students for College and Work* (Iowa City, IA: 2004); Serge Herzog, "Measuring Determinants of Student Return Versus Dropout/Stopout: A First to Second Year Analysis of New Freshmen," *Research in Higher Education* 40, No. 6 (2005): 883–927.

that racial/ethnic minority and low-income students are much less likely to leave high school with the qualifications (e.g., test scores, grades, and course work) that give them access to college, particularly to four-year colleges, and which are critical to college performance and persistence.[15] One analysis of national data in the 1990s estimated that less than half of African American and Latino graduates had test scores, GPAs, and course work that would even minimally qualify them for admission to a four-year college, compared to 68 percent of white graduates.[16]

A second explanation focuses on the rising cost of college, the declining real value of federal financial aid, and the resulting net price burden faced by low-income families.[17] The U.S. Department of Education report, *A Test of Leadership*, calculated the average percentage of family income needed to cover net college costs after grant aid increased substantially from 1992–1993 to 2003–2004, particularly for private four-year colleges. The report found that, even at public colleges, families in the lowest income quartile still had an unmet need of almost half of their family income, while families in the highest income quartile had an unmet need of less than 10 percent of their family income.[18] There is a rich literature demonstrating the extent to which these increases in costs create barriers to college enrollment and completion. Research finds that levels of and changes in financial aid and college costs are strongly associated with the likelihood of college enrollment, the likelihood of four-year college enrollment, and college persistence.[19] While there is evidence that targeted scholarship programs improve college enrollment and persistence for low-income students,

15. National Center for Education Statistics, *High School Academic Curriculum and the Persistence Path Through College: Persistence and Transfer Behavior of Undergraduates 3 Years After Entering 4-Year Institutions*, NCES 2001–163, by Laura Horn and Lawrence Kojaku, C. Dennis Carroll (project officer) (Washington, DC: U.S. Department of Education, 2001); American Diploma Project, *Ready or Not: Creating a High School Diploma That Counts*; Advisory Committee on Student Financial Assistance, *Mortgaging Our Future: How Financial Barriers to College Undercut America's Global Competitiveness*.

16. National Center for Education Statistics, *Access to Postsecondary Education for the 1992 High School Graduates*.

17. Advisory Committee on Student Financial Assistance, *Mortgaging Our Future*; The Secretary of Education's Commission on the Future of Higher Education, *A Test of Leadership*.

18. The Secretary of Education's Commission on the Future of Higher Education, *A Test of Leadership*.

19. Edward P. St. John, "Price Response in Persistence Decisions: An Analysis of the High School and Beyond Senior Cohort," *Research in Higher Education, 31*, No. 4 (1990): 387–403; Susan M. Dynarski, "Does Aid Matter?: Measuring the Effect of Student Aid on College Attendance and Completion," NBER Working Paper 7422 (Cambridge, MA: NBER, 1999); Thomas J. Kane, *A Quasi-Experimental Estimate of the Impact of Financial Aid on College-Going* (Cambridge, MA: NBER, 2003); Institute for High Education Policy, *Expanding Access and Opportunity: The Impact of the Gates Millennium Scholars Program* (Washington, DC: author, 2006).

evidence of the effects of the Pell Grant program on college enrollment and persistence is mixed.[20]

The Aspirations–Attainment Gap in Chicago

How do these dynamics play out in an urban school system? Since 2004, researchers at CCSR have been looking closely at the college readiness, college attendance, and college performance of CPS graduates. In 2004, CPS began to track and publicly report on its graduates' college enrollment using data from the National Student Clearinghouse (NSC). CCSR, in partnership with CPS, is using NSC data along with student and teacher surveys and high school transcripts to examine the link between students' high school experiences, college choices, and college outcomes. In this chapter, we draw on data from our first report, *From High School to the Future: A First Look at Chicago Public School Graduates' College Enrollment, College Preparation, and Graduation from Four-Year Colleges*, to examine how college qualifications shape college enrollment and performance.[21] We then present more recent analysis from our forthcoming report, *From High School to the Future: Potholes on the Road to College*, to examine the barriers that CPS students face, in addition to academic qualifications, in taking the steps necessary to translate aspirations into enrollment in a four-year college.[22]

Data Sources

In this chapter, we focus on CPS graduates. CPS is the third largest school system in the United States and serves a predominantly low-income, minority population. The student population is about 50 percent African American, 38 percent Latino, 9 percent white, and 3 percent Asian. Approximately 85 percent of CPS students are from low-income families. We draw on four main sources of data on CPS students: (1) Official school records, (2) an online Senior Exit Questionnaire (SEQ), (3) CCSR teacher and student surveys completed in 2005, and (4) college tracking data from the National Student Clearinghouse (NSC).

High school transcript, test score, and demographic data are drawn from CCSR's extensive data archive of complete administrative records on all CPS

---

20. Kane, *A Quasi-Experimental Estimate of the Impact of Financial Aid on College-Going*; Eric Bettinger, "How Financial Aid Affects Persistence," in *College Choices: The Economics of Where to Go, When to Go, and How to Pay for It*, edited by Caroline M. Hoxby (Chicago: University of Chicago Press, 2004); Institute for High Education Policy, *Expanding Access and Opportunity: The Impact of the Gates Millennium Scholars Program*.

21. Roderick et al., *From High School to the Future*.

22. Melissa Roderick, Vanessa Coca, and Eliza Moeller, *From High School to the Future: Potholes on the Road to College* (Chicago: Consortium on Chicago School Research, forthcoming).

students. High school transcripts allow us to identify course-taking patterns and course grades. Test score data include ACT scores for all CPS graduates. This test is taken by all juniors in Illinois as part of the state accountability system. Administrative records provide basic demographic information on students such as race/ethnicity, gender, age, and schools attended. Additional socioeconomic status indicators were developed by geocoding addresses and linking them to 2000 Census block data.

Data on students' college plans, such as number of applications submitted and number of acceptances, are drawn from the SEQ. Begun in 2004 as a part of CPS's postsecondary tracking system, the SEQ is an online questionnaire completed by seniors in May before high school graduation. Nearly 90 percent of CPS seniors complete the SEQ.

For our analysis of students' college aspiration and plans, we use data from CCSR's senior survey. The senior survey is administered as part of the CCSR biennial survey of all high school students, teachers, and principals in CPS. The senior survey was explicitly designed to focus on students' postsecondary plans, as well as the support, guidance, and information they receive from teachers, counselors, and parents in making postsecondary plans. In 2005, 84 percent of high schools participated in the senior survey, with an average response rate of 62 percent.

Since 2004, CPS has also tracked the college enrollment and college performance of its students using data from the NSC. The NSC is a nonprofit college tracking system that provides school districts and colleges with information on students' college enrollment, persistence, and degree completion. For the cohorts included in our analysis, the NSC covers approximately 91 percent of college enrollment in the United States, with higher coverage in more recent cohorts. Because most Chicago graduates enroll in colleges in Illinois and a high proportion of Illinois colleges and universities participate in the NSC, we estimate that the NSC covers approximately 95 percent of college enrollment for CPS graduates.[23] In addition, approximately 1 to 2 percent of students either block their records from being reported or attend a college that blocks sharing of data in the NSC. We identify these students as enrolled in college, but because we do not know more about what college they attend, we do not include them in further analyses. NSC data are linked to data from the National Center for Education Statistics' (NCES) Integrated Postsecondary Education Data System (IPEDS)

23. We determined this 5 percent undercount figure by comparing colleges that participate in the NSC to colleges that CPS seniors reported that they planned to attend on the 2004 SEQ. The colleges that CPS students planned to attend that do not participate in the NSC are primarily local proprietary and technical institutions (Roderick et al., *From High School to the Future*).

to characterize colleges by type (e.g., two-year versus four-year, public versus private). In addition, we link NSC data to Barron's competitiveness rankings in order to classify schools by selectivity.[24]

Samples

In our analyses, we draw on three different samples of CPS graduates. We begin by reporting the academic qualifications for college and college enrollment rates of the CPS graduating classes of 2002 and 2003. We define a student as a graduate if he or she was enrolled in a CPS high school at the beginning of the school year and graduated in June or August. We exclude from our analyses students who were enrolled in special education at the time of graduation and students enrolled in alternative high schools. In 2002 and 2003, 13,379 and 14,306 students, respectively, met these criteria. We count students as enrolled in college if NSC reported that they enrolled within a year after high school graduation.

Since 2002 and 2003 graduates have not yet had sufficient time to graduate from college, we use data from the CPS graduating classes of 1998 and 1999 to examine college completion rates. In this analysis, we only include students who enrolled in a four-year college within a year after high school graduation and who enrolled in a four-year college that both participated in the NSC at that point and reported graduation data.[25] Our analysis suggests that colleges for which we do not have data tend to have lower institutional graduation rates, suggesting that we likely overestimate six-year graduation rates for CPS students enrolled in four-year colleges.[26]

Finally, in looking at students' participation in the college application process, we use data from the CCSR senior survey and the SEQ completed by the 2005 graduating cohort. We again limit our sample to graduates who were not special education and

---

24. *Barron's Profiles of American Colleges* rates four-year colleges on the academic qualification (e.g., ACT or SAT scores, GPA, and high school class rank) of its students, as well as the percentage of applicants who are accepted. We grouped four-year colleges into four separate categories based on their 2002 Barron's ratings: nonselective, somewhat selective, selective, and very selective. In Illinois, very selective colleges include the University of Illinois at Urbana-Champaign, the University of Chicago, and Northwestern University. Selective colleges include the University of Illinois at Chicago, DePaul University, and Loyola University. Less selective colleges include several large public universities such as Chicago State University and Southern Illinois University at Carbondale. Finally, nonselective colleges include Northeastern Illinois University, Columbia College, and Roosevelt University.

25. Among CPS graduates who attended a four-year college that participated in NSC in these cohorts, 74 percent attended a college that reported diploma data to NSC (Roderick et al., *From High School to the Future*).

26. Roderick et al., *From High School to the Future*; Elaine Allensworth, *Update to: From High School to the Future: A First Look at Chicago Public School Graduates' College Enrollment, College Preparation, and Graduation from Four-Year Colleges* (Chicago: Consortium on Chicago School Research, October 2006).

not enrolled in alternative high schools. We also exclude from our sample students who graduated from charter high schools, since charter high schools in Chicago do not report high school transcript data to CPS. For this reason, we cannot examine the academic qualifications for college of these students. There were 17,608 CPS graduates in 2005. Ninety-three percent of those graduates (16,374) completed the SEQ and 55 percent (9,723) completed the CCSR senior survey. If we look only at students who completed the senior survey and SEQ, our sample size is reduced to 8,774. Excluding students enrolled in charter high schools, alternative high schools, and special education further reduces our sample to 6,185. The resulting sample is significantly more qualified than the broader population of CPS graduates. Our sample has an average ACT score of 18.3 and a cumulative core unweighted GPA of 2.5, compared to an average ACT score of 17.0 and cumulative unweighted GPA of 2.18 for the entire graduating class. Thus, as with our analysis of six-year graduation rates, we expect that we overestimate the proportion of CPS students who meet specific benchmarks of participation in the college planning and application process.

College Enrollment and College Completion Among Chicago Public High School Graduates

The College-Going Patterns of CPS Students

We described national college enrollment and completion rates; now we compare them to the college enrollment and completion rates of CPS graduates. Table 2 shows the percentage of CPS students from the graduating classes of 2002 and 2003 who NSC identified as enrolled in college in the fall after graduation compared to students in Illinois and across the nation. Of CPS graduates, 51 percent enrolled in a college that participated in the NSC. The college enrollment rates of African American, white, and Asian students who graduated from CPS are only slightly lower than estimates of the college enrollment rates of public high school graduates of the same race/ethnicity in the rest of Illinois and in the nation.[27] However, Latino graduates from CPS were significantly less likely than Latino students in the rest of Illinois and the nation to enroll in college by the fall

---

27. We do not have estimates from other large urban school districts that would allow us to compare the college outcomes of CPS graduates to a comparable group of students in a different city. There is also no national tracking system that provides comparable information for a nationwide cohort. We do have two important sources to help place these results in context. First, we can obtain an estimate of national college participation rates from a yearly survey conducted by the Census Bureau as part of the Current Population Survey. Second, we have an Illinois comparison based on data from the Illinois Education Research Council (IERC), which has followed the college participation rates of the Illinois graduating class of 2002 using data from NSC. Because national estimates are based on students' self reports, we expect that the difference in college enrollment between Chicago students and their race/ethnic counterparts nationally is overstated (Roderick et al., *From High School to the Future*).

Table 2. 2002 and 2003 CPS graduates' fall college enrollment rate compared to high school graduation rates in Illinois and across the country

	National estimates, 2002–2003	Non-CPS Illinois estimates, 2002	CPS estimates, 2002–2003
All students	64%	62%	51%
African-American	57%	52%	52%
Latino	55%	46%	41%
White	66%	67%	63%
Asian	74%	77%	75%

Note: National estimates are based on self-reporting of college enrollment by recent high school graduates from the Current Population Survey of the Census Bureau. Here, we report the average of 2002 and 2003. State estimates are based on college enrollment in the NSC for the Illinois class of 2002, from a study by the Illinois Education Research Council. CPS estimates for the classes of 2002 and 2003 do not include students in special education or in alternative schools.

after high school graduation. Forty-one percent of Latinos who graduated from CPS enrolled in college by the fall after high school graduation, compared to 46 percent of Latinos in Illinois and 55 percent of Latinos nationally.

Table 3 shows the distribution of CPS graduates by enrollment in two- and four-year colleges and, among those who attended four-year colleges, by college selectivity based on Barron's rating. In our previous analysis, we used fall enrollment numbers to make them comparable to national figures, here we use enrollment within a year after graduation to allow students more time to enroll. Using this more generous time frame, the percentage of CPS graduates enrolled in college increases from 51 percent to 59 percent.

We see large differences in college enrollment rates across racial/ethnic groups and gender. However, most of these differences are driven by differences across groups in enrollment in four-year colleges; CPS graduates across gender and racial/ethnic groups enroll in two-year colleges at similar rates. Among students who enroll in four-year colleges, moreover, CPS graduates tend to enroll in nonselective and somewhat selective four-year colleges. Only 20 percent of African American females and 13 percent of African American males who attended college enrolled in a selective or very selective college. Asian CPS graduates were the most likely to attend selective or very selective colleges. Finally, male graduates from CPS, regardless of race/ethnicity, were less likely than female graduates to enroll in college; this disparity is consistent with national trends in college enrollment.

Table 4 presents the estimated six-year graduation rates for CPS students who graduated in 1998 and 1999 compared to national six-year graduation rate estimates derived from the NCES's Beginning Postsecondary Students study. Nationally, 64

Table 3. The percentage of Chicago Public High School graduates from the classes of 2002 and 2003 who enrolled in college by college type and selectivity and race/ethnicity and gender

Percent of all graduates enrolled in a college by the spring after graduation[1]		African-American		Latino		White/ other ethnic		Asian	
	Total	Male	Female	Male	Female	Male	Female	Male	Female
Any college	59%	54%	63%	41%	49%	67%	72%	78%	83%
Two-year college	22%	21%	23%	18%	20%	24%	24%	21%	17%
Four-year college	34%	30%	37%	20%	27%	41%	46%	54%	64%

Percent of all college-goers by college type and Barron's selectivity ratings		African-American		Latino		White/ other ethnic		Asian	
	Total	Male	Female	Male	Female	Male	Female	Males	Female
Two-year college	39%	41%	38%	47%	44%	37%	34%	28%	20%
Four-year non- or somewhat selective	35%	45%	42%	28%	28%	29%	30%	21%	22%
Four-year selective or very selective	26%	13%	20%	24%	28%	34%	36%	51%	57%
• selective	17%	7%	12%	16%	21%	22%	24%	37%	44%
• very selective	9%	6%	8%	8%	7%	12%	12%	14%	13%

[1] The percentage of graduates enrolled in two-year plus four-year colleges does not add up to the percentage of seniors enrolled in college by the spring after graduation because "type of college" is missing for approximately 2–3 percent of students. Students whose college type is unknown are students whose records are "blocked" either by the institution or by the students. These students are identified as enrolled in college but are "blocked" by the NSC from identifying the college they are enrolled in.

Table 4. Estimated six-year graduation rates for CPS students enrolled full-time in four-year colleges within the year after graduation compared to national estimates

	Estimated six-year graduation rate from four-year colleges	n
Total		
National sample[1]	64%	
CPS graduates of 1998 and 1999	45%	
African-American		
National sample	46%	
CPS graduates female	39%	1815
CPS graduates male	28%	848
Latino		
National sample	47%	
CPS graduates female	50%	792
CPS graduates male	36%	570
White		
National sample	67%	
CPS graduates female	64%	550
CPS graduates male	58%	397
Asian		
National sample	71%	
CPS graduates female	68%	403
CPS graduates male	64%	424

[1] U.S. Department of Education, National Center for Education Statistics. 2002. Descriptive Summer of 1995-1996 Beginning Postsecondary Students: Six Years Later, NCES 2003-151. Lutz, Berkner, Shirley He, and Emily F. Cataldi, Paula Knepper (project officer). Washington, D.C.: U.S. Government Printing Office.
[2] See Allenworth (2006) and Roderick, et al. (2006) for a more detailed description of the CPS samples and analysis.

percent of students who enter four-year colleges graduate within six years, compared to 45 percent of CPS graduates. These lower graduation rates are driven by differences in graduation rates across racial/ethnic categories. CPS is a predominately minority school district and its lower graduation rates reflect the lower graduation rates of African American and Latino students. However, the racial/ethnic composition of CPS does not fully explain why it lags behind the nation. Male CPS graduates in particular were significantly less likely than their counterparts nationally to complete college within six years. In contrast, Latino and white female graduates from CPS were about as likely as their racial/ethnic counterparts nationally to complete college within six years, with Asian and African American female graduates lagging slightly behind. Thus, our estimates suggest that while CPS graduates from the classes of 2002 and 2003 attended college at rates slightly below their national counterparts, their likelihood of graduating college may be substantially lower if we use the experiences of prior cohorts as a guide.

These college enrollment and graduation rates highlight the central disjuncture between CPS students' college aspirations and their actual college-going experiences. In 2005, over 80 percent of CPS seniors stated that they hoped to complete a bachelor's degree or higher and fully 94 percent hoped to complete some college or technical education. Yet, only 59 percent of graduates in the previous class made the immediate transition to college and most were enrolled in two-year and nonselective colleges. The gap was largest among Latinos, whose aspirations do not predict such low levels of college participation.[28] And, once in college, less than half of students were able to graduate within six years, with graduation rates being particularly disappointing for African American and Latino males. To what extent are urban students making different choices about the path they will take to attain those aspirations? Or to what extent do these college-going patterns and low college graduation rates reflect the fact that CPS students face constrained choices upon graduation and face limited prospects for graduation once enrolled? Our analysis of the high school performance of CPS graduates suggests that few students leave high school with qualifications needed to attain their goals.

What Determines Access To and Graduation From College: The Role of Qualifications

Translating Aspirations into Qualifications and Access

How do we assess whether students have the skills they need to be successful in college? Different studies have asserted different answers to that question. Many reports now base their definition of college readiness on high school course work completed by students.[29] However, a recent study conducted by ACT

28. Latino seniors' reports of their own and their parents' aspirations do not suggest that Latino students in CPS have significantly lower aspirations. In the 2005 CCSR survey, Latino seniors were less likely to report that they hoped to complete a four-year degree (70 percent versus over 80 percent of African American and white seniors). Latino seniors were nearly twice as likely as African American and white seniors (21 versus 12 and 11 percent respectively) to state that they hope to complete two-year or technical degrees. Most importantly, Latino seniors were only slightly less likely than African American and white students to report that their parents wanted them to go to college (84 percent versus 89 percent, respectively).

29. Patte Barth, "A Core Common Curriculum for the New Century," *Thinking K–16* 7, No. 1 (Washington, DC: The Education Trust, 2003); Jay P. Greene and Greg Forster, "Public High School Graduation and College Readiness Rates in the United States," Working Paper No. 3 (New York: Manhattan Institute, 2003); Act, Inc. and The Education Trust, *On Course for Success: A Close Look at Selected High School Courses that Prepare All Students for College* (Iowa City, IA: Act, Inc., 2004).

(2007) questioned this characterization, instead basing their definition of college readiness on college admissions test scores. Other studies have found, however, that grades, even self-reported grades, are a more important predictor of college performance than college admissions tests.[30]

Another strand of work has suggested taking a step back from existing measures of college readiness and being more explicit about what sets of skills determine whether students are qualified for college.[31] In our work, we have identified three categories of skills that research has demonstrated are critical in determining college access and performance: (1) content knowledge and basic skills, (2) precollegiate academic skills, and (3) noncognitive skills. In order for students to move from high school to college-level work, they must have basic skills (mathematics and reading) and content knowledge in core academic subjects. Equally important is developing thinking, problem-solving, writing, and research skills across subject areas that will allow students to engage in college-level work. Finally, meeting the developmental demands of college requires students to have a set of behavioral and problem-solving skills, sometimes termed noncognitive skills, that allows them to successfully manage new environments and new academic and social demands. This understanding of the skills students need in order to be ready to enroll and succeed in college allows us to better assess how we should measure college qualifications.

College admissions tests are commonly used as a measure of qualifications because they provide a standardized indicator of students' college readiness—based on an independent measure of students' cognitive achievement, basic skills, content area knowledge, and analytic thinking ability—compared to peers nationwide. Additional work has claimed that college readiness can be better measured through college admissions tests such as the ACT than through other measures of performances such as GPA. Whether such tests accurately

---

30. Jomills H. Braddock II and Marvin P. Dawkins, Predicting Black Academic Achievement in Higher Education, *The Journal of Negro Education, 50*, No. 3 (1981): 319–327; Julie Noble and Richard Sawyer, Predicting Different Levels of Academic Success in College Using High School GPA and ACT Composite Score (Iowa City, IA: Act, Inc., 2002); Roderick et al., *From High School to the Future*; Saul Geiser and Maria Veronica Santelices, "Validity of High School Grades in Predicting Student Success Beyond the Freshman Year: High School Record vs. Standardized Tests as Indicators of Four-Year College Outcomes," Center for Studies in Higher Education Research and Occasional Paper Series (Berkeley, CA: University of California, 2007).

31. James Heckman and Yona Rubinstein, "The Importance of Noncognitive Skills: Lessons from the GED Testing Program," *American Economic Review 91*, No. 2 (2001): 145-149; George Farkas, "Racial Disparities and Discrimination in Education: What Do We Know, How Do We Know It, and What Do We Need to Know?," *Teachers College Record 105* (2003): 1119–1146; David Conley, *Toward a More Comprehensive Conception of College Readiness,* Prepared for the Bill & Melinda Gates Foundation (Eugene, OR: Educational Policy Improvement Center, 2007).

assess these skills, particularly for minority students, is hotly debated.[32] They do not, however, provide a measure of noncognitive skills that may matter as well. There is an emerging debate about whether test scores or grades are more accurate predictors of college readiness. On the one hand, grades are a more comprehensive measure because they indicate whether students have mastered the material in their classes and provide an indicator of a different kind of college readiness—whether students have demonstrated the work effort and study skills needed to meet the demands of college courses. Still, grades are sometimes seen as imperfect as they might be subject to inflation and do not have set standards for performance that allow measurement across high schools.[33]

There is now a growing body of research linking students' measured achievement in core academic subjects and level of exposure to a higher-level, rigorous curriculum to postsecondary performance. This work has found strong links between a student's high school GPA and achievement test scores and the likelihood of college graduation. These studies have documented strong associations between students' course work and course performance (e.g., the level of course work students take, participation in advanced mathematics, grades, and performance on standardized tests) and the likelihood of placement in college remedial course work and college performance.[34]

---

32. Jacqueline Fleming and Nancy Garcia, "Are Standardized Tests Fair to African Americans? Predictive Validity of the SAT in Black and White Institutions," *The Journal of Higher Education, 69*, No. 5 (1998): 471–495; Alfie Kohn, *The Schools Our Children Deserve: Moving Beyond Traditional Classrooms and "Tougher Standards,"* (Boston: Houghton Mifflin, 1999); John Cloud, "Should SATs Matter?" *Time, 157*, No. 10 (2001): 23–34.

33. Robert L. Ziomek and Joseph C. Svec, "High School Grades and Achievement: Evidence of Grade Inflation," ACT Research Report Series 95–3 (Iowa City, IA: ACT, Inc., 1995); David J. Woodruff and Robert L. Ziomek, "High School Grade Inflation from 1991 to 2003," ACT Research Report Series 2004–4 (Iowa City, IA: ACT, Inc., 2004); ACT, Inc., "Are High School Grades Inflated?," Issues in College Readiness, http://www.act.org/path/policy/pdf/issues.pdf (Iowa City, IA: 2005).

34. Karl L. Alexander and Aaron M. Pallas, "Curriculum Reform and School Performance: An Evaluation of the 'New Basics,'" *American Journal of Education, 92*, No. 4 (1984): 391–420; National Center for Education Statistics, *Bridging the Gap: Academic Preparation and Postsecondary Success of First-Generation Students*, NCES 2001–153, by Edward C. Warburton, Rosio Bugarin, and Anne-Marie Nunez (Washington, DC: U.S. Department of Education, 2001); Heather Rose and Julian R. Betts, *Math Matters: The Link Between High School Curriculum, College Graduation, and Earnings* (San Francisco: Public Policy Institute of California, 2001); National Center for Education Statistics, *Descriptive Summary of 1995-96 Beginning Postsecondary Students: Six Years Later*, NCES 2003–151, by Lutz Berkner, Shirley He, and Emily F. Cataldi, Paula Knepper (project officer) (Washington, DC: U.S. Department of Education, 2002); ACT, Inc., *Crisis at the Core*; National Center for Education Statistics, *First Generation Students in Postsecondary Education: A Look at Their College Transcripts*, NCES 2005-171, by Xianglei Chen (Washington, DC: U.S. Department of Education, 2005); ACT, Inc., *Rigor at Risk: Reaffirming Quality in the High School Core Curriculum* (Iowa City, IA: 2007).

How Do We Measure Up? A Look At Chicago Public School Graduates

We rely on two measures to assess whether CPS students graduate from high school ready to engage in college-level course work: ACT scores and unweighted grade point averages (GPAs) in core classes. Since 2000, Illinois has required all juniors to take the ACT as part of the state's high school assessment test, the Prairie State Achievement Exam (PSAE).[35] This puts us in a unique position to examine the ACT performance of almost all CPS graduates, not just those who plan to attend college. Like other studies of college-going, we also consider GPA to be an important measure of college readiness. Other studies, however, examine students' weighted GPAs, which reflect both students' performance in their courses and the difficulty of their courses, as students receive extra points for taking more difficult courses (e.g., honors and Advanced Placement Program® (AP®) courses). Since taking more difficult courses is related to college readiness independent of performance in those courses, we separate GPA and course difficulty by examining students' unweighted GPAs in their core courses (English, mathematics, science, social science, and world language.) We also differ from other studies, such as those produced by ACT, in that we do not base our definition of college readiness on completion of a minimal set of course requirements.[36] In 1996, CPS adopted more rigorous graduation requirements: four years of English, three years of mathematics, three years of science, three years of social science, and two years of foreign language. For this reason, we know that all CPS graduates have met basic curricular standards of college readiness. In other analysis, we use enrollment in more advanced course work, such as honors and AP, or participation in an IB program, to define higher levels of college readiness.

I.   ACT Performance of Chicago's Graduates

CPS graduates' ACT scores are considerably lower than both Illinois and national averages. For the 2002 and 2003 cohorts, the average ACT score of CPS graduates was 17.1, compared to 20.2 for the rest of Illinois' juniors and 20.8 for college-going juniors in the nation.[37] Only 18 percent of CPS graduates scored higher than the national average of 20.8 (see Table 5). Within CPS, we see large differences in

---

35. In our work we rely on students' ACT scores when they take the exam as a part of the Illinois state accountability system during their junior year. Some students take the exam additional times, and with these subsequent tries, their scores may increase, causing us to underestimate the ACT scores students use for admission to college.

36. In separate work, we are examining the role of more advanced coursework such as those offered through the Advanced Placement Program (AP) and International Baccalaureate (IB) programs in making students college ready.

37. The average Chicago ACT score is not directly comparable to the national average because we are comparing the performance of almost all Chicago juniors to a more select college-oriented group nationally.

Table 5. Average and distribution of ACT scores and unweighted GPAs of CPS graduates of 2002 and 2003 by race/ethnicity and gender

	Total	African-American		Latino		White/other ethnic		Asian	
		Female	Male	Female	Male	Female	Male	Female	Male
Average composite ACT[1]	**17.1**	16.2	15.9	16.5	16.8	19.9	20.5	20.3	20.3
Distribution of ACT scores									
<18	65%	73%	75%	68%	66%	39%	37%	33%	37%
18–20	18%	17%	15%	19%	19%	21%	17%	25%	20%
21–23	10%	7%	6%	8%	9%	18%	15%	19%	18%
>23	8%	3%	4%	4%	6%	22%	29%	24%	25%
Average unweighted GPA in core classes	2.33	2.35	1.97	2.45	2.12	2.78	2.44	3.05	2.66
Distribution of GPA									
<2.0	35%	32%	56%	28%	48%	17%	31%	7%	23%
2.0–2.5	24%	27%	24%	25%	22%	18%	21%	11%	17%
2.5–2.9	20%	24%	14%	23%	17%	22%	20%	23%	21%
3.0–3.4	14%	14%	6%	17%	10%	25%	18%	32%	22%
3.5–4.0	7%	4%	2%	8%	3%	20%	11%	29%	17%

[1] The average ACT score for Illinois juniors taking the exam as part of the state accountability system is 20.2. The national average for college-bound students is 20.8.

ACT performance by race/ethnicity. In their junior year, over 70 percent of African American and two-thirds of Latino graduates scored below 17 on the ACT, compared to less than 40 percent of Asian and white graduates. Racial/ethnic differences are just as extreme at the top end. Over 40 percent of Asian and white graduates scored above a 21 on the ACT, compared to only 10 percent of male and female African American graduates, and only 15 percent of female Latino graduates and 12 percent of male Latino graduates. In contrast to the racial/ethnic gaps, we see only moderate differences by gender. Using ACT scores as one measure of college readiness, it appears as though only a small proportion of CPS students graduate ready for college.

II. Course Performance of Chicago's Graduates

The low ACT scores of CPS graduates do not happen in isolation. Over one-third of 2002 and 2003 CPS graduates had unweighted GPAs below 2.0 in their core classes upon high school graduation, and 59 percent had less than a 2.5 (see Table 5). Only 7 percent of graduates had greater than a 3.5. As with ACT scores, we observe dramatic differences in GPAs by race/ethnicity. Over 57 percent of female African American and 78 percent of male African American graduates had less than a 2.5 unweighted GPA in their core classes and 52 percent of female Latino and 69 percent of male Latino graduates had a GPA that low. In contrast, 33 percent of female white, 17 percent of Asian female and 39 percent of Asian male graduates had GPAs that low. At the other end, over 60 percent of Asian female students graduated with a 3.0 GPA or higher in their core classes compared to only 18 percent of African American female graduates and 25 percent of Latino female graduates.

Poor performance in high school classes appears to be the norm among minority males. While we found only moderate differences between male and female graduates in average ACT scores, there were dramatic differences in their GPAs. Among the graduating classes of 2002 and 2003, around 50 percent of African American and Latino male graduates, compared with about 30 percent of their female racial/ethnic counterparts, graduated with unweighted GPAs below 2.0 in their core classes. Across all racial/ethnic groups, female graduates were much more likely to graduate with high GPAs.

CPS graduates' ACT scores and GPAs suggest that few African American and Latino graduates demonstrate the basic skills and content knowledge they need for college. The low GPAs and ACT scores of graduates, moreover, suggest that they struggle academically throughout high school and that simply enrolling students in a college-preparatory curriculum is not enough. It also appears that students are not challenged to work hard in their courses, and do not exhibit the study skills and engagement in course work that signal they are ready to complete college-level work.

III. The Impact of Preparation in Shaping Access to College

How important are ACT scores and GPAs in shaping students' access to college? We ran a series of multivariate analyses that estimated differences among CPS graduates by ACT score and unweighted GPA in their likelihood of attaining three outcomes: attending any college, attending a four-year college, and attending a selective or very selective college (see Table 6).[38] The samples for each of these outcomes differ. We estimated the probability of enrolling in college for all CPS graduates, the probability of going to a four-year college for all college-goers, and the probability of attending a selective or very selective college for graduates who enrolled in a four-year college. Table 6 shows the estimated probability of each of the three college outcomes for a student who attended an average CPS high school, had typical demographic characteristics and entering test scores, and was "average" on other high school indicators, including grades and test scores.

These results suggest that poor performance in high school is not a significant barrier to enrolling in college, but does considerably constrain students' range of college options. Students with ACT scores lower than 17 had only slightly lower probabilities of enrolling in college than their classmates with ACT scores over 24. But, these students were much more likely to enroll in two-year colleges instead of four-year colleges, and few enrolled in selective or very selective four-year colleges. Students' grades emerge, moreover, as a more important predictor of college enrollment than ACT scores. Among students with similar ACT scores, students with higher GPAs were significantly more likely to enroll in college, four-year colleges, and selective or very selective four-year colleges.

It is not surprising, given CPS graduates' low GPAs and ACT scores, that they are concentrated in two-year and nonselective four-year colleges. Within CPS, students who had ACT scores above 18 and GPAs above 2.5 were much more likely to enroll in four-year colleges, and those who had ACT scores above 24 and GPAs above 3.5 were much more likely to enroll in selective or very selective four-year colleges. But few CPS graduates have ACT scores and GPAs this high.

IV. Developing Access Categories

In this chapter, we define college access as not just "walking through the door," but as having access to colleges of varying selectivity based on students' ACT scores and GPAs. As shown in our analysis, poor qualifications are not a barrier to enrolling in college, but they do pose a barrier to enrolling in four-year colleges, particularly selective colleges. Table 7 shows the

---

38. In addition to unweighted GPA and ACT scores, we take into account participation in honors and AP courses, demographic characteristics, prior elementary school test scores, and the average demographic and achievement characteristics of the high school the student attends.

Table 6. The effects of unweighted GPA and ACT scores on college participation for Chicago Public School students in the graduating classes of 2002 and 2003

	Probability of attending college among all graduates	Probability of attending a four- versus a two-year college among students attending college	Probability of attending a selective or very selective college among students attending four-year colleges
ACT			
< 15	.57*	.40*	.06*
15–17	.57*	.50*	.12*
18–20	.62*	.64*	.17*
21–23 (omitted category)	**.67**	**.69**	**.20**
24–26	.68	.70	.25*
>26	.64	.71	.22
GPA			
< 2.0	.46*	.30*	.05*
2.0–2.4	.57*	.53*	.14*
2.5–2.9 (omitted category)	**.66**	**.67**	**.27**
3.0–3.4	.72*	.75*	.35*
3.5–4.0	.81*	.82*	.47*

Note: These predicted probabilities were calculated from a two-level hierarchical linear model. Each model included a student's ACT score, unweighted GPA, coursework (participation in honors and AP courses), dummy variables for race/ethnicity and gender, a measure of the average poverty level and socioeconomic status of the student's neighborhood, age of entry into high school, distance traveled to high school, and a measure of the student's 8th grade achievement on the ITBS in reading and mathematics. We include both the summary achievement measure and a squared term because of nonlinearity. At the school level, we include information on the average socioeconomic status, average achievement level, and the racial/ethnic composition of the student body.

* Statistically significant from the omitted category. The omitted category for ACT is 21–23, for GPA is 2.5 to 2.9.

Table 7. Categories for access to college types based on CPS graduates' GPAs and ACT scores and patterns of college enrollment

ACT composite scores	Unweighted GPA in core classes				
	<2.0	2.0–2.4	2.5–2.9	3.0–3.4	3.5–4.0
Missing ACT	Access to 2-year colleges	Access to Non-Selective 4-year college	Access to Somewhat Selective Colleges	Access to Selective Colleges	Access to Selective Colleges
<18	Access to 2-year colleges	Access to Non-Selective 4-year college	Access to Somewhat Selective Colleges	Access to Somewhat Selective Colleges	Access to Selective Colleges
18–20	Access to Non-Selective 4-year college	Access to Somewhat Selective Colleges	Access to Somewhat Selective Colleges	Access to Selective Colleges	Access to Selective Colleges
21–23	Access to Somewhat Selective Colleges	Access to Somewhat Selective Colleges	Access to Selective Colleges	Access to Selective Colleges	Access to Selective Colleges
>23	Access to Somewhat Selective Colleges	Access to Selective Colleges	Access to Selective Colleges	Access to Very Selective Colleges	Access to Very Selective Colleges

Note: Graduates without grade transcript data, including graduates of charter schools, are not categorized.

Table 8. The percentage of 2002 and 2003 CPS graduating classes who have GPAs, ACT scores, and coursework that would give them access to colleges by college type and selectivity

What Students Are Qualified To Attend	Total	African-American		Latino		White/other ethnic		Asian	
		Male	Female	Male	Female	Male	Female	Male	Female
A **2-year** college only	31%	49%	29%	42%	26%	29%	13%	18%	6%
A **nonselective** 4-year college only	21%	23%	24%	20%	22%	15%	13%	14%	8%
At least a **somewhat selective** 4-year college/university[1]	48%	28%	47%	38%	52%	63%	73%	68%	86%
At least a **selective** 4-year college/university									
GPA & ACT qualified	20%	7%	13%	13%	18%	36%	43%	41%	56%
GPA & ACT qualified and participated in a honors/AP sequence.	10%	4%	7%	5%	8%	22%	25%	28%	39%
At least a **very selective** 4-year college/university									
GPA & ACT qualified	4.0%	<1.0%	2%	2%	2%	14%	13%	15%	19%
GPA & ACT qualified and participated in an honors/AP sequence.	3.6%	<1.0%	1%	<1%	2%	11%	11%	12%	17%

[1] At least a somewhat selective includes students who are qualified to also attend a selective and most selective. The first two rows in the table are mutually exclusive and represent the proportion who could only go to a two-year college or who qualified only go to a nonselective college. All CPS seniors are qualified to attend a two-year college because of open admissions. Thus 100 percent of CPS students are qualified to attend a two-year college, but 31 percent have such low qualifications that they could not attend a nonselective four-year college. Many nonselective colleges also have open admissions but have some minimum criteria.

types of colleges to which CPS graduates from the classes of 2002 and 2003 would likely have had access given their high school performance. Our rubric indicates the minimum GPAs and ACT scores that CPS graduates would need to have a high probability of being accepted to and enrolling in certain classifications of colleges. We developed this rubric using the modal college attendance patterns of students with different GPA and ACT score combinations. In addition to our rubric, we further characterize students' qualifications by whether they took a course work sequence that included honors classes and at least 2 AP courses or were enrolled in an International Baccalaureate (IB) program.

For example, in Illinois, a student would have access to a *somewhat selective college* if he or she had at least a 2.0 GPA and an 18 on the ACT. Because all high school graduates have the option of attending a two-year college, we categorized graduates with ACT scores and GPAs that fall even below the level necessary for likely admittance to a nonselective four-year college as being limited to attending two-year colleges. The GPAs and ACT cutoffs we used are generally lower than the definitions used in college ratings such as Barron's and other existing rubrics to measure qualifications. This is because we base this rubric on the actual GPAs and ACT scores of CPS graduates who enrolled in these schools, not the average of the entering class of that college.[39]

Only half of CPS graduates had the ACT scores and GPAs that would give them access to the majority of Illinois' four-year public universities. Only 20 percent of CPS graduates had the ACT scores and GPAs that would allow them access to selective colleges. If we include in this characterization whether the student had taken an honors/AP course sequence, the rate falls to 10 percent. White CPS graduates were more than three times as likely as African American graduates and twice as likely as Latino graduates to leave high school with the ACT scores and GPAs that would qualify them to attend selective colleges. Once again, gender differences occurred within every racial/ethnic group, largely driven by the significantly lower GPAs of males. Nearly three-quarters of African American males graduated from CPS with such low GPAs and ACT scores that they would only likely be admitted to a two-year or nonselective four-year college.

---

39. We use a lower cutoff in our analysis for a variety of reasons. First, college ratings reflect median or average scores of the entering class, not the minimum students need, and CPS graduates may fall at the low end of each college's distribution of acceptable ACT and GPAs. Second, colleges may also weigh other factors more heavily when admitting low-income minority students. Third, we use students' junior year ACT scores and because some students may retake the ACT, we expect that we are underestimating some students' ACT scores. Our cutoffs also roughly align with the admissions requirements of in-state public universities.

V. The Impact of Preparation on Four-Year College Graduation Rates

Earlier in this chapter, we showed that only 45 percent of CPS graduates who begin at a four-year institution graduate within six years. As with college access, our analysis suggests that the low GPAs and test scores of CPS graduates are important contributors to this low four-year college graduation rate. Figure 2 presents the results of an analysis designed to disentangle how grades and test scores shape the likelihood of college completion among CPS graduates for the classes of 1998 and 1999.[40] The first bar for each indicator shows the predicted effect of each measure of preparation, not accounting for student characteristics, high school course-taking, and other measures of high school performance. Thus, students who entered a four-year college with a 3.0 unweighted GPA were

Figure 2. Predicted effect of unweighted GPA, high school test scores, and weighted GPA on the chances of graduating from a four-year college within six years for Chicago graduates from the classes of 1998 and 1999

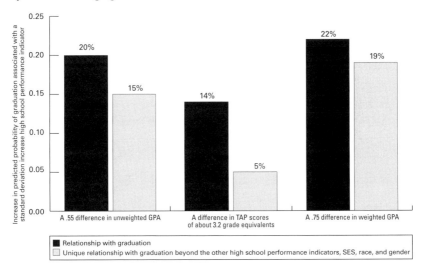

Each comparison represents a difference of 1 standard deviation in the high school performance variable. Difference in graduation rates were calculated for a student with typical preparation on the other indicators (GPA or TAP) as well as the number of honors and TAP refers to eleventh-grade test scores on the Test of Achievement Proficiency. The unique relationships were estimated using a logistic regression. Roderick et al. (2006)

---

40. Unfortunately because these earlier cohorts attended high school before the introduction of the new state tests, we do not have ACT scores for these students. We do have a measure of achievement based on the Test of Achievement Proficiency (TAP) which was given in 11th grade in the CPS prior to the new state exam. In 2002, juniors in CPS took the TAP in 10th grade and the ACT in 11th grade. This overlap in test administration allows us to gauge how similar students' performance would be on both these tests. Students' scores were highly correlated (.86), which suggests that TAP is a good proxy for students' overall achievement as would be indicated by the ACT.

20 percentage points more likely to graduate within six years than students who entered a four-year college with a 2.45 GPA. These students, of course, also had higher test scores and were more likely to take advanced course work. The second bar shows the independent effect of each measure of preparation when accounting for students' TAP scores (the only available achievement test scores for this time period), GPA, advanced course work, and demographic characteristics. Thus, among similar CPS students who entered a four-year college with similar TAP scores, students who entered with a 3.0 unweighted GPA were 15 percentage points more likely to graduate from a four-year college within six years than students who entered a four-year college with a 2.45 GPA.

We have painted a dire picture of the academic readiness for college and prospects for college graduation among CPS graduates. Clearly, closing the aspirations–achievement gap must begin with a focus on improving students' qualifications. Low GPAs, particularly among minority males, and low ACT scores seriously constrain CPS students' access to four-year colleges and undermine their chances of success once enrolled. The strongest predictor of graduation from four-year colleges was GPA; students who graduated from CPS high schools with less than a 3.0 unweighted GPA were very unlikely to graduate from college. Just over a third of students who enrolled in four-year colleges with GPAs between 2.6 and 3.0 graduated within six years and only about one in five students with GPAs below 2.5 graduated within the same time frame. On the other hand, CPS students with high GPAs (greater than a 3.5) had graduation rates from four-year colleges (75 percent) above the national average. Thus, urban students who do well in high school, as measured by their course performance, can be successful in four-year colleges. However, only 9 percent of CPS students in this cohort graduated with such a high GPA, having demonstrated that they had worked hard and mastered their course work in high school.

While this story of low levels of college readiness is compelling, it is also incomplete. First, levels of qualifications explain little of the differences we observe in the college enrollment of CPS Latino graduates and their African American counterparts. For example, in a multivariate analysis, we found that Latino graduates are approximately 14 percentage points less likely to enroll in a four-year college than African American and white students when we account for differences in their high school qualifications (GPAs and ACT scores). Adding information about students' family background (e.g., Socioeconomic Status (SES), immigration status, and mother's education) and background characteristics (e.g., age and timing of immigration) explains little of this observed difference. Second, as we will see later in this chapter, college qualifications alone do not explain the concentration of CPS students in two-year and less selective colleges.

These patterns suggest that CPS students may face additional barriers to college enrollment and graduation.

As discussed at the beginning of this paper, economists looking at these patterns in college enrollment tend to focus on the role of college costs and financial aid in creating barriers to college choice and enrollment. An equally important strand of research, largely drawing on social capital theory, highlights the importance of social support, the norms of students' environment, students' access to college information, and concrete guidance in shaping, aspirations, engagement in school, and college access.[41] The sociological research on college choice and selection posits that in urban environments translating aspirations into positive postsecondary outcomes requires that schools provide both strong academic preparation for college and the social supports (e.g., social capital) that guide students through the process. Urban and first-generation college students are especially dependent upon their teachers and other nonfamilial adults in making educational plans and decisions.[42]

Research points to two ways in which limited guidance, access to information, and norms for four-year college attendance shape urban students' college enrollment. First, without such supports, urban students with high aspirations often have difficulty taking the concrete steps needed to find colleges they are interested in, manage the application process, apply for financial aid, and enroll in college.[43] Moreover, urban students may not effectively participate in the college application process simply because they lack the information on what to do.[44] We call this "constrained college application." Constrained application not only applies to planning for and applying to college, it also applies to managing

41. McDonough, *Choosing Colleges*; Kohn, *The Schools Our Children Deserve*; Barbara Schneider and David Stevenson, *The Ambitious Generation: America's Teenagers, Motivated but Directionless* (New Haven, CT: Yale University Press, 1999); Alberto F. Cabrera and Steven La Nasa, "Understanding the College Choice of Disadvantaged Students," *New Directions for Institutional Research, 107* (2000): 5–22; James E. Rosenbaum, *Beyond College for All: Career Paths for the Forgotten Half* (New York: Russell Sage Foundation, 2001); Ricardo Stanton-Salazar, *Manufacturing Hope and Despair: The School and Kin Support Networks of U.S.-Mexican Youth* (New York: Teachers College Press, 2001); Kenneth P. Gonzalez, Carla Stoner, and Jennifer E. Jovel, "Examining the Role of Social Capital in Access to College for Latinas: Toward a College Opportunity Framework," *Journal of Hispanic Higher Education, 2*, No. 1 (2003): 146–170; Tyrone C. Howard, " 'A Tug of War of Our Minds': African American High School Students' Perception of their Academic Identities and College Aspirations," *The High School Journal, 87*, No. 1 (2003): 4–17.
42. Stanton-Salazar, *Manufacturing Hope and Despair*; George L. Wimberly, *School Relationships Foster Success for African American Students* (Iowa City, IA: Act, Inc., 2002); Howard, "A Tug of War for Our Minds."
43. Grace Kao and Marta Tienda, "Educational Aspirations of Minority Youth," *American Journal of Education, 106* (1998): 349–384; Avery and Kane, "Student Perception of College Opportunities."
44. Venezia et al., *Betraying the College Dream*.

the college finance system. The recent U.S. Department of Education report on higher education concluded that "our financial aid system is confusing, complex, inefficient, duplicative, and frequently does not direct aid to students who truly need it."[45]

Second, without strong access to information, many urban low-income students cannot determine to which colleges they could gain acceptance and could afford. Instead, they rely on their own familial and friendship networks that often only have limited college information. This results in many urban students focusing their entire college search within the traditional feeder patterns, largely public, two-year, or non- and somewhat selective colleges, and not participating effectively in the financial aid process.[46] Thus, many first-generation college students conduct what we refer to as a "constrained college search."

Participation of Chicago Students in College Search and Selection

How do CPS students manage the college search and application processes, and is there evidence that barriers other than qualifications shape their likelihood of enrolling in four-year institutions? Specifically, we will examine whether there is evidence of the two barriers identified in the previous section: constrained college application and constrained college search. Evidence of constrained application includes students experiencing difficulty in taking the necessary steps in the college application and financial aid process. Evidence of constrained search includes students enrolling in colleges that do not meet their qualifications and instead following the feeder patterns of their less-qualified peers. To answer these questions, we draw on the CPS postsecondary tracking system and CCSR senior surveys. In April of senior year, CCSR surveys asked students about their educational aspirations, whether they planned to attend college the next year, and whether they planned to attend a two- or four-year college. In late May, students completed the SEQ, which asked them whether

---

45. The Secretary of Education's Commission on the Future of Higher Education, *A Test of Leadership*, p. 3.

46. Hearn, "Academic and Nonacademic Influences on the College Destinations of 1980 High School Graduates"; McDonough, *Choosing Colleges*; Plank and Jordan, "Effects of Information, Guidance, and Actions on Postsecondary Destinations"; Ann E. Person and James E. Rosenbaum, "'Chain Enrollment' and College 'Enclaves'": Benefits and Drawbacks for Latino Students," Institute for Policy Research Working Paper WP-04-01 (Evanston, IL: Northwestern University, 2004); Doo Hwan Kim and Barbara Schneider, "Social Capital in Action: Alignment of Parental Support in Adolescents' Transition to Postsecondary Education," *Social Forces, 84*, No. 2 (2005): 1181–1205; Mari Luna De La Rosa, "Is Opportunity Knocking? Low-Income Students' Perceptions of College and Financial Aid," *American Behavioral Scientist, 49*, No. 12 (2006): 1670–1685.

they had applied to a four-year college and whether they had been accepted to a four-year college. In addition to this survey data, we examine college enrollment data from NSC to determine whether students ultimately enrolled in college, and if so, what types of colleges.

The Pathway to College

Figure 3 shows the pathway from aspiring to attain a four-year college degree to enrolling in a four-year college. On this pathway, we identify key benchmarks that students must meet to enroll in a four-year college. First, students must aspire to attain a four-year degree, next they must plan to continue their education, and then they must plan to enroll in a four-year college. After making these decisions, they must apply to a four-year college, be accepted, and finally enroll in a four-year college.

CPS students fall off this pathway at different benchmarks. Among CPS students who stated in their senior year that they aspired to attain a four-year degree, only 39 percent followed this pathway and enrolled in a four-year college within a year of graduation. An additional 8 percent of students managed to

Figure 3. The estimated percentage of 2005 CPS graduates that aspired to at least a four-year degree who applied to, were accepted at, and enrolled in a four-year college

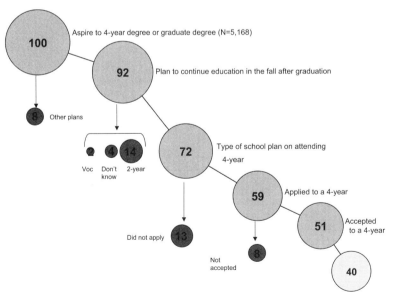

Note: This figure does not include CPS charter school graduates, alternative school graduates, or special education students. It only includes graduates who completed both the CCSR senior survey and Senior Exit Questionnaire. An additional 8 percent of students who aspired to a four-year degree ultimately enrolled in a four-year school.

enroll in a four-year college without following this pathway. While the previous section would suggest that the biggest barrier to enrollment faced by students was being accepted, our analysis indicates a much more complicated picture. Many CPS students who aspire to attain a four-year degree do not even consider enrolling in a four-year college in the fall after graduation, and even fewer apply. Only 71 percent of CPS seniors in our sample stated that they planned to enroll in a four-year college in the fall after graduation, and only 59 percent stated that they had applied to a four-year college. Over 80 percent of students who applied to a four-year college (or 51 percent of the entire sample) were accepted there, yet many of these students did not enroll.

Many CPS graduates make an early decision to attend a two-year college rather than a four-year college, and even among those who plan to attend a four-year college, many do not make it through the application process. Does this mean that students correctly judge their qualifications and decide that they are not qualified to attend a four-year college? Table 9 presents the proportion of CPS graduates who aspired to attain a four-year degree who ultimately enrolled in college by their levels of qualifications. We characterized qualifications using our rubric (see Table 7) of the type of colleges CPS students would likely be able to attend given their ACT scores, GPAs, and enrollment in advanced course work. Here we add another dimension to our qualifications rubric by moving students up one qualification category if they completed an honors sequence and at least 2 AP courses or participated in an IB program. Not surprisingly, students who were only qualified to attend a two-year or nonselective four-year college were not likely to plan to attend or apply to four-year colleges. They were also very unlikely to be accepted at a four-year college. What was surprising was that many students who were qualified to attend a four-year college did not plan to attend a four-year college or did not apply. Only 72 percent of students who were qualified to attend a somewhat selective university (the majority of four-year colleges in Illinois) planned to attend a four-year college and only 60 percent applied. Similarly, only 75 percent of students who were qualified to attend a selective four-year college applied and only 60 percent ultimately enrolled.

In sum, our look at CPS students' pathway from aspiring to attain a four-year degree to enrolling in a four-year college identifies three important points at which students who are qualified to attend at least a somewhat selective university fall off the path. First, many students opt to attend a two-year or vocational school instead of a four-year college. Second, many students who plan to attend a four-year college do not apply. Third, even students who apply to and are accepted at a four-year college often do not enroll.

Table 9. The estimated percentage of CPS graduates from 2005 who aspired to a four-year degree, ultimately applied to and were accepted at a four-year college, and enrolled by student's levels of qualifications for college

Of CPS graduates who aspired to at least a four-year degree, the proportion who:	Total	Pathway for students who are qualified to attend…					
		A two-year college only	A nonselective four-year college	A somewhat selective four-year college	A selective four-year college	A very selective four-year college
N	5188	1110	808	1388	988	841
Planned to continue education in the fall	91%	84%	89%	93%	96%	99%
Planned to attend a four-year school	72%	50%	59%	72%	83%	96%
Applied to a four-year college or university	59%	32%	43%	59%	75%	88%
Accepted at a four-year college or university	51%	19%	31%	50%	71%	88%
Enrolled in a four-year college or university	39%	9%	18%	38%	60%	77%

Note: The sample size for each qualifications category in our "college application sample" is based on graduates from 2005 who were not in special education, graduated from non-charter or alternative schools, and who completed both the Senior Exit Questionnaire and CCSR 2005 senior survey.

Barriers to College

What could explain why students who aspire to attain a four-year degree do not take the necessary steps to enroll in a four-year college? In our forthcoming report, *From High School to the Future: Potholes on the Road to College*, we use data from our qualitative study to show that many CPS students fall through the cracks due to lack of norms for college enrollment, lack of information on types of colleges, and lack of support in managing college search and application. Often CPS students do not understand what college options are available, the difference between two- and four-year colleges, and particularly what the real costs of college are and how to apply for financial aid. Thus, we find that financial cost has become a barrier to both college application and enrollment, not solely because of the cost itself, but rather because students lack the information and support they need to understand their financial aid options. While we do not have space in this chapter to present a full qualitative and quantitative analysis, this point can be made by looking at the school- and student-level predictors of enrolling in a four-year college for students who are accepted to a four-year college.

We conducted an analysis that estimated the likelihood of enrolling in a four-year college for students who had been accepted to at least one college.[47] We were particularly interested in how students' probability of enrolling was shaped by the college-going culture of their school and the degree to which they participated in the college application process. To measure the college-going culture of the school, we included several school-level variables: a measure from the 2005 CCSR teacher survey of teacher expectations for college attendance, school averages of the percentage of students who reported filling out their Free Application for Federal Student Aid (FAFSA) form, the percentage of students in the prior graduating class who attended a four-year college, and the percentage of students in the prior graduating class who were qualified to attend a selective or very selective college but enrolled in a two-year college. We gauged students' participation in the college application process based on the number of college applications completed and whether they had completed their FAFSA.

The pattern of these results capture the interplay among social guidance, access to information, and potential financial barriers that undermine college access, even for students who are admitted to college. Students who were accepted to a four-year college were much more likely to enroll if they attended a high

---

47. This analysis used a two-level logistic hierarchical model. The model controls for students' qualifications, demographic variables (race/ethnicity, gender, and age), family background (mother's education, timing of immigration, and measures of SES of the student's census block), students' involvement in school activities, whether students worked out of school, and student survey measures of the support they received from parents, teachers, and counselors in managing college search and application.

school that traditionally sent its graduates to four-year colleges. This suggests that access to norms, support, and information at the high school level is critical to college enrollment. One of the key pieces of this process is whether students get the support they need to navigate the financial aid process and complete a FAFSA. The strongest predictors of whether accepted students enroll in college were whether they had applied for financial aid and whether they attended a school with high proportions of FAFSA completion. We estimate that, controlling for family background, students' qualifications, and reported levels of teacher, parental, and counselor support, on average, accepted students who completed their FAFSA were almost 60 percent more likely (80 percent versus 51 percent) to enroll in a four-year college than students who did not complete a FAFSA. This finding may be a proxy for the overall level of norms and supports for college in the school environment. It may also indicate that failure to complete a FAFSA creates a significant barrier to college enrollment for low-income students.

More recent data suggest that FAFSA completion is a significant problem for many low-income students. This year, CPS began tracking FAFSA completion among seniors. As of late March 2007, when most students make their college decisions, only one-third of CPS seniors had completed a FAFSA. The students who did complete a FAFSA were very likely to receive substantial financial aid. Indeed, 47 percent of students who completed their FAFSA had zero expected family contributions and over three-quarters were eligible for a Pell Grant.

At the beginning of this section, we noted that qualifications alone are an insufficient explanation for the relatively low rate of college attendance among CPS Latino graduates. Research has consistently found that Latino students have the most difficulty managing the college application process and gaining access to guidance and support.[48] Our research generally confirms these findings. Table 10 presents the proportion of students who took the steps to enroll in a four-year college by race/ethnicity. Latino students were the most likely to make the initial decision to begin at a two-year college. Less than half of Latino students who aspired to a four-year degree even applied to a four-year college, compared to 63 percent of their African American and white counterparts.

We confirmed Latino graduates' lower rates of planning to attend and applying to four-year colleges in a more rigorous analysis that controlled for differences in academic qualifications and family background (e.g., mother's education, immigrant status, and measures of socioeconomic status). Not

---

48. Ricardo Stanton-Salazar and Sanford Dornbush, "Social Capital and the Reproduction of Inequality: Information Networks Among Mexican-Origin High School Students," *Sociology of Education, 68* (1995): 116-135; Gonzalez et al., "Examining the role of social capital in access to college for Latinas."

Table 10. The estimated percentage of CPS graduates from 2005 who aspired to a four-year degree, applied to and were accepted at a four-year college, and enrolled in a four-year college by graduates' race/ethnicity

Of CPS graduates who aspired to at least a four-year degree, the proportion who:	Total	Pathway for students by race/ethnicity:			
		African American	Latino	White/ other ethnic	Asian
N	5188	2440	1628	656	456
Planned to continue education in the fall	91%	92%	90%	94%	97%
Planned to attend a four-year college or university	72%	76%	60%	76%	82%
Applied to a four-year college or university	59%	63%	45%	65%	72%
Accepted at a four-year college or university	51%	53%	39%	61%	67%
Enrolled in a four-year college or university	39%	39%	29%	49%	62%

Note: The sample size for each qualifications category in our "college application sample" is based on graduates from 2005 who were not in special education, graduated from non-charter or alternative schools, and who completed both the Senior Exit Questionnaire and CCSR 2005 senior survey.

surprisingly, we found that lack of participation in the application process explains almost all the gap in four-year college enrollment between Latino students and students of other racial/ethnic groups. To restate, Latino students who aspired to attain a four-year college degree, planned to attend a four-year college, and applied to a four-year college were just as likely to enroll in a four-year college, controlling for their high school performance and family background, as African American and white CPS graduates. Thus, qualifications alone do not explain the lower enrollment of Latino students in four-year colleges. Rather their lower rates of enrollment may be attributed to the fact that so many Latino students do not plan to attend and do not apply to four-year colleges.

It appears that financial barriers to college may occur early, before students are deciding among financial aid packages and college options. The financial aid process itself poses one barrier. More importantly, the real and perceived costs of colleges, as well as a lack of information about financial aid options, seems to result in students, particularly Latino students, prematurely removing themselves from participating in the application process before they can make informed decisions about their college options.

The Role of College Mismatch

Our analysis so far has largely confirmed research findings that urban students often lack the social capital (i.e., norms, information, and supports) to take the steps needed to apply to and enroll in four-year colleges.[49] Research on the role of social capital in shaping college access also emphasizes how lack of information on colleges and college finance and lack of support in the college application process often results in urban students limiting their college search and enrolling in traditional "enclaves"— large public universities with lower levels of selectivity.[50] We look for evidence of this "constrained search" or "talent loss" hypothesis by comparing the types of colleges CPS students in our college application sample enrolled in to the kinds of colleges they would have access to given their levels of qualifications.

Table 11 provides evidence of significant mismatches for CPS students that occur among students at all levels of qualification. On average, less than one-third of CPS students enroll in a college that has a selectivity level that matches their qualifications based on ACT scores, GPA, and advanced course work. Students who had access to very selective colleges were as likely to end up in a very selective college as they were to end up in a college that was far below their match (e.g., a somewhat selective, nonselective, or two-year college). Students who had access to the majority of public four-year colleges in Illinois (somewhat selective or above) were equally likely to enroll in one of those institutions as they were to not enroll in college at all. In the final section of this chapter, we examine whether college choice, particularly for students who mismatch, mattered for their likelihood of attaining a four-year degree.

Does College Choice Matter?
A Look at Graduation Rates Across Colleges for CPS Students

The process of searching for a college can be daunting. There are over 2,500 four-year colleges in the United States, including over 100 in the state

---

49. Plank and Jordan, "Effects of Information, Guidance, and Actions on Postsecondary Destinations"; Christopher Avery and Thomas K. Kane, "Student Perception of College Opportunities."
50. Hearn, "Academic and Nonacademic Influences on the College Destinations of 1980 High School Graduates"; McDonough, *Choosing Colleges*; Plank and Jordan, "Effects of Information, Guidance, and Actions on Postsecondary Destinations."

Table 11. College match among CPS graduates: The estimated percentage of CPS graduates who enrolled in a college with a level of selectivity that matched the student's qualifications based on their GPA, ACT score, and participation in advanced coursework

	n	College enrollment as reported in the National Student Clearinghouse by whether the selectivity of the college the student enrolled in matched the student's qualification			
		Match or above match	Below match	Far below match college	Far below match no college[1]
Total	**6163**	31.3%	16.6%	13.8%	38.4%
Match by qualifications					
Access to very selective college	**859**	32.7%	22.2%	31.3%	13.7%
Access to selective college	**1060**	21.6%	32.6%	22.6%	23.3%
Access to somewhat selective college	**1591**	32.4%	11.5%	21.5%	34.6%
Access to nonselective four-year college[2]	**1048**	23.8%	28.8%	--	47.4%
Access to two-year college only	**1608**	40.7%	--	--	59.3%

Note: The sample size for each qualifications category in our "college application sample" is based on graduates from 2005 who were not in special education, graduated from non-charter or alternative schools, and who completed both the Senior Exit Questionnaire and CCSR 2005 senior survey.

[1] No college may be overestimated because not all CPS students enrolled in a college or university that participates in the National Student Clearinghouse. See our forthcoming report *From High School to the Future: Potholes on the Road to College* for estimates that are corrected for non-NSC college-enrollment.

[2] Below match for students who have access to a non-selective four-year college is a two-year college. Below match for students who have access to only a two-year college is no college.

of Illinois.[51] We have shown how CPS students struggle with the process of searching through these options and how ultimately, only 34 percent of graduates enroll in a four-year college. We have provided evidence that suggests students' access to norms, support, and information at their high schools shapes their likelihood of enrollment. Other research has shown how this lack of information and support for the college application process often results in urban students limiting their college search and enrolling in traditional "enclaves." Indeed, we find that CPS graduates follow this pattern of constrained enrollment in a small number of less selective institutions (see Table 12). Among CPS graduates who enroll in a four-year college, nearly two-thirds attend just seven institutions.[52]

This pattern of constrained enrollment is not necessarily surprising or troubling. Students make choices about college enrollment for a wide variety of reasons. The preference for a small number of local institutions may simply reflect the desire to live at home or attend college with friends. Perhaps students who attend local colleges will be more successful in college as they will have greater access to an existing network of support and have reduced living expenses. In addition, students with poor academic preparation may only be qualified to enroll in less selective institutions and thus their choices simply may reflect their reduced college options. However, research suggests that there are consequences to students' constrained college choices. The selectivity of institutions matters a great deal in shaping the likelihood of college graduation and in particular, undermines the chances of four-year degree attainment for urban and minority students.[53]

Should we be concerned about this constrained college enrollment pattern? Earlier in this chapter we demonstrated that CPS graduates have lower probabilities of attaining a four-year degree within six years than their counterparts across the nation. This is likely related to CPS graduates' constrained pattern of enrollment in a small number of local institutions that offer students very low probabilities of graduation, even when compared to schools in the same selectivity category. How much of these lower

51. National Center for Education Statistics, "Table 2. Title IV Institutions, by Level and Control of Institution and State or Other Jurisdiction: Academic Year 2005–2006," Integrated Postsecondary Education Data System, Institutional Characteristics Components (Washington, DC: U.S. Department of Education, 2005).

52. The seven four-year colleges in order of popularity are: University of Illinois at Chicago, Northeastern Illinois University, University of Illinois at Urbana-Champaign, Chicago State University, Northern Illinois University, Columbia College, and Southern Illinois University. See Table 12 for selectivity ratings.

53. Turner, "Going to College and Finishing College"; Alon and Tienda, "Assessing the 'Mismatch' Hypothesis"; Mortenson, "Institutional Graduation Rates by Family Income, Student SAT Scores and Institutional Selectivity."

Table 12. Six-year graduation rates for CPS graduates, all students, and underrepresented minorities at the 12 most commonly attended colleges

	Barron's selectivity rating	Institutional 6-year graduation rate	Institutional 6-year graduation rate for underrepresented minorities	CPS classes of 1998 and 1999 6-year graduation rate
University of Illinois, Chicago	Selective	46%	35%	48% (n=1353)
Northeastern Illinois University	Nonselective	18%	12%	13% (n=884)
University of Illinois, Urbana-Champaign	Very selective	81%	64%	72% (n=684)
Chicago State University	Somewhat selective	15%	15%	18% (n=560)
Northern Illinois University	Somewhat selective	53%	35%	n/a (n=508)
Columbia College	Nonselective	27%	17%	21% (n=443)
Southern Illinois University	Somewhat selective	43%	35%	n/a (n=409)
DeVry University	Nonselective	n/a	n/a	37% (n=375)
DePaul University	Selective	64%	54%	76% (n=321)
Illinois State University	Somewhat selective	59%	44%	40% (n=189)
Loyola University	Selective	68%	51%	67% (n=172)
Roosevelt University	Nonselective	25%	15%	42% (n=106)

probabilities can be attributed to the characteristics of the institutions themselves, and how much can be attributed to the individual characteristics of students, such as low levels of preparation or low financial resources? One way to evaluate the consequences of this enrollment pattern is to examine how CPS students fare in the most popular colleges. Table 12 compares the institutional six-year graduation rates of all students and underrepresented minority students, where available, to that of CPS students in the four-year colleges most attended by the CPS classes of 1998 and 1999.[54] Of the seven

---

54. Data on the graduation rates for all students including non-CPS graduates, which we call the institutional graduation rate, is based on data collected by U.S. Department of Education's National Center for Education Statistics, posted by the Education Trust (2005). Data are collected through the Graduation Rate Survey (GRS) through which institutions provide data about themselves. GRS graduation rates are based on the percentage of first-time, full-time, degree-seeking freshmen who earn a bachelor's degree from the institution where they originally enrolled (Education Trust, 2005). In one case, DeVry, the U.S. Department of Education does not report an institutional graduation rate, and in other cases, DePaul and Northern, we do not have data yet on graduation of CPS students.

most popular institutions for CPS graduates, only two had an institutional graduation rate at or above the national average of 53 percent, the highly selective University of Illinois at Urbana-Champaign and the somewhat selective Northern Illinois University. Two of the most popular colleges, Northeastern Illinois University and Chicago State University, had abysmal six-year graduation rates, below 20 percent. Furthermore, at many colleges, CPS students were less likely to graduate than students from other school districts.

It is clear that one of the primary reasons why institutional graduation rates vary is that different colleges enroll very different types of students. We would expect that very selective colleges would have higher graduation rates than nonselective colleges simply because their students begin with higher levels of college qualifications. To make a fairer comparison, we examine students who have the same background characteristics and high school preparation but attend different institutions. We can do this by using statistical models that adjust the college graduation rates for advantages and disadvantages associated with enrolling students with different levels of high school preparation.[55] We then pool graduation data on CPS students from all 103 colleges to show the average graduation rates at three types of colleges: the six most popular colleges,[56] other in-state colleges, and out-of-state colleges. As shown in Table 13, graduation rates at the most popular colleges for CPS students were substantially below

Table 13. Six-year graduation rates by in-state versus out-of-state status and popularity among CPS students

	Unadjusted	Adjusted for SES, demographic characteristics, and high school preparation
In-state, not one of the six most popular	47%	46%
Out-of-state	61%	56%
Most popular six	25%	26%

Note: These programs come from hierarchical linear models with students nested within colleges with dummy variables representing the most popular six schools and out-of-state schools. The unadjusted model included no variables at level 1, while the adjusted model included control variables for the students' economic status, race, gender, TAP score, high school GPA, and high school course rigor. Similar results are obtained if non-nested student-level variables are used instead of hierarchical ones.

55. Adjustments are made through two-level hierarchical linear models, with students nested within college ($n = 103$ colleges). Graduation rates were adjusted with level 1 variables including GPA, TAP score, honors/AP courses in high school, extra advanced math courses, socioeconomic status, race/ethnicity, and gender. No variables were entered at level 2, so the adjustments do not compensate for college characteristics.

56. Northern Illinois University was not included because it does not report graduation data to NSC.

those of other colleges in Illinois, even when adjustments are made to compare students with similar high school preparation and background characteristics. Students who attend college outside of Illinois had even higher graduation rates than students attending college in Illinois. Quite simply, CPS students who went to college someplace other than the most popular schools were more likely to graduate than students with similar preparation and backgrounds who followed the constrained path to college.

One explanation for the lower graduation rates for students who enroll in the most popular colleges is that these students did not fully participate in the college search process and as a result, ended up in institutions that were not a good match for their interests and skills. Enrollment in an enclave college could also be an indication of low levels of social capital, which also undermine students' likelihood of college success. Attending an out-of-state college and living on campus may allow students to more fully immerse themselves in the college experience. There are many possible reasons for these patterns, including both institutional and student characteristics.[57] To better understand the role of college choice in shaping graduation rates, we examine four-year college degree attainment rates among students with the same level of qualifications but who enrolled in different institutions.

Figure 4 demonstrates how college choice, in combination with high school GPA, was related to very different probabilities of attaining a four-year degree. Each of the lines in the chart represents a different college in Illinois, showing the graduation rates of the students who went to that college from CPS by their high school GPA. Again, to make a fairer evaluation, we compare students who have the same background characteristics but attend different institutions.

We can see three important factors in students' likelihood of attaining a four-year degree in Figure 4. First, students with very low GPAs were unlikely to graduate regardless of which college they attended. The range of institutions attended by students with about a "C" average was limited, but no matter where they attended, fewer than 20 percent graduated. Students with a high school GPA of about 2.5 attended a broader range of colleges, but less than one-third graduated. Second, regardless of the college, high school GPA mattered. Within

---

57. We examined indicators of college quality, such as selectivity (e.g., median SAT, admittance rate), the types of students they enroll (e.g., percent part-time, percent age 25 or older, percent receiving Pell Grants), their structure (e.g., size, reliance on part-time faculty, status as a historically black college/university, student-faculty ratio) and their costs and services (e.g., expenditures on students) to see their impact on college graduation rates. Once adjustments are made to account for different levels of high school preparation among students, only a few college characteristics show even moderate relationships with graduation, median SAT, educational expenditures per student, sector (private/public), and the percentage of students over age 25 (Roderick et al., *From High School to the Future*).

Figure 4. Six-year graduation rates at the most popular colleges by high school GPA

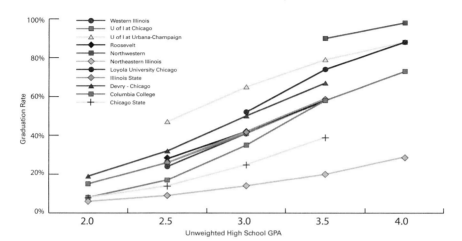

Note: These lines come from logistic regression models performed for each college, predicting graduation with GPA. The regression lines are based on data from all students based on their actual (not rounded) GPA. Points are included only if at least 20 students had that GPA within that school. Schools with fewer than 40 students were not included, nor were schools that had no variability in GPA.

each institution, students with higher high school GPAs were more likely to graduate. This suggests, once again, that GPA is not only important in gaining access to selective schools, but also in succeeding once there. Finally, we see that college choice mattered substantially for graduation, especially among high-achieving students. While CPS graduates with a 4.0 high school GPA had a 97 percent probability of graduating from Northwestern University within six years, this figure drops to 29 percent for similar students enrolled in Northeastern Illinois University. It is very likely that students who enroll in Northwestern differ from students who enroll in Northeastern in many ways that we have not taken into account in our analysis. However, we still expect students that manage to attain a 4.0 GPA throughout high school would have a high probability in succeeding in college, particularly at a nonselective college.

It seems counterintuitive that college choice would be most critical for high-achieving students. We would expect that the best prepared students would be able to succeed at any institution they attended. The students with the highest qualifications had the most options, yet where they enrolled still mattered greatly. It is possible that there are important unmeasured reasons underlying college choice that also have an impact on degree attainment. Still, the very large differences in graduation rates across colleges, even among students with the same high school GPAs, suggest that we need to pay attention to students' choices after high school. While it is clear that improving students' preparation for college is an essential step for increasing college access and degree attainment, the gains from these efforts can be rendered meaningless if students are not given the support they need to make good college choices.

Conclusion

Over the past several years, the Chicago Public Schools (CPS) have been engaged in a major initiative to address what has become a national policy question: How do we increase college access and attainment for low-income minority and first-generation college students? In 2003, the CPS administration established the Department of Postsecondary Education and Student Development, charged with ensuring that all CPS students have access to the courses, opportunities, and experiences that will prepare them for a viable postsecondary education or career. As part of this initiative, CPS became the first major school system in the country to begin tracking and reporting the college participation rates of its graduates using data from the National Student Clearinghouse (NSC). This initiative also includes new supports to build strong postsecondary guidance systems and accelerated efforts to expand participation in rigorous course work, such as AP courses. In collaboration with CPS, CCSR mounted a major research project to track the postsecondary experiences of successive cohorts of graduating CPS students, and examine the relationship between high school preparation and supports, college choice, and postsecondary outcomes. The goal of this research is to help CPS understand the determinants of students' postsecondary success and to identify key levers for improvement. This chapter presented analysis from our first two reports and in this conclusion we reflect on what we have learned so far.

First, efforts to increase students' likelihood of college enrollment and success must start with a focus on improving instruction and qualifications in high school. Preparation is particularly important in shaping access to four-year colleges. The low GPAs and ACT scores of CPS graduates constrain their access to and options among four-year colleges, and seriously undermine their chances of being successful once enrolled. The national policy debate has focused on increasing participation in rigorous curricula and improving students' measured college-readiness based on standardized achievement tests or college entrance exams. These are important policy steps. At the same time, research such as ours points to the importance of broadening our emphasis to include engaging students in developing the habits and skills, such as study skills and motivation to achieve, that are precursors to being successful in college.

In our work, we find that grades are a central determinant of college enrollment and completion. This should be no surprise. We cannot expect students with consistent patterns of poor performance in high school to perform well in college. It appears as though too many students in Chicago are "just getting by" in high school. Classes that allow students to "get by" versus those that require students to push themselves to learn and engage in the material enough to master and excel in it are those which are bridging the gap between students' aspirations to attain a college degree and actual degree attainment. This is the difference between developing and not developing the kinds of noncognitive skills—such as the ability to work independently, study, and engage deeply with problems—that are critical for academic success. It is not surprising, then, that GPA has emerged in our work and others' work as perhaps the most important determinant of students' access to and likelihood of graduation from college. Grades are not just a measure of what students have learned, they also indicate whether students have mastered the noncognitive skills that are essential for success in college.

If, as our work and many national reports suggest, the first strategy for improving college access in urban areas is to get students to work harder, engage in more rigorous course work, and achieve a high level of qualifications, how do we motivate students and their families to meet these new expectations? A focus on instruction is not enough. It must be accompanied by an equivalent emphasis on guidance and the development of normative environments and support structures. As we saw in this chapter, too many students who aspire to attend four-year colleges fall through the cracks, not taking the steps necessary to apply to and enroll in four-year colleges. And, too many CPS students enroll in colleges that are less selective than they are qualified to attend, suggesting that they actually could have worked less in high school and ended up at the same colleges. This is not a pattern that sets a high bar for students and pushes them to excel. Strong guidance programs and strong college norms, therefore, may be both a precursor to and an essential support for raising achievement. This includes helping students translate aspirations into concrete plans, defining clearly for students what preparation means, translating that into day-to-day expectations and experiences, and demonstrating that achievement pays off.

Second, high schools cannot ask students to work hard, engage in more rigorous course work, and develop specific sets of skills if students and their families do not understand why doing so matters and if they do not aspire to postsecondary experiences that demand high performance.[58] Raising

---

58. John Bishop, "Incentives for Learning: Why American High School Students Compare so Poorly to their Counterparts Overseas," *Research in Labor Economics, 11* (1990): 17–51; Rosenbaum, *Beyond College for All.*

achievement norms for students begins by working with students to make their aspirations concrete. College, for many students, is a path to a good job. These students do not see colleges as an array of educational institutions that differ in their quality and offerings. And they do not see college as an educational experience for which they need to be "ready." Unless they have siblings or relatives who attended college and have communicated that colleges differ from each other, to most urban students, college is college. James Rosenbaum has argued that open admissions policies have sent the message that all you need to do to go to college is to graduate from high school.[59] This is true; any high school graduate can go to college. However, not all colleges provide a path to a four-year degree. We also know that connecting performance in high school to college makes a difference in students' work effort. Rosenbaum found that 40 percent of urban students with college plans believed that how they performed in high school was irrelevant to their future. This belief was associated with less effort in high school and poorer college performance. Thus, raising students' achievement must begin by working to change students' view that college is an outcome, rather than an institution they need to plan and prepare for.

Third, high schools must provide the information structures and academic experiences that communicate to students and their families what "preparation" actually entails. Few minority students and their families understand what is needed to enter college.[60] Students must consistently hear messages about the skills they need to acquire to reach their goal, experience those expectations in their classrooms, and experience success in developing those skills. Many students, not just urban students, do not make the connection from effort and learning skills in high school to success in college. In a recent survey of college graduates, 65 percent of college students agreed or strongly agreed that, given their experience in college, they would have "worked harder and applied themselves more in high school" and "taken more rigorous courses" if they had known what college demanded.[61] Students at two-year colleges were more likely (75 percent versus 60 percent) than those at four-year colleges to agree that they would have changed what they had done in high school if they understood what college demanded, most likely reflecting the recognition that their high school performance limited their college access.

Fourth, as vividly illustrated in this chapter, educators must realize that preparation will not necessarily translate into access to college if high schools do not provide better structure and support for students in college search,

---

59. Rosenbaum, *Beyond College for All.*

60. Venezia et al., *Betraying the College Dream.*

61. Achieve, Inc., *Rising to the Challenge: Are High School Graduates Prepared for College and Work? A Study of Recent High School Graduates, College Instructors and Employers,* conducted by Peter D. Hart Research Associates, Public Opinion Strategies (Washington, DC: 2005).

planning, and application.[62] This may be critical in shaping motivation; students and their families need to believe that their high aspirations are attainable. In part, this belief is created when students feel well-supported and capable of achieving their goals.[63] They also believe that their high aspirations are attainable when high schools provide concrete structures and supports for college, so that students know they can rely on their school for information and guidance, and when their school demonstrates a track record of success. The need for guidance and information creates new roles for teachers and school staff and is as important a challenge for high school reform as raising achievement test scores. Part of this strategy must also involve a local strategy to help families and students manage college finance, along with a national and state strategy to break down barriers to college affordability. There is a growing body of evidence that efforts to make college more affordable, particularly efforts that link scholarship to performance, improve students' motivation and college enrollment and ultimately their performance in college. Early evidence from the evaluation of the Gates' Millennium Scholars program has found that, relative to a comparison group, Gates scholarship recipients were more likely to enroll in very selective colleges, more likely to be engaged in activities on their college campuses, and more likely to persist in and complete college.[64]

Finally, it is clear that the lack of academic preparation is not the only barrier to success in college. Another key component, as documented in this chapter, is to focus on college choice and to encourage students to attend colleges that offer high levels of support and environment conducive to student learning, particularly for underrepresented minorities. Our analysis on institutional differences in CPS students' odds of degree attainment is not conclusive. We do not adequately control for unmeasured selection effects and, unfortunately, do not yet have information on the net financial burden students faced across these various institutions. This is an area where our research will continue with more rigorous analysis. Nevertheless, other research has similarly documented the wide variation in college graduation rates we observe across institutions, suggesting that college choice matters a great deal. From an urban high school system's perspective, the strategy must be to ensure that students make college choices that maximize the quality of education they receive and their chances of completing a degree. But better sorting is not a high quality strategy for the nation. There is a significant need for research and policy attention in this final

62. McDonough, *Choosing Colleges*; Cabrera and La Nasa, "Understanding the College Choice of Disadvantaged Students"; Gonzales et al., "Examining the Role of Social Capital in Access to College for Latinas."

63. Ferguson, 1994; Wimberly, *School Relationships Foster Success for African American Students*; Howard, "A Tug of War for Our Minds."

64. Institute for Higher Education Policy, *Expanding Access and Opportunity*.

area—investigating the determinants of disparities in institutional graduation rates and finding what supports are needed to improve these rates. The bottom line is that four-year colleges and universities need to become part of the strategy for improving college graduation rates. Without changes in the higher education sector, efforts to reform high schools will not be enough to close the gap between students' college aspirations and their college attainment.

Financial Aid at Public Flagship Universities

Michael S. McPherson, Morton Owen Schapiro, and Francie E. Streich

Success in College

In recent decades, the benefits of higher education, for both the individual and society, have become strikingly clear. A simple look at earnings illustrates the benefits to the individual. Between 1980 and 2004, the median salary for males with a bachelor's degree grew from $46,300 to $50,700 while the median salary for those without a degree fell from $38,800 to $30,400. During these 24 years, the salary differential between the two groups grew from $7,500 to $20,300.[1] For the benefit of the entire society, higher education affords greater productivity, lower crime rates, and a better-informed populace.[2]

As the rewards for pursuing higher education and, more specifically, completing a degree, become more apparent, the field of higher education research has expanded its focus from issues of access and opportunity to those of persistence and success. While it is crucial to afford all willing and able individuals the opportunity to go to college, they should also be afforded the opportunity to succeed.

New Research Opportunity

The possibilities for research concerning "success" are greatly expanding thanks to the recent efforts of William Bowen and his research team at the Mellon Foundation. In 2005, Bowen commenced a massive data collection project that spanned an extensive set of public research universities. From a total of 21 flagship institutions, the Mellon Foundation acquired detailed information regarding the personal, family, financial, and academic characteristics of the entering class of the 1999 academic year.[3] These data form the basis of the Public University Database.

---

1. Salary statistics are in 2004 dollars. Source: U.S. Department of Education, National Center for Education Statistics. (2007). *The Condition of Education 2007* (NCES 2007–064), Indicator 20.

2. Stacy Dickert-Conlin and Ross Rubenstein, Eds., *Economic Inequality and Higher Education* (New York, NY: The Russell Sage Foundation, 2007).

3. The 21 institutions consist of Iowa State University; Ohio State University; Pennsylvania State University; Purdue University; Rutgers, The State University of New Jersey; State University of New York at Stony Brook; University of California: Berkeley; University of California: Los Angeles; University of Florida; University of Illinois at Urbana-Champaign, University of Iowa, University of Maryland: College Park; University of Michigan; University of Minnesota: Twin Cities; University of Nebraska-Lincoln; University of North Carolina at Chapel Hill; University of Oregon; University of Texas at Austin; University of Virginia; University of Washington; and the University of Wisconsin-Madison.

The utility of this new data set stems mainly from its size. While previous literature commonly addressed questions of persistence with data from a single school and/or a short time span, the Public University Database affords more thorough analysis by providing data on entering cohorts at 21 schools, nearly 90,000 individual students, for a six-year time span.[4] With such a large number of observations, the data can be broken down by gender, income, race, and/or family characteristics while still affording sufficient cell sizes upon which to run meaningful analyses. And, as opposed to addressing within-year or across-year persistence, we can address persistence to graduation, the ultimate goal of attending college.

Moreover, this database covers an important subset of influential institutions in the American higher education system: public flagship universities. While students have multiple options for postsecondary education—private colleges, community colleges, and technical schools to name a few—the public flagship institutions are responsible for educating a substantial portion of states' college-going population as well as serving as a role model for other institutions of higher education.

With this new resource, researchers at the Mellon and Spencer Foundations are jointly delving into the myriad questions surrounding persistence, departure, and attainment and the factors that may influence these outcomes. Work is currently under way to analyze the effects of high school characteristics, academic preparation, family circumstances, student characteristics, and financial aid on the academic outcomes of college-going individuals.

The last of these topics, financial aid, is of particular interest not only to the Mellon/Spencer research team, but to government policymakers, institutions of higher education, financial aid administrators, families of students, and students themselves. First of all, the financial aid nexus is constantly evolving. Aid programs are added and removed at the federal and state level on a regular basis. For example, the federal government recently instituted Academic Competitiveness Grants and Smart Grants to supplement funding of Pell recipients.[5] Before further changes are made to the already complex system, it is crucial to understand the effects of previous attempts at providing financial aid. Second, government support to institutions of higher education, as a share of higher education revenue, has decreased, leaving families and students to face

---

4. Stephen L. DesJardins, Dennis A. Ahlburg, and Brian P. McCall, "Simulating the Longitudinal Effects of Changes in Financial Aid on Student Departure from College," *The Journal of Human Resources* (2002): 653–679.; Larry D. Singell Jr. "Come and Stay a While: Does Financial Aid Effect Retention Conditioned on Enrollment at a Large Public University?" *Economics of Education Review* (2004): 459–71.; Edward P. St. John and Johnny B. Starkey, "An Alternative to Net Price: Assessing the Influence of Prices and Subsidies on Within-Year Persistence," *Journal of Higher Education* (Spring 1995): 156–186.

5. Sandy Baum, "It's Time for Serious Reform of the Student-Aid System," *Change, 39*, No. 2 (March/April 2007): 14–20.

higher tuition rates.[6] Financial aid plays a more important role for families and students as they witness such constant increases in price.

With the growing necessity of attaining a higher education, does the financial aid system, in its current state, provide the necessary support for all students to succeed? Does financial aid benefit certain subgroups of the college-going population more than others? Does the timing of financial aid or changes in aid received impact the likelihood of success? The Public University Database can help us answer these important questions.

Untangling Financial Aid

These questions seem simple enough, but, in reality, untangling the specific effects of financial aid is a challenging task; its relationship to success is complicated by an issue economists refer to as endogeneity—factors that determine aid are also likely to influence persistence and success through channels other than the aid itself. When aid is based on need, for example, low-income students will get more aid but low income may discourage college success in other ways. And when aid is determined by academic merit, the good grades and test scores that result in more aid are helpful to success through other channels as well. It is of course possible to control statistically for these confounding factors to some degree, but in the absence of perfect measurement of these factors, the causal link between aid and persistence remains in doubt.

In addition, financial aid involves choice, thus complicating the analysis. Students choose whether or not to apply. If aid is offered, they then choose how much to accept. Students' self-selection into the aid-receiving category may bias research findings. For example, if students who are more likely to apply for aid are also more likely to succeed in college (possibly due to an unobservable characteristic such as dedication or motivation), the effect of financial aid will be biased upward. Further, students can, and do, choose not to accept aid that is offered.[7] If students who are more likely to accept aid offers are also less likely to graduate, the influence of aid will be biased downward. Additional data denoting application for aid and offers of aid would improve the analysis. Unfortunately, these data are rarely available in research data sets, including the one we are using.

Clearly, there are several hurdles to jump when approaching questions about financial aid. Understanding aid and its effect on success requires sifting through the detailed processes by which students do, or do not, succeed in attaining a

---

6. Michael S. McPherson and Morton Owen Schapiro, *The Student Aid Game* (Princeton, NJ: Princeton University Press, 1998).

7. This is unlikely to happen in the case of grant aid; however, loan offerings are more likely to be declined.

higher education. Fortunately, the Public University Database affords us a new and improved opportunity to tackle this important and challenging issue.

Current Work

As we embark on the challenge of untangling the effects of financial aid, we must first recognize that it is not a random variable. It is generally determined by other factors that appear on the explanatory side of the causal relationship. In hopes of accounting for the endogeneity issue and appropriately identifying causal relationships, it is crucial to understand the extent of the endogeneity by clarifying the sources of variation in financial aid. The remainder of the paper focuses on doing just that.

Of course, the allocation of grant aid among students with differing characteristics is interesting in its own right. The question of the relative social value of providing aid to students with high financial need versus those with high academic promise has been much debated in recent years.[8] There is much interest as well in issues about the efforts universities undertake to recruit a diverse student body, and financial aid is one tool they can use in pursuing those objectives. The data presented below provide evidence on both issues.

Variations in Financial Aid

Financial aid is commonly categorized on a dichotomous basis: "need-based" or "merit-based." In reality, the delineation is not so tidy. Colleges and universities have been known to label aid allocations in one of these ways while distributing it for other reasons.[9] In this analysis, we eschew the common categorical distinction between "need-based" and "merit-based" aid. Instead, we approach the question by addressing differences in aid received based on family income and SAT® scores. These simple tabulations are expanded to include rough controls for tuition and race. In addition, we employ statistical analysis to formalize these general findings and specify, more precisely, the relationship among family, individual, and institutional characteristics and the receipt of aid.

---

8. Elizabeth A. Duffy and Idana Goldberg, *Crafting a Class: College Admissions and Financial Aid*, 1955–1994 (Princeton, NJ: Princeton University Press, 1998); Michael S. McPherson and Morton Owen Schapiro, *The Student Aid Game* (Princeton, NJ: Princeton University Press 1998); Richard D. Kahlenberg, Ed., *America's Untapped Resource: Low-Income Students in Higher Education* (New York, NY: The Century Foundation Press, 2004); William G. Bowen, Martin A. Kurzweil, and Eugene M. Tobin, *Equity and Excellence in American Higher Education* (Charlottesville, VA: University of Virginia Press, 2005).

9. Michael S. McPherson and Morton Owen Schapiro, "Watch What We Do (and Not What We Say): How Student Aid Awards Vary with Financial Need and Academic Merit," 49–73, in Michael S. McPherson and Morton Owen Schapiro, Eds., *College Access: Opportunity or Privilege?* (New York, NY: The College Board, 2006).

Our analyses show that family income and SAT scores are both significantly related to the receipt of financial aid at public research universities. When analyzed with appropriate controls, both students from higher-income families and those with lower SAT scores receive less aid than do others. Furthermore, after controlling for other sources of variation, race is found to influence financial aid significantly. Finally, variation based on income, SAT, and race differs across income quartiles and selectivity tiers. These conclusions are supported by both the tabular and statistical analyses.

Cross-Tabulations

The simplest way to approach these data is with descriptive statistics. Table 1 presents data on institutional aid, total grants, and net tuition of in-state students at 18 institutions in the Public University Database which provided financial aid data.[10, 11] All three categories are broken down by family income

Table 1. Tabulations of aid receipt for in-state students

Institutional Aid			
Income Quartile			
SAT	Q1	Q2	Q3	Q4
low	$1,654	$1,310	$579	$414
n	1,005	690	854	594
middle	$1,300	$1,012	$469	$263
n	2930	3,321	5,000	4,916
high	$1,687	$1,403	$818	$538
n	3,737	5,691	1,1278	1,6710
Total Grants			
Income Quartile			
SAT	Q1	Q2	Q3	Q4
low	$6,748	$3,512	$1,063	$738
n	1,005	690	854	594
middle	$5,993	$3,114	$1,140	$636
n	2,930	3,321	5,000	4916
high	$6,204	$3,788	$1,885	$1,203
n	3,737	5,691	1,1278	1,6710
Net Tuition			
Income Quartile			
SAT	Q1	Q2	Q3	Q4
low	$-2,876	$100	$2,371	$2,780
n	1,005	690	854	594
middle	$-2,396	$446	$2,379	$3,057
n	2,930	3,321	5,000	4,916
high	$-2,648	$-170	$1768	$2,660
n	3,737	5,691	1,1278	1,6710

10. Institutional aid includes all aid from the institution and Supplemental Educational Opportunity Grants (SEOG). Aid from the institution includes tuition waivers and, if the institution grants loans, possibly loan dollars. SEOGs are included despite the fact that they are federal dollars because their distribution is at the discretion of the school. While one might expect that institutional aid would necessarily amount to less than total grants, the inclusion of tuition waivers and possible loans prevent this inequality from holding on a few occasions. This only applies to 1,617 of 56,726 observations in this analysis, so the effect is minimal. However, it is important to note that there is more certainty about the contents of total grants than that of institutional aid. Total grant aid refers to all grants and scholarships received by a student from any source. Net tuition is defined as in-state tuition less total grant aid.

11. The analysis presented here does not treat loans as a source of financial aid (unless the institution granted loans and included these dollars in the value "institutional aid") for two reasons. First, loans need to be repaid, making them quite different from grants. Second, the amount of debt a student accrues is essentially determined by the student and his or her family (subject of course to constraints). Work-study is also excluded because students determine the amount of hours they work (up to the limit offered). In contrast, the amount of grant aid received is determined essentially by the university and other providers of aid.

and SAT scores.[12] Family income is categorized by nationally representative income quartiles.[13] SAT scores (which include ACT equivalents) are separated into three categories: low, middle, and high.[14] The average grant amount received is provided for each category; students with no aid are included in the average.

The basic statistics show that income plays an important role in determining financial aid. Within each SAT category, institutional aid and total grants consistently decrease as income increases. However, the differences in aid are much more striking at the total grant level. This suggests a greater degree of income sensitivity at the state and federal level, clearly the case of means-tested aid like federal Pell Grants.

As expected, net tuition increases with income.[15] This relationship suggests that, even when controlling for the cost of attendance, families with higher income pay more for their children's college education.

When looking across SAT categories, a somewhat unexpected pattern appears. One would anticipate a positive relationship between SAT scores and aid received, due to the influence of "merit-based" aid, yet these calculations do not consistently meet this expectation. For example, the low SAT scorers, within the lowest income quartile, receive the highest average total grant aid. However, in the other three income quartiles, the largest average aid receipt does occur in the high SAT category.

Furthermore, the middle SAT scorers typically acquire the lowest amount of institutional aid and total grants while paying the highest net price within their designated income quartile. It is surprising that universities would offer more aid to students with low test scores than to those with mid-level test scores. Analyses reported below, however, suggest that these unexpected findings do not survive the incorporation of more controls.

To enhance the tabular analysis, a rough control for race is included. Table 2 presents these statistics for white and black students alone. (The analysis reported below incorporates other racial/ethnic groups.)

Including rough controls for race resolves the concerns from Table 1. Those whom we would expect to receive the most aid, low-income and high SAT

---

12. Family income comes from the Free Application for Federal Student Aid, FAFSA. Missing observations are predicted from census tract and self-reported income data. For a more detailed description of the prediction methodology, contact the authors. SAT scores also include ACT equivalents.

13. The income data consists of family income reported on the FAFSA as well as predicted incomes. The income quartile cutoffs are $28,861, $51,854, and $82,283.

14. ACT scores were transformed into their SAT equivalents. The scores are categorized as follows: low—below 900, middle—between 900 and 1100, and high—above 1100.

15. A negative value for net tuition means that financial aid covers some living expenses in addition to tuition.

Table 2. Tabulations of aid for white and black in-state students

White Students				Black Students			
Institutional Aid				Institutional Aid			
	Income Quartile				Income Quartile		
SAT	Q1	Q2	Q3	Q4	SAT	Q1	Q2	Q3	Q4
low	$1,108	$1,059	$409	$294	low	$2,095	$1,950	$1,198	$1,159
n	240	343	573	463	n	422	188	171	80
middle	$962	$778	$352	$202	middle	$2,093	$1,989	$1,345	$836
n	1,407	2,255	3,984	4,052	n	536	421	368	329
high	$1,488	$1,258	$715	$465	high	$2,945	$3,136	$2,505	$2,407
n	2,321	4,361	9,383	1,3956	n	193	223	275	327
Total Grants				Total Grants			
	Income Quartile				Income Quartile		
SAT	Q1	Q2	Q3	Q4	SAT	Q1	Q2	Q3	Q4
low	$5,026	$2,372	$627	$541	low	$7,460	$5,094	$2,496	$1,850
n	240	343	573	463	n	422	188	171	80
middle	$4,764	$2,490	$932	$542	middle	$7,450	$4,885	$2,573	$1,622
n	1,407	2,255	3,984	4,052	n	536	421	368	329
high	$5,646	$3,424	$1,766	$1,138	high	$8,110	$6,480	$4,004	$3,476
n	2,321	4,361	9,383	13,956	n	193	223	275	327
Net Tuition				Net Tuition			
	Income Quartile				Income Quartile		
SAT	Q1	Q2	Q3	Q4	SAT	Q1	Q2	Q3	Q4
low	$-1,433	$1,041	$2,710	$2,900	low	$-3,562	$-1,261	$1,117	$2,054
n	240	343	573	463	n	422	188	171	80
middle	$-1,252	$998	$2,557	$3,129	middle	$-3,846	$-1,207	$1,018	$2,172
n	1,407	2,255	3,984	4,052	n	536	421	368	329
high	$-2,167	$172	$1,859	$2,701	high	$-4,573	$-2,783	$-228	$465
n	2,321	4,361	9,383	13,956	n	193	223	275	327

students, receive exactly that. The highest SAT category within each income quartile receives the largest amount of institutional aid and total grants while facing the lowest net price. Occasionally, it is still the case that middle SAT scorers receive less financial assistance than their lower SAT counterparts; however, this occurs with less frequency than when race controls were excluded.

The cross-tabulations leave open the possibility that the correlation between aid and SAT comes about because higher SAT students attend more expensive institutions and, therefore, receive more need-based aid. However, the net tuition cross-tabulations, which provide a control for tuition, show that high SAT scorers face substantially lower net prices. This suggests that the observed positive relationship between grant awards and SAT cannot be fully explained by high SAT students having higher need as a result of attending more costly institutions.

Finally, one should note the consistent and substantial discrepancy between aid received by white students and black students. Black students in each SAT/income category receive more institutional aid, more total grants, and face a lower net tuition. These results suggest race is an important factor when explaining variations in financial aid. Again, one must not place too much weight on such basic examination. While these findings suggest that institutions, as well as state and federal governments, are working hard to attract and assist black students, it may alternatively be the case, based only on these cross-tabulations, that black students are concentrated in states or institutions with more generous financial aid policies.

Econometric Analysis

The simple tabulations presented above give us a better understanding of the data at hand and an initial sense of variations in the distribution of financial aid. That said, there is a clear need for statistical corroboration. Thus, we turn to a more sophisticated approach, Tobit analysis.

Unlike the tabular approach, econometric analysis allows for simultaneous control for a wide array of factors. Ideally, one would control for all factors that influence variations in aid, thus isolating the specific influence of the variables of interest, family income and SAT score being central to the investigation at hand. This analysis seeks to understand the influence of family income and SAT scores by estimating financial aid receipt as a function of family income, SAT score, race, gender, and institution of attendance.[16]

As indicated in the earlier tabulations, family income is expected to correlate negatively with financial aid. With greater ability to pay should come more expectation to do so. The opposite expectation holds for SAT scores. Students with stronger test scores are expected to receive aid that reflects their greater desirability to the institution.

The influence of race and gender is harder to predict. If certain races or a particular gender are desired, this would be illustrated by the tailoring of aid packages to benefit the targeted group. The previous tabulations suggest this is the case. Similarly, institutions offer individualized sticker prices and maintain

---

16. Despite the extensive offerings of the Public University Database, this analysis faces a data limitation. The estimation could be improved by controlling for the number of siblings a student's family is concurrently putting through college. This factor is given significant weight in determination of Pell Grant allocation, a portion of total grants, and other need-based awards. These data are not available to us. Thus, the estimates in the total grants analyses may suffer from omitted variable bias.

distinct financial aid strategies; thus, they warrant inclusion as categorical "dummy" variables to control for such differences.[17]

Within the relevant sample, 57 percent of students receive some grant aid. This leaves a good many students receiving no such aid. Thus, grant aid is a limited dependent variable—a collection of observations occur at $0, and the remainder is distributed across positive dollar values. To account for this type of dependent variable, Tobit analysis is the statistical method of choice.[18] To spare the reader the mathematical detail of such analysis, it suffices to say that Tobit is effectively a combination of two statistical techniques, multiple regression and probit analysis. Thus, it estimates the effect of changes in the independent variables (income, SAT, gender, race, and institution) on the dependent variable (grant aid) as a combination of the probability of being above the limit ($0) and the changes that result when the observation is above the limit.

Consequently, one cannot simply interpret Tobit coefficients as changes in the dollar amount of grant aid that result from a one unit increase in each respective independent variable. To avoid the difficult interpretation of Tobit coefficients, we present marginal effects. The marginal effect of the continuous variables, income and SAT, suggest the change in grant aid that would result from a one-unit increase from the mean of the independent variable. The marginal effect of the categorical variables, gender and race (institutional marginal effects are not presented), suggest the difference in grant aid that would result if a student was female instead of male or black, Asian, Hispanic, Native American, or other instead of white.

Another important admonition regarding the following analyses is the potential for selection effects. As mentioned earlier, this concern arises because students choose whether to apply for aid and whether to accept it. Within this data set, only aid received is observed. If, for example, white students or male students are less likely to apply for aid and frequently appear in the raw data as having received $0, regardless of whether they would have qualified, then the Tobit results will indicate that being white or being male results in receiving less aid. Selection effects of this sort will bias down the coefficients of those subgroups that have lower probabilities of even applying for aid (other things equal). Analogously, observed financial aid awards depend on the awards students accept. So if some group of students (say, for illustration, white women) is more

---

17. The Public University Database consists of essentially one school per state. Therefore, school controls may be operating as state level fixed effects. With confidentiality restrictions in mind, the estimates for the individual schools are not reported in the discussion of results.

18. James Tobin, "Estimation of Relationships for Limited Dependent Variables," *Econometrica* (January 1958): 24–36.

likely to decline attendance if they receive low offers of aid, the data will indicate that these students tend to receive higher aid awards than others because those who received lower aid offers disproportionately declined attendance. In sum, we have to be careful in assuming that these data simply reflect the quality of the aid offers made to students with different characteristics.

Table 3 presents marginal effects from Tobit estimates of total grant aid.[19] The marginal effects in Table 3 meet the prestated expectations. The marginal effect of -0.032 on family income suggests that an increase in income of $1,000, holding all other variables constant, is associated with a $32 decrease in total grant aid. Responsibility to pay appears to increase with ability to pay. (It is important to remember that this analysis averages the effect over all students, including nonneedy students for whom a small variation in income will have no effect. Later in this paper, we will provide an analysis of the size of the effect for different income groups.)

SAT scores are positively correlated with financial aid. The marginal effect of 3.143 on SAT suggests that a 100-point increase in a student's SAT score earns them $314 of additional grant aid. Ceteris paribus, students with better standardized test scores receive more financial assistance.

Gender plays a significant role in these variations as well. All else equal, females garner more aid than their male counterparts; their marginal effect is $265. This finding is a bit surprising considering the recent feminization of the academy. One might suppose that this trend would result in greater aid being directed toward men. However, a plausible explanation is that women generally

Table 3. Tobit of total grants for all in-state students[1]

Variable	Marginal Effect	Variable	Marginal Effect
Family Income	-0.032	Hispanic	$1,833.602
	[0.000]**		[68.075]**
SAT	3.143	Native American	$1,719.105
	[0.076]**		[205.24]**
Female	$264.928	Other	$331.075
	[21.548]**		[108.15]**
Black	$2,578.518	Observations	56,457
	[63.868]**		
Asian	$651.354		
	[41.854]**		

[1] Standard errors are presented in brackets. ** indicates significance at the 1 percent level.

19. These are unconditional marginal effects calculated at the means of the continuous independent variables and at the discrete change from 0 to 1 of the categorical "dummies."

perform better than men on other measures of high school academic achievement (grades, AP* courses, etc.). Our analysis here does not control for these other factors that influence "merit," and thus may attribute this difference to being female.[20]

Last, these Tobit results lend support to the earlier conjecture that race plays a significant role in determining aid. All race/ethnicity categories experience a positive marginal effect on grant dollars compared to their white counterparts. The marginal effects suggest that a black student will receive $2,579 more in grant aid than an otherwise similar white student.

The results of the samplewide analysis are quite enlightening. However, to capitalize on the potential of the Public University Database, we turn to an income quartile-specific analysis. Table 4 summarizes the marginal effects from this analysis in which the four income quartiles are considered separately.[21]

Clearly, students in the second income quartile are affected the most by increases in income. On average, a $1,000 increase in income reduces their grant aid by $109. Students in the top and bottom quartiles do not experience much shift in grant aid as a result of changes in income. One might speculate that many students in the highest income quartile are ineligible for grant aid, and therefore changes in income of this magnitude hardly have an effect on their aid. Alternatively, many students in the bottom quartile have already maxed out the amount of grant aid they can receive; changes in income have minor repercussions here as well.

Changes in SAT scores have stronger effects on grant aid for higher income quartiles. A 100-point score increase for students in the lowest quartile only earns them $129 while a similar increase for students in the top quartile earns them $343. It is plausible that this trend represents schools' mechanisms for attracting desirable students. If students from higher income families are not

Table 4. Marginal effects of grant aid by income quartile

Income Quartile	$1,000 Increase in Family Income	100-Point Increase in SAT
Q 1	-$10	$129
Q 2	-$109	$292
Q 3	-$36	$374
Q 4	-$1	$343

20. The significance of the gender variable in fact disappeared when high school GPA was included as a control. This provides support for the hypothesis that the gender variable is capturing the effects of other ability measures. We chose not to proceed with analyses that include GPA as a control throughout our analysis because it reduced the size of the sample by nearly 50 percent. We are also concerned that the group of students for whom GPA is not reported may differ systematically from the others.

21. The complete set of Tobit results for this analysis is available from the authors.

going to receive much in the way of "need-based" aid, schools may be more likely to shower them with "merit-based" aid as a means of inducement. However, if students are likely to receive a good deal of need-based aid, the institution may be less inclined to supply additional merit-based dollars.[22]

Clearly, practices around the distribution of aid vary across family income levels. The following analysis highlights differences across institutional selectivity levels. The subset of institutions within this analysis can be divided into four selectivity tiers based on Barron's Rankings from the 1999–2000 academic year. The average SAT scores of the entering full-time first-year class are 1257, 1191, 1147, and 1111 at tiers 1, 2, 3, and 4, respectively. Table 5 summarizes marginal effects from Tobit estimates broken down by selectivity tier.[23]

An increase in income of $1,000 is associated with a reduction in grant aid of $38 for students at tier 1 schools and $25 for students at tier 4 schools. More selective schools tend to be more expensive; thus, the monotonic relationship between changes in grant aid and selectivity tier is not surprising. That said, the differences are quite small. Evidently, changes in family income do not have substantially different effects on grant aid across selectivity tiers.

On the other hand, the response of aid allocation to SAT scores varies quite a bit across selectivity tiers. A 100-point increase for a student at a tier 1 school earns him or her $102 while the same increase for a student at the tier 4 level earns him or her more than four times as much. It is likely that tier 1 schools are able to attract high-SAT students without offering much merit aid. However, at the tier 4 level, institutions are likely to make larger aid contributions on the basis

Table 5. Marginal effects of grant aid by income quartile

Selectivity Tier	$1,000 Increase in Family Income	100-Point Increase in SAT
Tier 1	-$38	$102
Tier 2	-$33	$186
Tier 3	-$31	$372
Tier 4	-$25	$472

22. Although the results are not presented here, the effects of race and ethnicity across income quartiles are also interesting. Black students, on average, garner approximately $2,000 more grant aid than their white counterparts in all quartiles. Hispanic and Native American students also acquire more grant aid than white students in all quartiles. The most variation appears for Asian students. *Ceteris paribus*, they receive less aid as they move up the income quartiles. Asian students in the lower quartiles still acquire significantly more aid than similar white students, but the trend reverses in the highest quartile where Asian students receive significantly less.

23. Again, the complete set of Tobit results for this analysis is available from the authors.

of merit in hopes of attracting stronger students and improving the institution's academic standing.[24]

Conclusions

The preceding analyses confirm the expected correlations among family income, SAT scores, and financial aid. Other things equal, an increase in family income is associated with a decrease in total grant aid. The opposite is true for increases in SAT scores.

The findings regarding race are also of interest. As seen in the simple tabular analyses, black students are receiving more institutional aid and more total grant aid than their white counterparts for all income and SAT levels. Even after controlling for the effects of tuition, gender, and institution, the Tobit estimates suggest that black students receive more grant aid on average than students in other racial categories. While black students appear to garner the largest benefits, Asian, Hispanic, and Native American students also receive more total grant aid than similar white students.[25]

A few cautionary notes regarding these findings should be noted. First, this analysis does not definitively establish causal relationships between student characteristics and receipt of aid. It simply outlines, in a predictive manner, the variations in aid that are correlated with such characteristics.

In addition, this study is based on observations of aid received, not offered. Thus, each observed aid award represents a deal between the student and the school. If students found the schools' offers to be acceptable, then they accepted and enrolled. The data we have do not explicitly convey the school's response to student characteristics, but instead those among the schools' responses that the students accepted.

These findings suggest that colleges and universities, state and federal governments, and private sources (in aggregate) are directing funding to needy and academically deserving students as well as students of color. These findings are particularly important because of the schools they represent. The public

---

24. Similar to the findings in the income quartile-specific analysis, the effects of race and ethnicity (though not presented) are of interest. Minority racial and ethnic groups received amounts of grant aid significantly different from those of similar white students at all tiers. With the exception of the "other" category, all groups receive significantly more aid than their white counterparts. Interesting variation occurs in the Asian category. Asian students at tier 1 schools receive approximately $200 more grant aid than similar white students. This amount increases as you move down the selectivity tiers, peaking in tier 3 at $1,400. This suggests that there may be a greater supply of Asian students applying to tier 1 institutions; thus, these schools do not need to offer as much monetary incentive from them to enroll.

25. This trend did not hold across income quartiles, but for the Asian category as a whole, average aid is higher.

flagship institutions present in this analysis wield great influence within their states and across the nation. It is important to understand their practices and, in turn, to understand the outcomes of their practices.

This leads us back to the bigger question. Keeping these variations in mind, what is the impact of financial aid on persistence and eventually success in college? Do the variations in aid across gender, race, income level, and selectivity tier manifest in variations in persistence into the second year (a time when high levels of attrition occur), completion of a degree, and the time it takes to complete a degree? Analyses that employ the Public University Database to explore these questions are forthcoming.

What the Gates Millennium Scholars Program Can Tell Us About Success in College[1]

▥

William T. Trent

The American Council on Education's 2002 *Increasing the Success of Minority Students in Science and Technology* reports that:

- Completers [of degree programs in science, technology, engineering or mathematics fields—STEM] were better prepared for postsecondary education because a larger percentage took a highly rigorous high school curriculum.
- Nearly all completers were younger than 19 when they entered college in 1995-96, compared with 83.9 percent of noncompleters.
- Completers were more likely to have at least one parent with a bachelor's degree or higher.
- Completers came from families with higher incomes.
- Noncompleters were more likely to work 15 hours or more a week.

The report, based on longitudinal data for 12,000 undergraduate students, also highlights other information pertaining to minority-student persistence in the STEM fields. African American and Latino/a students displayed levels of interest in majoring in the STEM fields similar to white students, but the time to degree completion is longer for those who persist, which the authors partly attributed to a difference in the rate of credit-hour completion.[2]

The current literature concludes that although great improvements have been made over the last few decades, further research must be conducted to identify additional factors that may influence a student's major choice, how these choices differ across gender, racial and ethnic lines, and what changes can be made through programs and policies to improve minority participation

1. The research reported in this chapter was supported by the Bill & Melinda Gates Foundation, support that is gratefully acknowledged. The opinions expressed in this chapter are those of the author and do not represent policies or opinions of the foundation.

2. Eugene L. Anderson and Dongbin Kim. *Increasing the success of minority students in science and technology* (Washington, DC: American Council on Education, 2006).

in the STEM fields.[3] Elaine Seymour[4] calls for coordinated reform that must occur in K-12 and higher education in an effort to expand access to the sciences for minority students, while Edward P. St. John and others[5] contend that revisions to financial aid policies and academic programs are key to attracting and retaining more minority students to fields previously dominated by whites.

In most ways, the above results regarding access and persistence in STEM fields are fundamentally no different from what we would expect the results to be for success in college, regardless of major field choice. The Gates Millennium Scholarship is not focused solely or even primarily on STEM fields but rather on increasing the pool of talented students of color regardless of field. At the same time, Gates Millenium Scholarship (GMS) applicants will have many of the academic attributes of students most likely to pursue STEM fields. When we examined the results from the ongoing research on Gates Millennium Scholars, we found that they do indeed share many of the academic credentials of students who pursue STEM fields. We also found that many of the factors that are important for success in STEM fields are just as important for success in college more generally. Paramount among the results of the GMS research thus far is very clear evidence about the primacy of preparation and the significance of quality financial aid. Other factors that tend to dominate research on retention and persistence appear to be more endogenous, meaning dependent at least in part on both preparation and quality of aid. Moreover, there appear to be both cultural differences and similarities that contribute significantly to the postsecondary success(es) of students of color.

This chapter reports the results of studies that examined college success outcomes for Gates Millennium Scholars and nonrecipient applicants, and

---

3. Jeannie Oakes. Opportunities, achievement, and choice: Women and minority students in science and mathematics. *Review of Research in Education, 16* (1990): 153–222.

Jayne E. Stake and Kenneth R. Mares. Science enrichment programs for gifted high school girls and boys: Predictors of program impact on science confidence and motivation. *Journal of Research in Science Teaching, 38* (10) (2001): 1065–88.

Elaine Seymour. Tracking the processes of change in U.S. undergraduate education in science, mathematics, engineering, and technology. *Science Education, 86* (2001): 79–105.

Edward P. St. John, Shouping Hu, Ada Simmons, Deborah Faye Carter, and Jeff Weber. What difference does a major make? The influence of college major field on persistence by African American and white students. *Research in Higher Education, 45* (3) (May 2004): 209–232.

4. Elaine Seymour. Tracking the processes of change in U.S. undergraduate education in science, mathematics, engineering, and technology. *Science Education, 86* (2001): 79–105.

5. Edward P. St. John, Shouping Hu, Ada Simmons, Deborah Faye Carter, and Jeff Weber. What difference does a major make? The influence of college major field on persistence by African American and white students. *Research in Higher Education, 45* (3) (May 2004): 209–232.

discusses the implications of these findings for higher education policy. The paper begins with an overview of the Gates Millennium Scholars program, followed by a discussion of selected research examples based on recent and ongoing research. I close with a discussion of educational and policy implications.

The Gates Millennium Scholars Program

The Gates Millennium Scholars (GMS) program seeks to increase the representation of low-income, high-ability minority students in colleges, both at the undergraduate and graduate levels. By increasing access to those who have been underrepresented in higher education over a 20-year period (2000–2020), the program seeks to diversify colleges and universities, as well as shape community and workforce leaders by administering $1 billion in scholarships established by the Bill and Melinda Gates Foundation (The Gates Foundation).

This is a multiyear, $1 billion commitment to increase access to higher education for talented students of color from low-income households who demonstrate leadership potential. To launch the program, the first cohort of recipients, funded in 2000-01, was composed of 1,430 entering freshmen, 2,406 continuing undergraduates, and 217 graduate students. Thereafter, approximately 1,000 scholarships are given each year to freshman cohorts to attend the college of their choice. Scholarships are not fixed-dollar amounts but instead are awarded to individual recipients based on "last-dollar need," which provides recipients (i.e., Gates Scholars) with greater choices in where they choose to enroll. In addition to reducing the costs of going to college (up to five years of full-time undergraduate study), the program offers funding to Gates Scholars for graduate study in one of six areas: education, library and information studies, computer science, engineering, science, and public health. In this respect, the GMS program contributes to the production of college students of color with attention to those with financial need, many of them in fields where they are underrepresented. The program also provides activities and other supports to enhance the development of minority students as future leaders. The Gates Foundation undertook a bold initiative in setting aside one billion dollars to support the college-going aspirations and interests, and success in college for our nation's underrepresented students.

Below is a bulleted description of the beneficiaries of the program, the selection criteria, and the Gates Foundation's aspirations for the recipients and the intervention. It is very important to note that the initial gift establishing the scholarship was accompanied by a commitment to learn as much as possible from the intervention in order to share the successes of the model within the philanthropy community, develop a deeper understanding of the resources students have and need in order to achieve postsecondary success, and gain insights into how better to generate leadership among a diverse set of learners. The GMS Scholarship was also intended to be "pipeline enhancing" rather than an expansion of opportunities in the traditional sense. The focus was on making a difference in the quality of the postsecondary experience.

The Gates Scholars are easily described as follows:

- Gates Scholars are students of color
  - African American, Hispanic, American Indian, Asian American, and Pacific Islanders
- Gates Scholars are talented students
  - Recipients must have a minimum GPA of 3.2
- Gates Scholars are financially needy students
  - Recipients must be eligible for a Pell Grant
- Gates Scholars must show cognitive and key noncognitive strengths as a basis for selection, including demonstration of leadership abilities and potential

The Gates Foundation's aspirations for more proximate outcomes from the intervention include:

- Increasing applicants' awareness of the "promise" of college
- Increasing the likelihood that Gates Scholars will defer loans and work while enrolled in college
- Increasing opportunities to acquire and exhibit leadership skills
- Increasing opportunity for both academic and community engagement

There is an explicit set of aspirations on the part of the Gates Foundation to facilitate the development of leaders who will impact their communities as well as the institutional and work contexts—fields—that they enter. That aspiration is manifested in a set of experiences in which the program immerses Gates Scholars, beginning with their selection as a recipient and continuing throughout their tenure as Gates Scholars.

In addition to these more proximate or short-term outcomes, the Gates Foundation has aspirations for long-term outcomes for the Gates Scholars, their institutions, government higher education policies, and ultimately the key fields into which the Gates Scholars enter and their communities. The most specific of these include:

- Gates Scholars will demonstrate:
  - High achievement
  - Optimal attainment
  - Meaningful social and civic engagement
- Colleges attended by Gates Scholars will have increased:
  - Attendance by students of color and high-need students
  - Persistence by students of color and high-need students
  - Graduation rates for students of color and high-need students
- More equal representation of low-income minority scholars in selected majors
- Change in institutions' admissions and financial aid policies
- Change in government higher education and financial aid policies
- Ultimately:
  - Communities will have more diverse leaders
  - America will have a more competitive, more diverse, more inclusive global democracy

The aspirations set forth in the framing of the intervention present a substantial challenge to determining whether both the short-term and long-term outcomes that are hoped for are being achieved. Beginning with the effort to identify the pool of potential applicants, the nature of the research and evaluation task is substantial. Fortunately, the scope and depth of the research effort needed to address the myriad questions that such an intervention generates was embraced and supported by the Gates Foundation.

The Research Challenge

The Gates Foundation recognized the critical need for research to address both basic and applied questions. Essentially, what was needed was to try to conceptualize a study and to develop a research framework that would stand the test of time; that would enable the Gates Foundation to answer the kinds of questions that, in many instances, have not been addressed before because there has been no database quite like this one, composed solely of students of color. The framework is structured in terms of basic research that addresses discipline-generated questions that are important for the subareas of sociology of education, higher education and social psychology, including questions on gender, race, class, language, and ethnicity. The framework also focuses on issues of applied research that address the following topics: questions of practice, implementation, and operation of an intervention of this magnitude; and data that would be needed to inform issues of both immediate and ongoing service delivery. The research has two broad contexts: understanding the effects of existing and newly conceptualized and measured factors that impact access, and understanding how the mechanisms of the program operation and its administration facilitates access and success.

The initial focus for this research, for both the basic and applied issues, has been to understand the treatment itself; to understand the selection process and selection criteria; to learn as much as possible about the targeted populations; and to identify technical and discipline-based matters related to the science of the research activity itself. In some instances the research employs some nontraditional questions and measures, and we don't have strong validation of those measures in the prior literature.

Following are some of the constructs comprising the research focus:

- Social, cultural, linguistic, and economic background
- Gender patterns
- Academic preparation
- High school achievement and educational contexts
- Rigor of high school curriculum
- Relevance of civic and other extracurricular leadership opportunities
- The GMS selection process
- The role of financial aid
- Mentoring
- College choice
- Transition to college
- College attendance: type and level
- Major field choice and persistence
- Undergraduate academic, cultural, and social experience
- The development of and the role of leadership
- Academic engagement
- Civic and community engagement
- Values, opinions, attitudes, and perceptions
- College graduation
- Transition to graduate school
- Graduate education: academic, cultural, and social experience
- Employment experience: high school through postgraduate career

Most of these are the standard correlates and outcome measures that are prevalent in the higher education literature. Extending beyond these traditional measures, the framework includes increased emphasis on the relevance of civic and other extracurricular leadership activities, mentoring, understanding better the transition to college, issues of major field choice, civic and community engagement, as well as on values, opinions, attitudes, and perceptions.

With the National Opinion Research Center (NORC) as the contractor for the survey-based data collection, the Gates Foundation had the opportunity to build on the kind of work that NORC is known for executing, given their tradition of working with large-scale surveys including the federal national surveys. The GMS survey conducted for the Gates Foundation contains data for both recipients and nonrecipient applicants for the award. The research findings presented are noted to indicate when they reference comparisons between recipients and nonrecipients or to a national sample.

A particularly difficult challenge for researchers striving to understand the effects of the Gates Millennium Scholars program is that the students who receive scholarships are very carefully selected, with the selection based on qualities that tend to forecast strong college performance. It is very hard, therefore, to distinguish the effects of the scholarships from the effects of being selected into the program. Much of the research described here uses sophisticated analytical and statistical techniques in an effort to address this problem. While these methods are too technical to be explained in these pages, and while they can never eliminate all uncertainties in the interpretation of these findings, the consistency of the results deriving from a range of data and approaches gives us considerable confidence in the principal conclusions. Obviously, more work on these issues would be desirable.

Correlates of Success in College: Lessons Learned

The main findings from the Gates Foundation research include the following:

- Attending a high-quality high school, taking challenging courses, and taking AP® courses matters greatly and has positive implications for persistence in college.
- Receiving the Gates Millennium Scholarship is critical for persistence overall and particularly in STEM fields.
- Receiving the Gates Millennium Scholarship is critical for choice of major and college.
- Being academically engaged is a major contributor to success in college.

- Being socially engaged is supportive of success in college.
- Receiving the Gates Millennium Scholarship enables and allows recipients to be academically and socially engaged.
- Receiving the Gates Millennium Scholarship enables and allows recipients to be more socially integrated into the college experience, which facilitates the transition to college and persistence.

The findings thus far are not very surprising. Attending a high-quality high school and taking AP courses matter greatly and have positive implications for college persistence and graduation. Receiving the Gates Scholarship is critical for persistence overall, and particularly in STEM fields. Receiving the Gates Millennium Scholarship is also critical for choice of major and for choice of college. Being academically engaged is a major contributor to success in college and being socially engaged is also supportive of success in college. Receiving the Gates Millennium Scholarship enables and allows recipients to be both academically engaged and socially engaged. I revisit the importance of this finding in the more detailed discussion of the findings below.

The *quality* of financial aid is absolutely essential. These are last-dollar scholarships that take work and loans off the table. The importance of that cannot be overestimated, especially for these students. Moreover, while we have traditionally thought of financial aid as having a largely direct effect on college access and success, the evidence here is that there are substantial indirect effects of high-quality financial aid.

We're also finding that mentoring matters, as does the campus climate. And these findings emerge in our survey results, but mainly through our focus group data collection with students. In the students' own voices they talk about the ways in which both mentoring and campus climate matter. In the pages that follow we elaborate on the above summary for selected findings.

First, the levels of success achieved by Gates Scholars from cohorts 1 and 2 are presented in Charts 1-3 on the following pages. The focus here is on graduation and retention rates. These are students who are doing quite well in terms of their persistence. Chart 1 shows the overall distribution for cohort 1 freshmen after five years in terms of actual numbers for the currently enrolled students in undergraduate school, those currently in graduate programs, alumni, and those who have deferments. In addition, there are 180 inactive students. So, the graduation rate is substantial—out of 1,423 scholars, 839 are alum—suggesting that there is reason to think that we can learn something important from studying the students and the intervention.

Chart 1. Cohort 1 Graduation and Retention Distributions

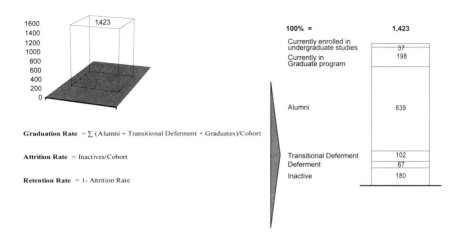

Graduation Rate = ∑ (Alumni + Transitional Deferment + Graduates)/Cohort

Attrition Rate = Inactives/Cohort

Retention Rate = 1- Attrition Rate

100% =	1,423
Currently enrolled in undergraduate studies	37
Currently in Graduate program	198
Alumni	839
Transitional Deferment	102
Deferment	67
Inactive	180

Chart 2. Cohort 1 Graduation and Retention Rates, Overall and by Gender

GMS Graduation and Retention Rates

cohort 1	All Gender	
	4-year	5-year
Graduation Rate	55.17%	80.04%
Attrition Rate (5 year)	12.09%	13.00%
Persistence Rate	87.91%	87.35%

By Gender Cohort 1	Female	Male
4YR-Graduation Rate	59.23%	45.83%
4YR-Attrition Rate	10.29%	16.67%
4YR-Persistence Rate	89.71%	83.33%

By Gender Cohort 1	Female	Male
5YR-Graduation Rate	81.74%	76.16%
5YR-Attrition Rate	10.60%	17.36%
5YR-Persistence Rate	89.40%	82.64%

ACT 2005*	
Graduation Rate- 5 year National Average	51.80%
Attrition Rate- Freshman to Sophomore (1 yr)	31.70%
Persistence Rate- Freshman to Sophomore	68.30%
2005 Retention/Completion Summary Tables, ACT	

*ACT presents results regarding five year graduation rates and freshman to sophomore retention rates at traditional "four-year" baccalaureate colleges/universities across the United States. The graduation rate information is based on the responses of 1,644 baccalaureate institutions, while the retention rate information is based on the responses of 1,450 baccalaureate institutions. *ACT News Release: College Graduation Rates Steady despite Increase in Enrollment, ACT 2005*

As reflected in Chart 2, the graduation rate for cohort 1 after four years was 55.2 percent approximately and after five years, 80 percent. The attrition rate at four years was 12 percent, rising to 13 percent after five years, yielding a persistence rate of about 88 percent. These are fairly impressive figures for students who comprise these four race/ethnic and income categories from that first cohort. Note that the Gates Scholars graduate at a rate substantially higher than the national five-year graduation rate of about 52 percent for 2005 reported by ACT. By gender, you also see the male and female four-year and five-year graduation rates were greater than those of males; 59 percent versus 46 percent at four years, but 82 percent versus 77 percent at five years. Again, females have a distinct advantage with respect to the five-year graduation rate, graduating at a rate about 5 percent higher than their male counterparts, but males have closed the gender gap by more than half, from 13 percent at the four-year mark to about 5 percent at the five-year mark. This is a substantial gain and may be a reflection of the value of the quality of financial aid.

Chart 3. GMS Cohort 2 Graduation and Retention Rates, Overall and by Gender

Graduation and Retention Rates- Cohort 2

All Gender	
cohort 2	4-year
Graduation Rate	49.80%
Attrition Rate	11.70%
Persistence Rate	88.30%

By Gender Cohort 2	Female	Male
Graduation Rate	53.32%	42.41%
Attrition Rate	10.64%	13.93%
Persistence Rate	89.36%	86.07%

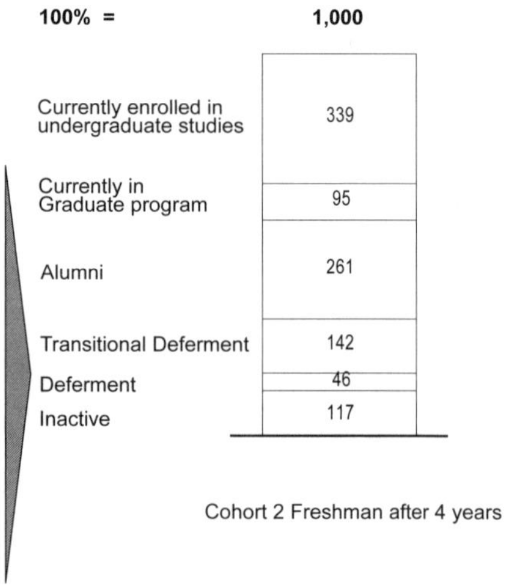

100% =   1,000

Currently enrolled in undergraduate studies	339
Currently in Graduate program	95
Alumni	261
Transitional Deferment	142
Deferment	46
Inactive	117

Cohort 2 Freshman after 4 years

Graduation and retention rates for cohort 2 shown in Chart 3. GMS Cohort 2 Graduation and Retention Rates, Overall and by Gender to those for cohort 1. The four-year graduation rate is just under 50 percent, and the attrition rate is just under 12 percent, yielding a persistence rate of about 88 percent. The female advantage at the four-year graduation mark is still quite evident, but at 11 percent is somewhat smaller in cohort 2 than in cohort 1. The graduation rates observed thus far provide strong evidence of the capabilities of the targeted student populations and strong evidence for supporting the scholarship intervention. At the same time, the female advantage enjoyed at graduation is in addition to the female advantage in initial receipt of the GMS award. Overall and across each race/ethnic category, more females than males are recipients of the award. Chart 4 presents the advantage that females enjoy as recipients, which hovers near a 70-30 split. In order to dramatically impact the gender gap at graduation, substantial progress will have to be made in addressing the gender gap in preparation for males in order for them to compete more successfully without encumbering the learning outcomes for females.

Chart 4. Distribution of Gates Scholars by Gender, by Cohort Year

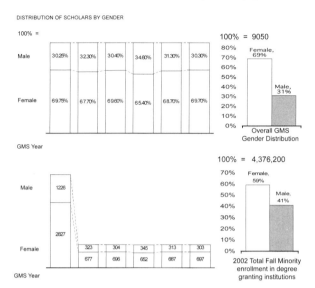

DISTRIBUTION OF SCHOLARS BY GENDER

Preparation matters

Gates Scholars mainly attend good high schools and take a challenging selection of courses. Trent examined high school attributes for GMS applicants in cohort 1.[6] That study reported that cohort 1 scholars attended high schools that generally offered four or more AP courses and that among all Gates Scholars and recipients, Asian students were more often in schools that had as many as seven or more AP courses and consequently took more AP courses. Gates Scholars and Nonrecipients were much more likely to take AP courses if they attended magnet schools but few Gates Scholars were actually enrolled in magnet schools.[7] Figures 1 through 4 provide additional details on the course-taking patterns of Gates Scholars, highlighting their precollege academic preparation.

Nearly all the Gates Scholars took three or more years of math while in high school. A large majority took four or more years (Figure 1). A substantial majority of Gates Scholars also took three years of science in high school, and many took four or more (Figure 2).

---

6. William T. Trent, Yugin Gong, and Dawn Owens-Nicholson. The relative contribution of high school origins to college access. In Edward.P. St. John, Ed., *Readings on Equal Education 20* (2004), 45–70.

7. William T. Trent, Dawn Owens-Nicholson, and M. McKillip. Looking for love in all the wrong places: High school racial composition and becoming a GMS Scholar: The implications of strategic recruitment. In William T. Trent and Edward P. St. John, Eds., *Resources, Assets, and Strengths Among Success Diverse Students: Understanding the Contributions of the Gates Millennium Scholars Program. Readings on Equal Education, 23* (New York: AMS Press Inc., forthcoming, 2008).

Figure 1. Percent of scholars taking four or more years of math in high school by minority group

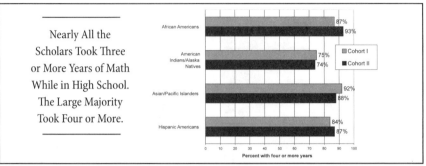

Close to 99 percent of the Scholars took at least three years of math in high school. The large majority took four or more, but the proportions vary somewhat by cohort and minority group. In the first cohort, Asian/Pacific Islanders were the most likely of any group to take four or more years of math in high school. In the second cohort, African American Scholars were the most likely of any minority group to take four or more years of math.

Source: A Portrait of the Inaugural and Second Cohorts of Gates Millennium Scholars and Nonrecipients. Michelle F. Zimkowski. The National Opinion Research Center. 2006.

Gates Scholars also took their share of AP courses while in high school. More than three out of every four Gates Scholars took at least one AP Exam while in high school; more than one out of every four scholars took four or more AP Exams. More than a fourth of the scholars in both cohorts took four or more AP Exams while in high school, but the proportions vary considerably by race/ethnic group, which is what might be expected based on prior research. The least likely to have taken as many AP Exams among the four groups in the pool of scholars are American Indians. They are most likely not to have had access to AP courses in the high schools they attended.[8]

While one proper policy response might be to create greater access to AP and other challenging courses, doing so without attending to the quality of the instruction in such courses is not likely to yield the necessary quality of preparation that will sustain success at selective institutions or in a challenging major. For example, the Illinois Education Research Council (IERC) has recently issued a report, using data on the Illinois high school class of 2000, showing the disparities in the distribution of teacher quality across Illinois high schools. The report clearly shows the very small percentages of African American and low-income students who have access to teachers in the top quartile of their teacher

8. William T. Trent, Dawn Owens-Nicholson, and M. McKillip. Looking for love in all the wrong places: High school racial composition and becoming a GMS Scholar: The implications of strategic recruitment. In William T. Trent and Edward P. St. John, Eds., *Resources, Assets, and Strengths Among Success Diverse Students: Understanding the Contributions of the Gates Millennium Scholars Program. Readings on Equal Education, 23* (New York: AMS Press Inc., forthcoming, 2008)

quality index.[9] The study also reports that students who take challenging courses like AP courses from teachers in the bottom two quartiles of the index do not reap comparable benefits compared to students who take such courses from teachers in the top quartile.

Figure 2. Percent of scholars taking four or more years of science

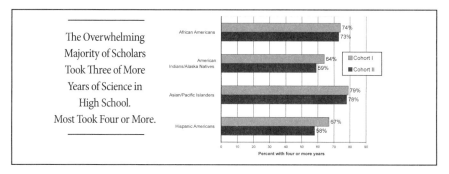

Close to 96 percent of the Scholars took at least three years of science in high school. Most took four or more. The shares vary somewhat by minority group. In both cohorts, Asian/Pacific Islanders were the most likely of any minority group to take four or more years of science in high school.

Source: A Portrait of the Inaugural and Second Cohorts of Gates Millennium Scholars and Nonrecipients. Michelle F. Zimkowski. The National Opinion Research Center. 2006.

Sylvia Hurtado posed the question regarding how these students came to know and engage in the process that would lead to their readiness for a challenging high school curriculum.[10] These are Pell-eligible students who live in largely segregated communities where the kinds of capital and networks that are often associated with taking the right courses as early as middle school are generally assumed not to be present. The Gates Scholars are mainly from families in which neither parent holds a college degree, and families where home ownership is the exception rather than the rule compared to home ownership rates for the nation.[11] We are unable at this time to explain how they became informed about making the right choices in early middle school that would allow them access to and prepare them effectively for taking the more rigorous high school classes, and we cannot rule out the possibility that the schools themselves are the source of guidance. Future research will be useful in finding out how the preparation process information was acquired.

---

9. Jennifer B. Presley, Bradford R. White, and Yugin Gong. *Examining the distribution and impact of teacher quality in Illinois.* Illinois Education Research Council. Policy Research Report: IERC 2005-2 (2005).

10. Sylvia Hurtado. The next generation of diversity and intergroup relations research. *Journal of Social Issues, 61* (3) (2005): 595–610.

11. Michelle F. Zimkowski. *A portrait of the inaugural and second cohorts of Gates Millennium Scholars and nonrecipients* (The National Opinion Research Center, 2006).

Figure 3. Percent of scholars taking one or more Advanced Placement Exams in high school by minority group

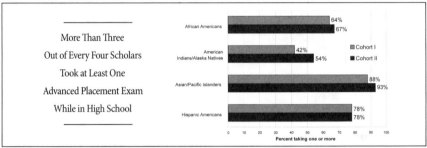

The majority of Scholars in both cohorts took at least one Advanced Placement Exam while in high school, but the shares vary considerably by minority group. In both cohorts, Asian/Pacific Islanders were the most likely of any minority group and American Indians/Alaska Natives the least likely of any minority group to take at least one Advanced Placement Exam while in high school.

Figure 4. Percent of scholars taking four or more Advanced Placement Exams in high school by minority group

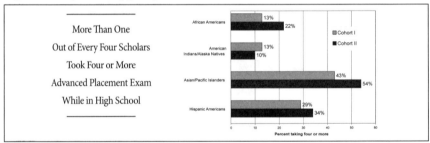

More than one-fourth of the Scholars in both cohorts took four or more Advanced Placement Exams while in high school, but the proportions vary considerably by minority group. In both cohorts, Asian/Pacific Islanders were far more likely than the other minority groups to take four or more Advanced Placement Exams. In the first cohort, American Indians/Alaska Natives and African Americans were less likely than the other minority groups to take four or more exams. In the second cohort, American Indians/Alaska Natives were the least likely of any minority group to take four or more, followed by African Americans.

- With respect to the number of Advanced Placement Exams and years of math and science taken while in high school, Asian/Pacific Islander Scholars, on average, tend to have the strongest academic backgrounds, American Indians/Alaska Natives the least strong, with African American and Hispanic American Scholars somewhere in between.

Succeeding in college and what it means

Receiving the GMS Scholarship is essential for reducing or eliminating work during undergraduate school. Not working or reducing the amount of time spent working increases time for studying and for academic and community social engagement. Overall, scholars were less likely to work than other undergraduates in the nation and their nonrecipient counterparts. Figures 5 and 6 present the descriptive findings for Gates Scholars.

Figure 5. Working for pay while in college

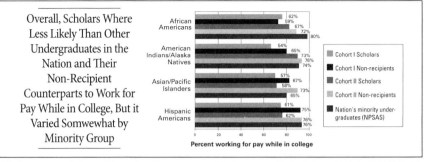

Overall, Scholars Where Less Likely Than Other Undergraduates in the Nation and Their Non-Recipient Counterparts to Work for Pay While in College, But it Varied Somwewhat by Minority Group

Percent working for pay while in college

Scholars as a whole and by minority group—with the exception of American Indian/Alaska Natives in the second cohort—were less likely than undergraduates nationwide and their respective undergraduate minority counterparts to work for pay while in school. Scholars as a whole and by minority group—with the exception of African Americans and American Indians/Alaska Natives—were also less likely than their non-recipient counterparts to work for pay even though their socioeconomic backgrounds tend not to be as strong.

Figure 6. Hours worked per week by minority group

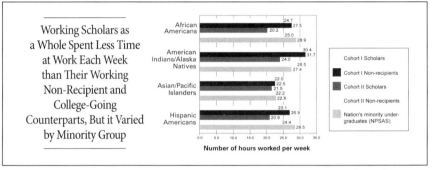

Working Scholars as a Whole Spent Less Time at Work Each Week than Their Working Non-Recipient and College-Going Counterparts, But it Varied by Minority Group

Number of hours worked per week

Working African and Hispanic American Scholars in both cohorts worked fewer hours per week than other working African American and Hispanic American undergraduates in the nation and in their respective non-recipient populations.

In the second cohort, working American Indian/Alaska Native Scholars also worked fewer hours per week than working American Indian/Alaska Native non-recipients.

It is important to understand that while many of these students are exemplary students and leaders, they may also be the healthiest individuals in their respective households and indeed in their immediate or extended families. In such cases, when these students leave their families or households to enroll in college, serious problems might be created by their absence. Many of the students may be most effective at communicating for family members who are English language learners or nonnative speakers. In addition, these are students who are responsible and can negotiate the larger civic public and private arenas. Perhaps equally or most important, the students themselves recognize the role(s) they serve in their communities and families. One of the more penetrating quotes from a recent study captures the strong sense of awareness:

"I've got to learn to stop worrying about my family. If I don't stop, I'm going to drown with them."

That's a substantial personal decision and sacrifice for any student to make, and many of these students must resolve this personal conflict by removing themselves from the family context to pursue their individual goals. Educators, especially as university-based leaders, need to understand the kinds of personal value-commitment challenges and changes that many of these students are making. I am reminded of the essay by Herbert Kohl, "I Will Not Learn from You" where the message is that some of what we might take to mean an inability to learn might better be understood as an unwillingness to discard or dismiss essential value commitments.[12] When these students make what seem to be irrational choices, a more careful consideration might yield a very different conclusion—one that is entirely rational.

Working scholars as a whole spent less time at work each week than their working nonrecipients and college-going counterparts, but patterns of working varied by minority group again. These are students who do work. The research shows that some scholars have taken out loans because they are assisting their families in meeting household expenses because their enrollment in college has taken their contribution of income out of the household. Working African American and Hispanic Gates Scholars in both cohorts, however, worked fewer hours per week than other working African American and Hispanic undergraduates in the nation and in comparison to their respective cohort nonrecipients.

Lee provides a very clear explanation of the relationship between the GMS aid and work from one of the scholars:[13]

"Before"—this is a direct quote from one of the scholars. "'Before, without the scholarship, I made work more of a priority and then school second. Although I knew school was something that was equally challenging, it's just that I needed to work, you know.' So, this puts off the focus and school is my number one priority now, you know, studying. And, you know, work is more like, you know, secondary to me now. It's more like, okay, if I really need to, I will, and I don't stress over, you know, my job as much. And it's allowed

---

12. Herbert Kohl. *I won't learn from you: and other thoughts on creative maladjustment.* (New York: New Press, 1994).

13. Malisa Lee. Achieving the impossible dream: Reflections from Gates Scholars. In William T. Trent and Edward P. St. John, Eds., *Resources, Assets, and Strengths Among Success Diverse Students: Understanding the Contributions of the Gates Millennium Scholars Program. Readings on Equal Education, 23* (New York: AMS Press Inc., forthcoming, 2008).

*me more time on my hands to be with family or even to do volunteer
work in the community, so it's great.'"*

Academic engagement by scholars compared to nonrecipients is much
higher when you examine the increased times per week when students report
being academically engaged, whether it's studying, reading, working in groups,
or meeting with a faculty member (see Figure 7). You see the set of items we
use; work with other students on schoolwork outside of class, discuss ideas from
the readings or classes with students outside of class, discuss ideas with faculty,
worked harder than you thought you could to meet an instructor's expectations,
worked on creative projects that you helped design, research or artistic. At the
high-end of time invested in academic engagement, clearly the Gates Scholars,
are advantaged in comparison to the nonrecipients. Compared to nonrecipients,
Gates Scholars are significantly more likely to report being academically engaged,
have higher grade point averages, spend more hours studying per week, have at
least one faculty member who took an interest in their development, receive
support from peers, find support in their own ethnic group, and attend to issues
of diversity on campus.

Figure 7. Self-reported academic engagement—Year 1

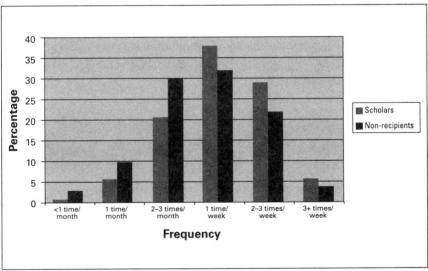

The GMS Scholarship–Quality of Financial Aid

Receiving the GMS scholarship reduces the use of loans for the recipients and
thereby reduces long-term debt. When scholars do borrow, they borrow less.
Receiving the GMS Scholarship supports the choice of a more expensive, private

four-year college. Scholars as a whole and by minority group were much less likely than their nonrecipient counterparts to take out loans for the current academic year, and when they did, they borrowed less. Chart 8 presents a summary of the findings on borrowing.

Figure 8. Loans for the current academic year by minority group

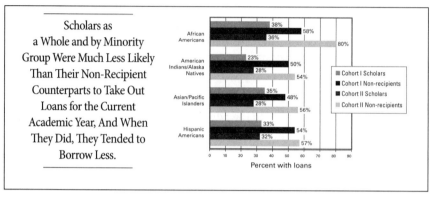

Less than one in three Scholars took out a loan for the current academic year compared to more than one out of every two non-recipients. The amount borrowed by Scholars, on average, was also considerably less than that of their non-recipient counterparts.

Scholars were also much less likely than non-recipients to report that their parents helped them out with their college expenses, especially in the first cohort.

K. L. Williams, Shouping Hu, and Edward P. St. John report that receiving the GMS award increased the probability for a low-income, high-achieving African American student to enroll at a private institution versus a public four-year college by about 8.6 percentage points.[14] Receiving this award also decreased the probability of attending a public two-year compared to a four-year public by 3.6 percentage points. These analyses confirmed that receiving the GMS award removed the financial barrier to enrollment in more expensive colleges. The implication here is that the quality of the financial aid package has a great deal to do with facilitating choice on a number of different outcomes. For example, we have fairly consistent evidence that retention, persistence, and graduation rates are greater for underrepresented students at more selective institutions. Thus, if the findings here reflect that GMS aid increases the likelihood of attending more selective institutions, then the aid has an added benefit.

---

14. K.L. Williams, Shouping Hu, and Edward P. St. John. The influence of public funding strategies on college choice: A study of low-income, high-achieving African American students. In William T. Trent and Edward P. St. John, Eds., *Resources, Assets, and Strengths Among Success Diverse Students: Understanding the Contributions of the Gates Millennium Scholars Program. Readings on Equal Education, 23* (New York: AMS Press Inc., forthcoming, 2008).

Scholarship and college reputation not only influence college destination, but also student involvement. St. John argues that the important finding from his reanalysis of cohort 1 data is that the GMS scholarships are significantly and positively associated with social integration, academic integration, and persistence.[15] Research that considers any of these measures as indicators of academic success must also consider the role and quality of finances. If there are inequalities in integration and persistence across income groups or race and ethnic groups, it is important to consider whether financial inequalities are the best explanation of differences. Failure to consider the possibility could affect findings in a more problematic way and result in blaming victims of economic policies and poverty for the consequences of those policies.

Lee provides an example here from one of the GMS respondents:[16]

> *"If you pretty much have some kind of path or goal to work towards, and you won't have to worry about well, what's going to happen next, or you know, so it's pretty much planned out and you can pretty much should be content that once you do undergrad you will continue with your education. And in the long-term you will end up accomplishing your goals and if not, it won't be due to financial reasons."*

The Gates Millennium Scholarship has been very powerful in assisting students with this notion of predictability. One of the things that economic disadvantage limits the ability to do is predict the future or, particularly, to predict a dependable future. That has a lot to do with the level of comfort and/or decrease in stress that one could have. The above quote makes clear this difference. On the one hand, quality financial aid provides the relief of knowing that things are taken care of; on the other hand, aid structured like the GMS award provides the possibility of constructing a plan for the future.

Walter R. Allen et al. have used the qualitative data generated from focus groups to explore scholars' perceptions of campus climate and their college

---

15. Edward P. St. John. Financial inequality and academic success: Academic integration, social integration, and persistence. In William T. Trent and Edward P. St. John, Eds., *Resources, Assets, and Strengths Among Success Diverse Students: Understanding the Contributions of the Gates Millennium Scholars Program. Readings on Equal Education, 23* (New York: AMS Press Inc., forthcoming, 2008).

16. M. Lee. Achieving the impossible dream: Reflections from Gates Scholars. In W.T. Trent & E.P. St. John, Eds., *Resources, Assets, and Strengths Among Success Diverse Students: Understanding the Contributions of the Gates Millennium Scholars Program. Readings on Equal Education, 23* (New York: AMS Press Inc, forthcoming, 2008).

experiences.[17] They report that roughly one-quarter of African American GMS scholarship recipients reported positive relationships with faculty at their respective universities. Concerning interaction with faculty, 27 percent of recipients indicated they discussed their ideas outside of class with faculty, at least once a week compared to 24 percent of nonrecipients.

In general, African American GMS scholarship recipients and nonrecipients expressed sizable ambivalence concerning the conduciveness of their campuses' racial climates. A slight majority of respondents felt their campuses provided an educationally conducive and racially sensitive environment. For example, in cohort 1, 54 percent felt that their university was supportive academically of students of color; however, only 46 percent indicated that their social climate was supportive. Forty-eight percent of nonrespondents reported that their campuses were encouraging academically, and 48 percent indicated that their respective social climates were supportive of students of color.

Because these conditions of climate and racial sensitivity are aspects of social integration, they are critical aspects of students' success in college. These can no longer be treated as incidental events that are soon forgotten, but rather as critical aspects of the learning environment that enhance the benefits of diversity on campus and increase the likelihood of student accomplishments.

Conclusion

There are valuable insights to be gained from the research on the GMS scholarship intervention. The easy takeaways from the current work can be quickly summarized by emphasizing the centrality of preparation and the significance of scholarship aid.

Preparation matters greatly. Attending a good school and taking a challenging curriculum supports a stronger, more successful transition to college; greater persistence to degree; and greater persistence within major, and in STEM fields in particular. Strong preparation also supports enrollment and persistence in selective colleges. Current efforts at school reform will be essential in increasing the number of high schools that can provide the high-

17. Walter R. Allen and Daniel G. Solórzano. Affirmative action, educational equity, and campus racial climate: A case study of the University of Michigan law school. *Berkeley La Raza Law Journal, 12* (2) (2001): 237–363.

Walter R. Allen and Allan M. Cartter. Saving grace: A comparative analysis of African American Gates Millennium Scholars and non recipients. In William T. Trent and Edward P. St. John, Eds., *Resources, Assets, and Strengths Among Success Diverse Students: Understanding the Contributions of the Gates Millennium Scholars Program. Readings on Equal Education, 23* (New York: AMS Press Inc., forthcoming, 2008).

quality curriculum offerings that will sustain such outcomes. It is also likely that reform in urban contexts will be even more important given the recent Supreme Court decision regarding the use of race in school assignments. Because of the strong association between high poverty, high minority concentration enrollment and deeply underresourced schools, the effort to ensure quality in the current school placements becomes much greater. At the same time, results from the GMS study also show that the majority of GMS scholarship recipients actually matriculate from majority-minority schools,[18] meaning that there are a significant number of urban schools where quality education happens daily. The results also underscore an unreported statistic here about the GMS research. For every GMS scholarship recipient in the 2006 cohort there were just under 10 candidates. In short, there are a significant number of students of color out there about whom we know very little regarding their educational attainment outcomes. Stated differently, we don't have a reliable estimate of the potential Gates Scholars, and that could be a much greater number than we are currently able to assist.

Money matters. Quality financial aid reduces worry, reduces the amount of time that students devote to working a part-time job, and reduces debt. By reducing work and worry, quality aid increases the opportunity and time for sustained academic engagement. By reducing concerns about the cost or affordability of college, quality financial aid supports the choice of a more challenging—selective—college and a more challenging college major. The evidence here is compelling in showing the broad effects of quality aid. In my estimation, the findings on engagement and its ramifications are most impressive. Many of our prior and ongoing studies of retention and persistence too often leave a disconnect between aid adequacy and the opportunity for engagement in learning, engagement in communities, or in adjusting to the new contexts. Having the time to process all that comes with the transition to college and to new ideas is an important element of intellectual growth and of individual development.

While in the main sense financial aid pays for the costs of attending college, we still have to acknowledge what economists identify as the hidden costs and social costs, some of which escape easy pricing. Kassie Freeman's study shows

---

18. William T. Trent, Dawn Owens-Nicholson, and M. McKillip. Looking for love in all the wrong places: High school racial composition and becoming a GMS Scholar: The implications of strategic recruitment. In William T. Trent and Edward P. St. John, Eds., *Resources, Assets, and Strengths Among Success Diverse Students: Understanding the Contributions of the Gates Millennium Scholars Program. Readings on Equal Education, 23* (New York: AMS Press Inc., forthcoming, 2008).

that African American students' economic barriers to higher education include insufficient funds to pay for college.[19] Similarly, Laura W. Perna's research suggests that African American students are less likely to enroll in college if they receive loans as their form of financial aid from colleges instead of scholarships or grants.[20] Jackson's research reveals that financial aid is a crucial factor for African American and Latino students' enrollment in college.[21] It is also questionable to build access on loan packages that for some—African American and Latino males in particular—may be unacceptable, based on their rational calculation about their future ability to cover the repayment based on current labor market employment patterns.[22]

The role of the GMS scholarship in opening the opportunity for students of color to attend four-year over two-year colleges and to attend more selective institutions is also compelling. The ability to do so is associated with higher completion rates and potential access to qualitatively different opportunity networks and social capital. These benefits, in turn, suggest a greater return on one's investment in education. The evidence here showing five-year completion rates hovering around 80 percent for this population of students is very compelling in regard to the benefits of the scholarship combined with high-quality preparation. It argues for a strong reconsideration of state and federal aid policies that have for nearly three decades turned disproportionately toward loans. Such policies, while perhaps steeped in the best intentions and logic, simply do not properly account for the social and economic inequalities that have hindered the populations that most need the financial aid for postsecondary education.

In closing, it remains necessary to emphasize that colleges and universities attend to the importance of engendering and nurturing a campus climate that is both welcoming and supportive to a diverse student body. This is still the case with very talented students whom we too often assume are quite capable of negotiating an academic and social space of their own, on their own. The current research on Gates Scholars suggests a different pattern, one that requires concerted effort and attention to increase the probable success of the greatest variety of students. For example, recent research supports the findings presented

---

19. Kassie Freeman. Increasing African Americans' participation in higher education: African American high school students' perspectives. *Journal of Higher Education, 68* (1997): 523–50.

20. Laura W. Perna. Differences in college enrollment among African Americans, Hispanics, and whites. *Journal of Higher Education, 71* (2000): 117–41.

21. Gregory A. Jackson. Financial aid, college entry, and affirmative action. *American Journal of Education, 98* (1990): 523–50.

22. William T. Trent, Heather Sophia Lee, and Dawn Owens-Nicholson, D.O. (2006). Perceptions of financial aid among students of color: Examining role(s) of self concept, locus of control and expectations. *American Behavioral Scientist, 49* (12) (2006): 1739–59.

above on campus climate reporting that African American students believe it is easier to approach faculty members if they are of the same race or gender; if the student has previously interacted with the professor by taking a course; and if the student's academic major is in the faculty member's department.[23]

23. Julie R. Ancis, Otis T. Griffin, Alan M. Schwitzer, and Celeste R. Thomas. Social adjustment experiences of African American college students. *Journal of Counseling and Development, 77* (1999): 189–97.

Section II:
What Do We Know About Succeeding in College?

Questioning Our Assumptions About College Requirements

James E. Rosenbaum and Lisbeth J. Goble

Each of us holds many assumptions about college based on our own observations and experiences, and we make decisions based on those assumptions. Yet American higher education has changed enormously over recent years, and many of our assumptions are no longer valid. Research can help us to question whether our most important assumptions continue to be valid, and if not, what kinds of changes to make.

This paper presents research findings that question basic premises about succeeding in college. First, it presents findings that question the assumption that college-bound students understand what colleges are and what they require. Second, it presents findings that question the assumption that colleges have a single set of requirements. These findings indicate that colleges follow different models, which are based on different assumptions about students.

This paper makes five points:

- Higher education has changed in amazing and inspiring ways.
- While many barriers have fallen, other barriers remain, and misperceptions prevent students from taking actions to overcome these barriers.
- Although the paradigm shift from blaming students to blaming colleges is probably too simple, it forces policymakers to notice abysmal degree completion rates at many colleges (both two year and four year). Multivariate analyses indicate the influence of both individual and institutional attributes.
- Despite much talk about innovations in private colleges and many studies of private college effects, research has not described these innovations. This paper summarizes some findings contrasting procedures in private and public two-year colleges which may account for higher completion rates at private colleges.
- Although these discoveries suggest hopeful directions for policy, we suggest some reasons why heavy-handed one-size-fits-all policies are not likely to encourage such innovation, but may instead create harmful unintended consequences.

Amazing Change

First, it is important to understand the revolutionary changes that have occurred in higher education. These changes have greatly increased access and led to entirely new groups of students attending college. Although percentages are often mind-numbing, these statistics are mind-blowing:

- 95 percent of high school seniors plan to attend college.

- Over 80 percent of high school graduates attend college in the eight years after graduation.

- There is little race gap in college attendance; 83 percent of white high school graduates attend college, 80 percent of blacks and Hispanics do.[1] While there are big gaps in getting high school diplomas, and big gaps in getting college diplomas, there are not big racial gaps in college attendance.

For anyone aware of college realities just one or two decades ago, these results are truly amazing and inspiring. However, big problems remain in terms of degree completion, as we note below.

Many Students Need a Reality Check

New opportunities often create new problems. College degree completion is a big problem, and there is a great chain of blame: reformers blame high schools and schools blame families. However, the evidence suggests that the problem partly arises from the poor articulation between high school and college, which prevents students from seeing incentives for high school effort.

Analyses of national data and detailed interviews in local areas indicate that students have many misperceptions.

Students believe that when they enter college, they will take college classes immediately. Since half of high school seniors have academic skills below the tenth-grade level, it's not surprising that over 60 percent of community college students and 25 percent of four-year college students are in at least one remedial class.[2] Many community colleges offer remedial classes for "college students" with academic skills below the eighth-grade level. Many students are enrolled in three or more remedial classes; they are barely in college. They are taking high school classes but getting no college credits, and often they do not realize this.[3]

---

1. Adelman, Clifford. 2003. "Principal indicators of student academic histories in postsecondary education, 1972–2000." Washington, DC: US Department of Education. Table 2.7

2. Cohen, A.M. and F. Brawer. 2003. *The American Community College* (4th edition). San Francisco: Jossey Bass.

3. Rosenbaum, James E., Regina Deil-Amen, and Ann E. Person. 2006. *After Admission: From College Access to College Success.* New York: Russell Sage Foundation.

Community colleges give placement tests which determine whether students are in college credit classes and how long it will take to get a degree. Many students don't anticipate this test, either in high school or on the day they arrive at college. These students don't spend even a minute preparing, and many don't realize its importance even after taking it. Often, students show up to register and are told to fill out many pieces of paper, including the placement test. One student took the test with a baby on her lap and her ride urging her to finish quickly. In an effort to hurry, she shaved minutes off the test, which potentially added months or years to her time in college.

Students don't know how long their degree will take. How long does it take to get a two-year degree? Three and a half years for full-time students to complete an associate's degree is typical in local studies and national data.[4]

Students believe that if they enroll in college, they are likely to get college degrees. This is not true. Degree completion is a problem. Only 23 percent of students at two-year colleges graduate in three years and less than 46 percent graduate in six years.[5]

High school seniors' understanding may not be improved by state exit exams. Exit exams often add to the misunderstanding. Exit exams required for high school diplomas are usually set at levels that most students can pass. New York State tried higher standards, but caved in because it is politically untenable to stop 60 percent of seniors from graduating.[6] As a result, exit exams' standards are far below what college classes require. Students think they are prepared for college because they pass state exit exams in May, but many of them will fail college placement exams three months later.[7]

Why Bother to Study?

Many students do not see incentives for high school achievement. Two different studies found that 40 percent of college-bound students say that high school is not relevant.[8] While many low-achieving seniors plan college degrees, 80 percent fail to complete any degree in the next eight years.[9] Many get few college credits,

4. Ibid. 2006.

5. Bailey, Thomas, Davis Jenkins, and Timothy Leinbach. 2005. "Is student success labeled institutional failure?" Working Paper No. 1, Community College Research Center, Teachers College, Columbia University, New York City.

6. Arenson, Karen. 2003. "New York to lower the bar for high school graduation." *New York Times*, October 9, 2003, p.1.

7. Rosenbaum, James E., Regina Deil-Amen, and Ann E. Person, *After Admission: From College Access to College Success* (New York: Russell Sage Foundation, 2006).

8. Ibid; Steinberg, Lawrence. 1996. *Beyond the Classroom*. New York: Simon & Schuster.

9. Rosenbaum, James E. 2001. *Beyond College for All: Career Paths for the Forgotten Half.* New York: Russell Sage Foundation Press.

and others get zero credits. However, because they aren't aware of placement tests, remedial classes, or poor graduation rates, students don't anticipate these risks, don't see incentives for effort, and don't take advantage of the opportunity to prepare academically in high school. Even ambitious students aiming for selective four-year colleges may be tempted by the easy route which requires less sacrifice of time, effort, and social life.

What reforms can fix these misperceptions? Reformers often try to threaten high school staff to improve students' achievement. But these reformers rarely notice that students don't see incentives. Can teachers improve achievement when students see no incentives to exert effort? Ironically, incentives do exist, but students don't see them. The solution requires systemwide policies that inform students.

Three Reforms

There are three elements for reform:

1. Articulation between high school and college—high school students need clear information about what college requires.
2. High school students also need advanced notice of how they are doing. Students take many tests, but none tell them whether they are prepared for college credit classes. If college placement tests were given in high school, students could tell if they will be taking high school courses when they get to college.
3. Students also need to know how the standards for college credit classes vary across different colleges and programs. An associate's degree in health, business, or technical fields prepares graduates for jobs with good pay, steady employment, and advancement potential, and these programs may have different academic prerequisites.

In sum, vastly expanding opportunity has created new problems. The changes have been systemwide, so the solutions must be systemwide. Accountability reforms which narrowly blame specific institutions don't fix the system, and they don't address the widespread problem of student misunderstanding. Colleges need to work together to create clarification of these issues.

Who Is Responsible, Institutions or Individuals?

The third topic is to examine how institutions vary in their degree completion rates for various groups of students. Traditionally, research has been concerned with college degree completion, however most of the focus was on which individuals succeeded in completing degrees, with an implicit presumption that failure was largely the fault of individuals. In recent years, some reformers have turned this upside down; they place the entire blame on colleges, and ignore individuals' contribution to their own outcomes. This is an amazing paradigm shift—from totally blaming students to totally blaming colleges. Some reformers want to hold colleges accountable for getting all students to graduate. Other reformers want students to choose colleges based on their graduation rates. They argue that colleges with poor graduation rates will be forced to improve or few students will choose to enroll there.

The reformers certainly have a point, the traditional focus on blaming individuals exclusively was clearly too narrow. However, the opposite is also too narrow and the unfairness of either position is obvious. The reformers say nothing about student attributes. They do not consider the possibility that graduation rate targets might push colleges to avoid enrolling high-risk students, especially if high stakes are attached. Yet the former exclusive focus on blaming students is probably mistaken—colleges may have some influence, and colleges could probably take some actions to improve students' degree completion.

Despite flaws in the blame attribution, the reformers are right to be concerned about college responsibility. Degree completion rates at some colleges are abysmal. Analyzing degree completion rates, those completing degrees in 150 percent of the expected time, for the universe of colleges with federal institutional data (the Integrated Postsecondary Education Data System or IPEDS), we find that one-fifth of two-year colleges have less than a 17 percent graduation rate in three years (for associates' degrees, which are intended to take two years). Four-year colleges are only a little better. One-fifth of four-year colleges have less than a 33 percent graduation rate in six years (where a bachelor's degree is intended to take four years). Analyzing a national sample of high school seniors (the National Education Longitudinal Study or NELS:88-00), we are able look at individual degree completion for a longer period (up to eight years after entering college). While rates improve, they still remain below 50 percent for many colleges attended by these students. Moreover, many students expect degrees on the traditional timetables, and colleges don't generally correct these expectations.

In addition, institutional differences have a strong impact even on well-prepared students. Restricting our analysis only to higher achieving high school seniors (top third of high school achievement), we find that their degree completion rates eight years later vary greatly according to the colleges they attended. The institutional graduation rate (calculated based on all students) strongly predicts degree completion for high-achieving students. Table 1a shows that of the high-achieving students starting at four-year colleges, only 38 percent of those at colleges in the bottom quintile of graduation rate complete a bachelor's degree or higher. For a high-achieving student in the middle quintile colleges, the number increases to 62 percent and for those in the top quintile colleges, 89 percent attain a bachelor's degree or higher. For high-achieving students who start in two-year colleges, the comparable rates are 43 percent, 64 percent, and 90 percent (see Table 1b). In other words, even for high-achieving students, who are relatively well-prepared for college, colleges' average degree completion rates strongly predict these students' degree completion.

Obviously, one cannot necessarily infer causality. These colleges may be doing something different which affects students' completion or they may be attracting students who have some other disadvantages that impair their completion.

There are other reasons why we must be cautious about taking actions. While the average four-year college has 18 percent underrepresented minorities, the colleges with the worst graduation rates have 36 percent underrepresented minorities. Clearly we don't want high-stakes accountability policies to shut down the colleges that offer the most opportunities to these students. More generally, if forced to get better graduation rates, colleges will shift to admitting students with fewer disadvantages, and students who attended weaker high schools will be offered less access to college.

Moreover, multivariate analyses that examine individuals' degree completion find that both individual and institutional attributes have significant impact.[10] Individuals' gender, socioeconomic status (SES), background, academic achievement, and sometimes race have significant impact in most models. However, even after controlling for these individual attributes, some institutional aspects (including college size and resources) have strong significant impact on individuals' chances of completing degrees.

Unfortunately, these national data lack indicators of institutional procedures that may influence individuals. We must turn to institutional studies to get more detailed understanding of what procedures colleges may use to improve students' success.

Innovation in College Procedures

Finally, we consider alternative college procedures that might improve outcomes. While studies have tried to test whether private colleges have better outcomes, there has been little effort to learn what innovations are used in private

---

10.   Bailey, Thomas, Davis Jenkins, and Timothy Leinbach. 2005. "Is student success labeled institutional failure?" Working Paper No. 1, Community College Research Center, Teachers College, Columbia University, New York City; Goble, Lisbeth Ann, E. Person, and James E. Rosenbaum. 2007. "Institutional Characteristics and Degree Completion Across Student Types." Paper presented to the American Education Research Association.

colleges that could be adopted in community colleges. We conducted carefully controlled statistical studies using propensity score methods on national data which found much higher degree completion rates at private colleges.[11] We also did detailed studies to examine whether private two-year colleges used different procedures to improve students' college success. Although we studied two-year colleges, our results may help four-year colleges consider their assumptions and alternative procedures.

We focused on two-year colleges because they are heavily attended by disadvantaged students. They are also increasingly chosen by middle-class students. About half of all college students attend two-year colleges. Although public two-year colleges, commonly called "community colleges," enroll 90 percent of two-year students, private two-year colleges offer an interesting alternative model. We studied what we call "occupational colleges": accredited private two-year colleges that offer occupational programs. These colleges are unlike most private two-year colleges which are not accredited, but they are like community colleges in offering similar accredited occupational programs and enrolling highly similar students. We tried to learn whether any procedures might explain why the occupational colleges we studied have higher degree completion rates, and whether these procedures might be applicable in community colleges.

We studied seven community colleges and seven occupational colleges in a large metropolitan region. Analyzing interviews with administrators, teachers, and students, as well as surveys from 4,400 students, we discovered many kinds of student problems at our community colleges that were much less common at the occupational colleges. In addition, the occupational colleges in our sample used innovative procedures designed to reduce these student problems. We suspect the average community college and other colleges could benefit from some of these procedures, especially in assisting disadvantaged students.

First, while the community college students struggle to pay tuition, we found that the occupational colleges devise procedures that allow low-income students to pay their higher tuitions. How can low-income students attend more expensive private schools? While few of the community colleges helped students get financial aid, nearly all of the private two-year colleges provide such help. The tuition difference between public and private colleges averages $9,000; however, federal Pell Grants and state grants can substantially reduce that difference—in Illinois, the difference is entirely eliminated. However, the application forms

---

11. Stephan, Jennifer L. and James E. Rosenbaum, 2005. "College Degree Completion: Institutional Effects and Student Degree Likelihood" Paper presented to the Annual Meetings of the American Sociological Association, Philadelphia, PA. August 12, 2005.

are complex, and many students cannot complete the forms by themselves. One to two hours of staff time helping students apply for financial aid produces $9,000 per year over the next two years. Community colleges could use the same procedures, but they don't.

Second, we find that the community colleges created barriers by not offering any structure to guide students' choices. In our interviews, many students report that they mistakenly choose courses that don't count for their degree, risk failure in courses that are too hard, waste time in courses that are too easy, waste time because required courses are not offered when needed or conflict with their job or childcare time schedules. This is made worse because class schedules change every term, creating new time conflicts.

In contrast, our occupational colleges offered highly structured package-deal programs that avoid poor choice and wasted time. These programs set clear goals, skill requirements, and a package of courses for each goal. They also make sure the right classes are offered when needed. For students with spotty preparation, common class schedules give all students a shared background for detailed class discussions, and also permit clear promises to employers about what all program graduates know. Part of the package deal is that when students sign up for a program, they commit to a package of courses and also to predefined time slots that don't change each term. They know from the outset exactly which hours are devoted to school.

Obviously, community colleges can't do this for every little niche program, but they could do it for a few programs in major areas. These programs would require adequate preparation and full-time studies; in return, they could promise dependable degree progress and cohort support.

Third, we find that many of the community colleges also create barriers by letting students make choices on their own without adequate advice. They assume college students can get information on their own, so they skimp on counselors. Typical counseling ratios are 1,000:1.[12] We find that students make mistakes because they don't realize they need advice, they can't get advice in time, or they get mistaken advice. Students get to make their own choices, but the result is misinformed choice, many mistakes, and serious delays in progress.

In contrast, the private colleges we studied tend to invest a lot in counseling, even though they are very cost-conscious. Instead of relying on students to initiate advising, their occupational colleges have frequent mandatory group counseling which makes sure students take appropriate courses. These sessions also create peer cohorts which provide information and support. In addition, these colleges

---

12. Rosenbaum, James E., Regina Deil-Amen, and Ann E. Person. 2006. *After Admission: From College Access to College Success.* New York: Russell Sage Foundation.

have student information systems which detect problems quickly, and advisers contact students at the first sign of difficulty before problems become serious. Also, the counseling office is centrally located so students can drop in easily on the way to class.

Although this advising does not require professional training, it does have costs. However, community colleges need to realize the costs of students' mistakes on students' progress.

This point brings us back to the issue of unwarranted assumptions. In all areas, while many community colleges mistakenly assume students can handle these tasks, the occupational colleges in our study do not. The occupational colleges devise college procedures that make success more likely in each domain. The average community college offers traditional procedures for nontraditional students, but these procedures don't match students' needs.

This makes us wonder whether four-year colleges' traditional procedures match the needs of their students, including their nontraditional students. Do students know how to choose a major and career path? Do they understand the course catalog, their major requirements, how they are progressing, and what they must do to complete their degree? Do they see options? If students fail a math class because they are not good with proofs, do they realize that applied math doesn't require proofs? Can they seek out help from counselors on their own, and are counselors available and knowledgeable on their major and career requirements? Do course offerings get in the way of timely completion?

These questions are important, but rarely asked. Although the focus on specific occupational goals doesn't always apply to four-year colleges, a structural approach (structured freshman curriculum and structured guidance process) may help students to make appropriate choices when they have difficulty getting good advice at home. Even liberal arts curricula can be structured. St. John's College provides an example of highly structured liberal arts curriculum that is likely to reduce students' mistakes and give all students a common background to build on.

Conclusion

In sum, a lot of evidence suggests that poor articulation between K–12 and college contributes to poor incentives. We have suggested giving placement exams in high school to warn students about the standards they will face and in what areas they need work. Since we currently have little knowledge about whether placement standards differ in different colleges and different programs, some research is needed before we can implement this.

We have some evidence that community college students make many mistakes which hamper their progress. We have strong evidence that the best occupational colleges have much better completion rates than community colleges, and we have some evidence that these occupational colleges' procedures may reduce these mistakes. We suspect the procedures and underlying philosophies may translate to community colleges, but we don't know this for sure.

The accountability movement suggests actions which can make big changes, but can also do unintended harm. Accountability threats by themselves are not likely to encourage the kinds of innovations we have noted, because currently they're not even recognized as options, and no one knows exactly how to implement them in new settings or how they will work. However, if accountability punishes colleges for not meeting achievement goals or "growth targets," then colleges may take fewer risks with students who have shown poor growth in the past. In other words, accountability threats may only curtail opportunities for students from poor high schools. No one wants that.

Moreover, since half of high school seniors have achievement below the tenth grade level, the accountability goals for colleges are not likely to exceed twelfth grade skills. Do we want to push colleges to be high schools, and reward them only for strong remedial programs?

Currently, various kinds of colleges enroll different kinds of students, with different levels of prior achievement and different goals. We desperately need to learn more about this variation, and how to serve the various kinds of students and the various goals.

The United States has the best universities in the world and has a bold second chance system that has accomplished revolutionary changes. Both of these can be improved, but until we understand the variation among colleges, a one-size-fits-all accountability model that ignores key distinctions is likely to do more harm than good.

Colleges as we have known them for the last 40 years were primarily designed for middle-class students who got advice from informed parents. Today most students are not like that and even traditional four-year students are not completing degrees within six years. The traditional college system doesn't work well for this new kind of student and perhaps even for many traditional students. When we talk about college, we think about the colleges we attended years ago or the colleges we work at now, but "college" means something different to students, parents, and policymakers who deal with the colleges attended by most students today. We have to increase our awareness of the problems that arise, and we have to consider other options that might work better. Comparisons between four-year colleges and colleges in other sectors may shed light on common problems and may even suggest possible solutions.

Table 1a. Percent of individuals completing a B.A. or higher by high school achievement status and institutional graduation rate at the student's college—4-year colleges (*n*=4130)

	Low Achievers	Middle Achievers	High Achievers
Bottom Quintile	15%	20%	38%
Second Quintile	28%	50%	60%
Third Quintile	37%	50%	62%
Fourth Quintile	54%	72%	72%
Highest Quintile	64%	73%	89%

Table 1b. Percent of individuals completing an A.A. or higher by high school achievement status and institutional graduation rate at the student's college—2-year colleges (*n*=2730)

	Low Achievers	Middle Achievers	High Achievers
Bottom Quintile	22%	33%	43%
Second Quintile	22%	42%	55%
Third Quintile	13%	44%	64%
Fourth Quintile	17%	41%	75%
Highest Quintile	32%	50%	90%

Measuring College Success: Evidence and Policy Challenges[1]

Sarah E. Turner

Answering the question, "Why is understanding college success so hard?" begs the fundamental question of what is "success in college." Surely "success in college" is much richer and more complicated than simply receiving a degree, ideally in four years, and the measure should capture the breadth and depth of academic accomplishment as well as broader personal growth in areas like leadership.

Still, putting aside the larger philosophical questions, it is expeditious to adopt a simple definition focused on measurable collegiate attainment expressed as the B.A. completion rate and the time taken by students to complete their degrees. On both counts, the data are clear in pointing to some erosion in outcomes over the last three decades, with the rate of college completion conditional on enrollment falling and the time taken to finish a B.A. degree on the rise. What is more, there is considerable variation in expected outcomes depending on where one starts college, with these differences increasing somewhat in recent years. In the first section of this paper, I review some of the basic evidence.

Even as the descriptive data on outcomes are relatively uncontroversial, if somewhat sobering, the social science task of explaining differences among individuals and across collegiate institutions is a daunting challenge. In the second section of this paper, I "round up the usual suspects" including differences in student achievement, changes in the capacity of individuals to finance college, and changes in the level of resources at collegiate institutions. Yet, at the end of the day, one is bound to regard the evidence as far from complete or definitive.

So, one might ask why is understanding the determinants of college completion or time to degree so difficult? One answer is "selection." Why some individuals succeed and others do not may have more to do with hard-to-observe individual differences in motivation or preparation than collegiate services. Absent pure random assignment,[2] it is hard to know whether institutional differences in

---

1. This paper was prepared for the Spencer Foundation Conference "Succeeding in College: What It Means and How to Make It Happen." I thank the participants for their helpful comments. Many of the empirical results presented in this paper are from the paper "Understanding the Increased Time to the Baccalaureate Degree," which is coauthored with Michael Lovenheim and John Bound.

2. Even at the extreme of random assignment, it may be hard to infer the causal effect of college as it is hard to imagine a true double-blind experiment of sufficient scale to allow for the variation in how college affects different groups.

completion rates are caused by programmatic differences among institutions or preexisting differences in student characteristics. Moreover, the complexity of the collegiate production process makes it very difficult to understand what policies really change outcomes. The final section of this paper explores these challenges and discusses some potential research and policy strategies to overcome them.

The State of Play: Completion Rates and Time to Degree

Overall completion and time to degree

Starting college is far from an assurance of college completion. For the cohort graduating from high school in 1992 and observed in the National Education Longitudinal Survey (NELS:88) panel, only 45.3 percent of initial college participants completed a degree, with this number down somewhat from the 51.1 percent completion rate observed for the class of 1972 (Bound, Lovenheim, and Turner, 2007).[3]

In presenting completion rates, note at the outset that not everyone entering college sets out to complete a B.A. degree, though expectations tend to far exceed the actual results.[4] What is more, it would not be a desirable policy objective to promote increased B.A. attainment as a goal unto itself. Surely some attrition from college is desirable if individuals have different rates of return to investments in college and, perhaps, some discover early on that college is not for them. Yet, it remains something of a puzzle that the economic rate of return to college and, particularly, completion of a B.A. degree has increased to such a high level in recent years without compensating improvements in completion rates.

In referencing the completion of a B.A. degree, the reference period is generally a four-year norm, corresponding to approximately 120 credit hours. But, for recent college graduates, less than half (43.6 percent for the 1992 high school cohort) completed in this period, which is down appreciably from the level of about 57 percent observed for the 1972 cohort (Table 2). What is visible in Figure 1 is the shifting of the distribution of completion times to a greater concentration in years five, six, and seven for the most recent cohort.

---

3. John Bound, Mike Lovenheim, and Sarah Turner. 2007. "Understanding the Increased Time to the Baccalaureate Degree." Mimeo.

4. Avery and Kane (2004) compare expectations for college enrollment and collegiate attainment in Boston area high schools. Measured in the fall of senior year, they found that students in both an inner-city Boston school and a suburban high school had very high expectations for attainment, with more than 70 percent of the students in the urban school and about 81 percent of students in the suburban school expecting to complete at least a B.A. degree.

Chris Avery and Thomas Kane, 2005. "Student Perceptions of College Opportunities" in C. Hoxby, Ed. *College Decisions: How Students Actually Make Them and How They Could.* University of Chicago Press for National Bureau of Economic Research.

Completion and degree by type of institution

Given the heterogeneity in U.S. higher education, it is a mistake to focus too much attention on a "single number" summarizing outcomes for all students at all institutions. The empirical point needs to be stated very clearly: there are substantial differences among students and different types of collegiate institutions in completion rates and measured time to degree.

Organizing the data by where students start college, completion rates for the 1992 cohort range from 78.2 percent for private colleges and universities to 56.7 percent for four-year public colleges and universities to 17.4 percent at community colleges. As is apparent in Table 1, these differences have widened over time with completion rates for students starting at private institutions improving since the 1972 cohort while the completion rates for students starting at community colleges have eroded. What is not clear from these data and will be the focus of discussion in the subsequent section is whether these changes are driven by changes in the operation of colleges and universities or changes in the characteristics of students entering college.

Turning to the time-to-degree outcomes, there are also sharp differences by institution type in the distributions of time to degree, with substantial erosion in four-year completion at public institutions at both the four-year and two-year levels. For students starting at public four-year institutions, the proportion of B.A. recipients receiving degrees within four years dropped from 54.6 percent to 37.1 percent between the 1972 and 1992 cohorts. For students starting at community colleges, the four-year completion rate declined from 35.9 percent of B.A. recipients in 1972 to 21 percent in 1992.

Making yet finer distinctions among colleges and universities within sectors, Bound, Lovenheim, and Turner (2007) show that the most selective public universities actually reduced time to degree and increased completion rates over this interval. But substantial variation in outcomes also exists among broadly similar types of schools. Looking at outcomes at institutions likely chosen by students from the Chicago Public Schools, Roderick and coauthors (2006)[5] show substantial differences in six-year graduation rates for students from similarly regarded high schools. To illustrate, while 52.9 percent of students graduate in six years from Northern Illinois University, the comparable rate is 15.2 percent at Chicago State University.

---

5. Melissa Roderick, J. Nagaoka, and E. Allensworth. 2006. *From High School to the Future: A First Look at Chicago Public School Graduates' College Enrollment, College Preparation, and Graduation from Four-Year Colleges.* Consortium on Chicago School Research.

Explaining Collegiate Outcomes

In thinking through the determinants of time to degree, there are multiple forces affecting outcomes including both student preparation and course offerings at the institutional level. In this section, I consider the alternative theoretical explanations combined with the available empirical evidence.

Student Characteristics

Precollegiate student achievement affects the extent to which college students will require remediation, the number of courses students will likely be able to manage during a term and, ultimately, the optimal level of collegiate attainment. Differences in precollegiate achievement likely explain much of the differences across institutions in outcomes. What is more, as the economic benefits of college education have increased in recent decades, more students find it worthwhile to attend and complete college. These students drawn into college may be less prepared than students from earlier cohorts, and therefore may have somewhat lower completion rates and longer time to completion.

While explanations focusing on the changes in the characteristics of new entrants to the collegiate pool have some theoretical appeal, there is little empirical evidence to suggest that these changes in characteristics are of sufficient magnitude to explain the observed deterioration in time-to-degree and completion-rate outcomes. Bound, Lovenheim, and Turner (2007) use data from the 1972 and 1992 cohorts to address the counterfactual question of what would have been the expected pattern of completion if the distribution of achievement and other characteristics for the 1992 cohort was reweighted to reflect characteristics observed in 1992. The results of this analysis are clear in rejecting the hypothesis that changes in the level and timing of completion can be explained by changes in student characteristics.

Institutional Resources

An alternative explanation for changes in collegiate outcomes looks to changes in the supply-side of the higher education market. At issue is whether the distribution of students among institutions of different resource intensities has changed or whether, within institutions, there have been reductions in resources per student.

Observing that tuition payments cover only a fraction of the total cost of providing undergraduate education and that public subsidies are unlikely to adjust fully to changes in demand, Bound and Turner (2007) posit that "crowding" may have increased in higher education as institutions enroll more students at lower resource intensity.[6] The result is that queuing and enrollment limits affect the pace of degree receipt and overall college completion rates.

Using changes in the size of a college-age cohort within a state as indicators of demand shifts, Bound and Turner (2007) and Bound, Lovenheim, and Turner (2007) provide convincing empirical evidence of the link between cohort size and increased time to degree and reductions in completion rates. Less formally, there is a growing set of examples from states experiencing significant growth in enrollment demand of the degree to which public supply of opportunities has not responded in full, generating demonstrable queuing and excess demand. Consider the following press accounts from the high population growth states. Writing about constraints in California in the *Chronicle of Higher Education*, Blumenstyk (1991) summarizes the collision between open access policies and high student demand:[7]

> Under a law passed more than 30 years ago, qualified students in California are promised admission to the University of California, to California State University, or to a community college.

> The law remains in effect. But already this academic year, eight institutions in the state-university system have announced they will not accept any new applicants in the spring semester, and the president of the University of California has said that system may soon start rejecting qualified applicants.

> Community colleges have yet to turn students away, but a legislative staff member says the absence of formal enrollment caps is "just a facade."

> Students are being admitted, "but when they go to register for classes there just aren't any," says Ann Blackwood, who works for the Assembly Committee on Higher Education.

States like Utah, Florida, and North Carolina have also faced conditions of considerable excess demand in recent decades manifested in the absence of physical space sufficient to provide the necessary course offerings as illustrated by the case from Utah below:

---

6. John Bound and Sarah Turner. 2007. "Cohort Crowding: How Resources Affect Collegiate Attainment." *Journal of Public Economics, Vol. 91* (5–6): 877–899

7. Goldie Blumenstyk. 1991. "Public Colleges Battered by Recession Turn Away Thousands of Students Higher admissions standards among the methods employed" *The Chronicle of Higher Education.* (November 13)

Last year's dilemma was finding enough faculty members to open extra classes. This year, lack of space is the main constraint, said Lynn Cundiff, president of SLCC [Salt Lake Community College], which is reporting a 14 percent hike in the head count. Last year at this time, SLCC counted 19,759 students. This year, 22,533 have registered.

"We've got cars parked everywhere," even on the soccer field, said Cundiff. "We don't have classrooms to put [students] in."

The college is renting space from the LDS Institute on campus and even has held one class in an outdoor amphitheater—a quick fix that works now, said Cundiff, "but not when winter rolls around." (*The Salt Lake Tribune*, Stewart, 2001)[8]

To the extent that time to degree has increased and completion rates have decreased because public colleges and universities are stretched too thin, it is worth asking why there are not market adjustments to eliminate queuing. The observation of students waiting in line for classes might be taken as a first-order indication of inefficiency. Adjustments often don't occur because public college and university administrators have few degrees of freedom with which to maneuver. First, with limited public funding—and little inclination to increase resources for colleges at the state and federal levels—it is simply not possible to add additional course offerings or accommodate more students without increasing class sizes. Secondly, college and university managers have little control over price, as tuition levels at public universities are often set through political process at the state level. Finally, at many of the institutions with low completion rates and high time to degree, "open access" or admission of all students meeting basic criteria is part of the stated institutional mission, with administrators likely to face objections from political constituencies if the college ceased to be seen as "accessible."

Potential Credit Constraints

The third and, perhaps, more difficult to assess explanation for changes in the timing and rate of college completion is the role played by increases in college costs, combined with stagnation in family income for families below the median. With college tuition and the associated costs of room and board rising over the last several decades, it is plausible that students are increasingly constrained and

---

8. K. Stewart. 2001. "Utah Colleges Brace for High Enrollment; With double-digit increases, some schools may be forced to restrict their admissions." *The Salt Lake Tribune*. September 1, 2001, Saturday.

thus unable to make optimal investments in collegiate attainment. With full access to credit markets and the capacity to borrow to finance full-time study, we would expect students to attend college full-time, providing more years to accrue the returns to college education. Yet, in the presence of some limits in access to credit markets, employment needed to pay for living expenses and tuition may crowd out collegiate attainment, reducing completion rates and extending time to degree.

To be sure, the family incomes of those attending college increased less rapidly than the rise in college costs during the 1980s and 1990s. While tuition and room and board expenses at public four-year colleges increased by a factor of three in nominal terms from 1986 to 2005, family incomes—particularly below the median—increased much less rapidly.[9] Such shifts are predicted to lead to a reduction in college enrollment among students from relatively low-income families and an increase in the fraction of college costs paid by students relative to parents, with increased student employment resulting from limited credit markets. Belley and Lochner (2007) show that family income has become a more important determinant of college enrollment and attainment over the last two decades while student employment among high–achieving, low-income youth has increased.[10]

The evidence is unambiguous that employment and hours worked among college students have increased in recent decades. Figure 2 uses data from the Current Population Survey to show the steady rise in employment rates among 18- to 21-year-old college students by type of institution. The top panel shows the employment rate while the bottom panel shows the average hours worked. Clearly, employment and hours worked are on the rise over the last three decades. What is more, the expansion in employment has been concentrated among students enrolled in the public four-year sector.

While employment increases are consistent with the hypothesis that increased difficulties in financing college are part of the explanation for increased time to degree, the causal mechanism linking employment and the pace of college completion is not well understood. Because it seems unlikely that all of the increase in employment can be explained by credit constraints as many students who are employed have not fully exhausted student loans, it may be that students

---

9. Combined tuition, room and board at public universities rose from $4,146 to $12,604 , a change of over 300 percent, at public universities (Table 31, *Digest of Education Statistics*), while nominal family incomes for those enrolled in college increased more modestly, with increases of 40 percent and 73 percent and the 25th and 50th percentiles (author's tabulations from the March CPS).

10. Philippe Belley and Lance Lochner. 2007. "The Changing Role of Family Income and Ability in Determining Educational Achievement." Mimeo.

work because they are adverse to borrowing for college, either because they fail to understand the student loan options or because they are rationally adverse to borrowing. An alternative explanation is that increased employment is not displacing collegiate attainment, but is rather a response to the availability of hours if course-taking is limited by institutional constraints. It may also be that colleges are increasingly responding to the preferences of students by offering courses of study that allow them to attend school while working. Finally, younger students may be working while in school to gain on-the-job skills and experience valued by employers. Understanding the nexus between employment and college attainment is of significant importance and represents an open area for future research.

What can be done? What should be done?

In reflecting on the differences in college completion rates and time to degree, a not too uncommon reaction among my colleagues in economics is "so what?" The skepticism deserves a serious answer. If individuals are making fully-informed choices about the intensity and type of investments in collegiate education with full access to credit markets to finance college, then the very heterogeneity in outcomes observed is, in some sense, a tremendous "success" of the U.S. higher education system.[11]

Still, given limitations in the availability of financial aid, restrictions and constraints on the funding mechanism in higher education, and less than full information about college choice, it seems plausible to consider whether reductions in completion rates and increased time to degree may be indicative of market failures in higher education. To the extent that these problems are most acute for the college students from lower socioeconomic groups, there is particular cause for concern.

Broad claims for public policy actions that do not follow from substantive understanding of the student and institutional factors contributing to collegiate success are likely to be misguided and, potentially, counterproductive. Political efforts to keep tuition low without compensating increases in public support are likely to exacerbate the inefficiencies of crowding and queuing in those institutions charged with offering access to college to many young people.

In thinking through research approaches that will help to improve understanding of the determinants of these outcomes, and ultimately, policy, I

---

11. There is a subtle point to ponder if one views the extension of time to degree as a form of individual consumption. Given that individuals pay appreciably less than the full cost of financing higher education with substantial subsidies from public and private sources, those who choose to take longer to complete do not bear the full cost of extended time to degree.

want to emphasize two margins of analysis. First, we know far too little about how individuals make choices about the intensity of investments in college (and work) and how these outcomes are affected by the availability of different types of aid, including both grants and loans. Secondly, while recognizing the complexity of the collegiate production process, we know far too little about "what works." New initiatives intent on improving outcomes are introduced with fine intentions and often much zeal, but despite the commitment of higher education to "research," comprehensive evaluation is rare.

Finally, there is much to be said for transparency and accountability in outcome measures. Surely there have been substantial improvements in the reporting of completion rates in the last decade, due in no small measure to the efforts of the NCAA. Such information holds the promise of not only serving as an important research tool, but also as a tool to improve the choices of students and their families.

In writing about completion rates and time to degree as outcomes representative of college success, it is important to place these indicators in the appropriate context. Time to degree and completion rates are visible measures of achievement yet should be seen as complimentary to other rich dimensions of success in college and beyond.

Table 1. Eight-year completion rate by type of first institution

Initial Institution Type	Completion Rate: 8 Years	
	NLS72 Cohort	**NELS:88 Cohort**
Four-Year Public	60.1%	56.7%
Four-Year Private	68.4%	78.2%
Two Year	23.2%	17.4%
Total	**51.1%**	**45.3%**

Source: Bound, Lovenheim, and Turner. (2007). Calculations from the NLS72 and NELS:88 surveys. Cohort high school graduation is defined as June 1972 for the NLS72 sample and June 1992 for the NELS:88 sample. NLS72 calculations were made using the fifth follow-up weights included in the survey. Fourth follow-up weights were used for the NELS:88 survey calculations. Only those participating in these follow-ups are included in the tabulations.

Table 2. Time to B.A. degree completion

	Years Out of High School				
Full Sample	**4**	**5**	**6**	**7**	**8**
NLS72	56.8%	83.8%	92.4%	97.0%	100.0%
NELS:88	43.6%	76.2%	89.6%	95.9%	100.0%
Difference	-13.2%	-7.6%	-2.8%	-1.1%	0.0%
Four-Year Public					
NLS72	54.6%	84.6%	92.9%	97.0%	100.0%
NELS:88	37.1%	76.6%	90.3%	95.7%	100.0%
Difference	-17.5%	-8.0%	-2.6%	-1.3%	0.0%
Four-Year Private					
NLS72	71.7%	89.9%	94.9%	98.4%	100.0%
NELS:88	66.4%	88.4%	95.4%	98.9%	100.0%
Difference	-5.3%	-1.5%	0.5%	0.5%	0.0%
Two-Year					
NLS72	35.9%	67.7%	85.2%	93.8%	100.0%
NELS:88	21.0%	49.8%	75.4%	90.3%	100.0%
Difference	-14.9%	-17.9%	-9.8%	-3.5%	0.0%

Source: Bound, Lovenheim, and Turner (2007). Calculations from the NLS72 and NELS:88 surveys. Cohort high school graduation is defined as June 1972 for the NLS72 sample and June 1992 for the NELS:88 sample. NLS72 calculations were made using the fifth follow-up weights included in the survey. Fourth follow-up weights were used for the NELS:88 survey calculations. Only those participating in these follow-ups are included in the tabulations.

Figure 1. Distribution of time to degree

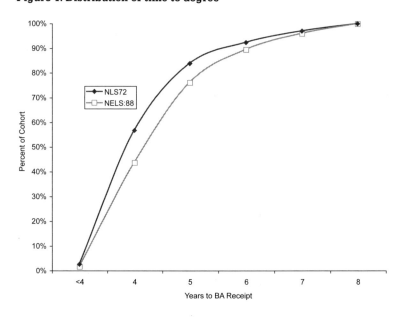

Figure 2. Employment and hours among those enrolled in college by type of institution, October CPS

Panel A. Percent of Enrolled Students Employed

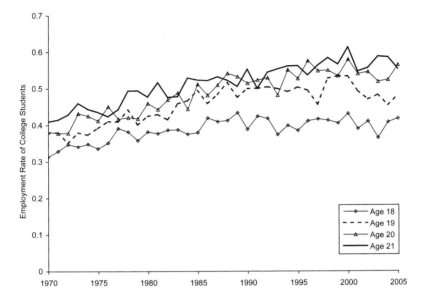

Panel B. Percent of Students Working 20+ Hours Enrolled

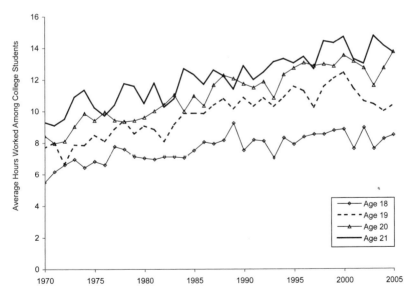

Source: Data are from author's tabulations using the October CPS. Individual weights are employed.

Heterogeneity and Higher Education[1]

Jeffrey A. Smith

Introduction

The higher education sector embodies a remarkable diversity of students, colleges, and programs within colleges. This essay makes the case that this heterogeneity matters for how we think about success in higher education for individuals and colleges, for what research questions we ask and for how we go about answering them.

This paper uses the terms diversity and heterogeneity as synonyms to refer to the wide variation among students, colleges, and programs within colleges. My conception of diversity at the student level goes well beyond its frequent use as shorthand for the representation of certain racial and ethnic groups. Instead, I have in mind diversity on many dimensions, including race and ethnicity but also ability and precollege achievement in math, reading, writing, the arts and athletics, effort level, study skills, ambitions for life, religious background, and so on. All these characteristics affect the optimal match between student and college and student and program. They also affect the nature and likelihood of success in college and the extent and nature of any effect of college on later life.

Colleges also exhibit extraordinary heterogeneity. They vary by the size of the student body, by expenditures per student (and available resources more broadly), by the quality of their faculty (on dimensions such as teaching, research, and service), by the extent of the intramural and intercollegiate athletic programs they offer, by location (contrast Columbia and Berea), by the amount of hand-holding they provide to students (or to helicopter parents!), by the student atmosphere they provide (contrast Reed and Hillsdale) and so on. Some colleges provide two-year degrees and others four-year degrees. Some specialize in the great books and others in engineering or science, like Purdue and Cal Tech. While some college characteristics, such as selectivity, fit reasonably well on a simple numerical scale, no single scale or ranking can hope to capture the relevant information on all or even most of these dimensions.

1. I am grateful for discussions about higher education with John Bound, Paul Courant, Mike Lovenheim, Lock Reynolds, and Sarah Turner that have shaped my thinking on the issue. Sarah Turner also provided detailed comments on an earlier draft and pointed me to the speech by Bill Bowen that I quote in the conclusion. Sadly, though inevitably, I retain all of the blame for both my outrageous opinions and for any errors.

Finally, programs within colleges and universities vary widely in availability, type and quality. Majors often vary widely in terms of number of students, faculty size and quality, and the type and amount of work required for successful completion. Some programs feature work opportunities as part of their curriculum. Others focus on writing and so on.

This amazing diversity among students, colleges, and programs within colleges has implications for how we think about the outcomes associated with college attendance and completion and for how we think about related policy issues. To see this, consider a couple of quick examples.

First, suppose that a particular college decides to adopt an income-contingent student loan program. Some students will now apply to this college who before did not apply to any college. These students will be differentially risk averse and differentially interested in majors that lead to jobs with low earnings, which are effectively subsidized under such schemes. Some existing students at the college will migrate toward majors that imply lower earnings as well. The students who migrate will generally be the ones with the lowest expected pecuniary and nonpecuniary benefits from the majors they leave (the marginal students, as economists like to say). Similarly, some particularly risk-averse current students will migrate toward majors that lead to jobs with a higher variance in earnings, which become more attractive due to the implicit insurance provided by the scheme.

Second, suppose that a college expands the number of majors graduating each year in its computer science program from 30 to 100 by lowering entry requirements for the major. The marginal students will likely come from other majors with weaker entry requirements but still with a lot of technical content, such as business, economics, or applied math, and not from English literature or general studies. Classes in computer science will get bigger, and the material in them will be aimed lower. As a result, the 30 students who would have gotten in under the old regime will now likely learn less while the 70 students on the margin will have different, and likely more lucrative, career tracks.

In both examples, policy changes introduced in the context of heterogeneous students, colleges, and programs leads to very specific changes in the behavior of certain decidedly nonrepresentative groups of students. They also lead to different outcomes even for students who do not change their behavior. As a result, such policy changes require careful analysis to trace out who wins, who loses, and what the net result is for students and for the institutions involved. The following sections amplify this argument and apply it in a variety of higher education contexts.

Students, Colleges, Programs, and Outcomes

We can think about college success in a number of ways: Does the student finish a degree? Does the student do well in the labor market relative to what he or she would have experienced without going to college? Does the student have better health outcomes as a result of attending college? Does the student contribute more to society in other ways, such as civic participation,[2] as a result of having attended college?

In each case, we can think about students having a variety of possible outcomes that depend on their own characteristics (measured and unmeasured), the particular college they attend and its characteristics (and the characteristics of its student body as a whole), and the particular program or programs they undertake. At the broadest level, each choice of school and program implies a different distribution of possible outcomes for each student, and no single college represents the best match for all or even most students.

Economists and other social scientists know surprisingly little about the nature of the relationships that govern student outcomes. Most of what we do know represents mean effects for all students or for subgroups of students defined by a single variable, such as males and females. For example, we know for both men and women that starting at a two-year college rather than a four-year college increases the probability of getting a two-year degree (no surprise there) but decreases the probability of getting a four-year degree, even among students who say they intend to do so before starting.[3] This aggregate result, however, hides a wealth of variation relevant to both policy and to individual decision making. For some students, the ability to live at home while attending a community college may improve school outcomes while for others it limits their ability to focus on their studies. Some two-year schools surely do a much better job of greasing the track to a four-year degree than others. Some students may learn in a two-year school that they really like particular programs offered at that level, and so on. Keeping heterogeneity in students, colleges, and programs in mind in interpreting the aggregate result leads to more nuanced thoughts about how to react in terms of institutional and governmental policies and also leads immediately to ideas for useful additional research to guide those policy (and individual) choices.

---

2. See the paper by Thomas Dee in this volume.
3. Lockwood Reynolds, "Where to Attend? Estimating the Effects of Beginning at a Two-Year College," University of Michigan (2007).

Matching students to colleges (or no college)

Economists sometimes talk about a mythical social planner with complete information and infinite processing capacity; in the land of economic theory, this planner makes optimal choices about resource allocation given the available inputs and known relationships between student, program, and college characteristics and later life outcomes such as earnings and civic participation. Given the (potential or actual, depending on how one reads the literature) role of peer effects, which cause the best choice for each student to depend on the choices of all of the other students, this represents a daunting task indeed. Access to deeper knowledge concerning what programs and college characteristics fit best for particular types of students than we currently possess would complicate the allocation problem still more.

The United States, a country whose residents tend not to revere would-be social planners, implicitly takes the opposite approach via a highly decentralized system. Students apply to individual colleges. Each college makes admissions and aid decisions about individual students (though at many public universities most students face a fixed and known and highly subsidized price per credit or per term with little chance of aid). Information enters the system via commercial college guides, high school counselors, paid admissions consultants, parents, siblings, and many other sources. Students from families with more resources, either monetary or informational, or both, may well make better choices and some evidence suggests that students from disadvantaged backgrounds sometimes do not end up very well matched.[4]

In general, the social science literature provides less systematic information than it should regarding the sources of information that students and colleges rely on in making their choices about where to apply or attend, in the case of the students, or whom to admit and how much financial aid to give them, in the case of the colleges. The literature on college quality does suggest that the various commercial rankings, such as those produced by *Barron's* and by *U.S. News & World Report*, provide valuable information, in the sense that these rankings (and the variables that underlie them) predict later labor market outcomes even after controlling for the nonrandom matching of students to colleges.[5]

In contrast, I am aware of no formal studies of the value added in match quality by high school guidance counselors and admissions officers at selective

---

4. Sara Goldrick-Rab, "Following Their Every Move: An Investigation of Social Class Differences in College Pathways," *Sociology of Education, 79* (2006): 61–70; Melissa Roderick, Jenny Nagaoka and Elaine Allensworth, *From High School to the Future* (Chicago: Consortium on Chicago Schools Research at the University of Chicago, 2006).

5. Dan Black , Kermit Daniel, and Jeffrey Smith, "College Quality and Wages in the United States." *German Economic Review, 6* (2005): 415–443.

colleges. The related literature on the value of caseworkers in assigning clients to particular treatments within the context of active labor market programs for the unemployed does not inspire much confidence. For example, Michael Lechner and I compare the performance of Swiss caseworkers in assigning unemployed individuals to different types of subsidized classroom and on-the-job training and find that they do about as well as random assignment.[6] In contrast, an automated system that assigns each individual to a training type based on a statistical model (what economists call a "statistical treatment rule") and their individual characteristics performs better than random assignment.

It would be a very interesting and worthwhile exercise for one or more selective colleges to choose to admit some small fraction (say 10 percent) of their applicants in the following way: First, define a simple rule involving cutoff values on the SAT® and on high school GPA. Second, randomly admit students who exceed the cutoff values to fill the slots available for this purpose. Then compare the academic and labor market outcomes of the two groups. Of course, one could also use more complicated rules in such an automated system; indeed, one way to obtain such a rule would consist of summarizing the behavior of the existing admissions system via a statistical model. In the event that the simple admissions rule does as well (or better) than existing admissions procedures, the college gains access to additional instructional resources. In the event that it does not, the college has produced some useful knowledge (and earned the undying gratitude of its admissions officers) at a fairly low cost.

Our understanding of the matching process would also benefit from further systematic qualitative and quantitative research on how counselors and admissions officers do what they do, and on how students combine the information from counselors and other sources to produce choices about application and acceptance. In addition, comparative work on alternative, more centralized application and allocation systems such as those in some European countries would help to illustrate alternatives and would highlight the costs and benefits of the present system.

College As an Experience Good

Many students know very little about college in general, and even less about their best match among the wide variety of colleges and programs available to them. College life, particularly when it involves living away from home, involves major changes in social networks, responsibility, supervision, and academic intensity. Because of all the uncertainty surrounding them, college in general as well as

---

6. Michael Lechner and Jeffrey Smith, "What Is the Value Added by Caseworkers?" *Labour Economics, 14* (2007): 135–151.

specific colleges and programs represent what economists call "experience goods." Students cannot really know how well they match to a particular school or program without enrolling and experiencing it, at least for a while.

Thinking about colleges and programs as experience goods leads naturally to thinking about how students learn. They begin at one particular college with some idea about programs of interest. Over time, as their studies continue, they learn about how well their initial choices of college and program of study suit them, and likely gain more information about the characteristics and outcomes associated with other colleges and, even more so, other programs of study. At some point, they may acquire enough information to cause the perceived benefits of changing college or changing program to exceed the costs. All else equal, we would expect the amount of such switching to decrease in proportion to the quality and quantity of information underlying the initial choice and to increase in proportion to the number of choices available. Note that switching as used here includes dropping out (i.e., "switching" from college to work). Thinking about college as an experience good suggests an optimal dropout rate different from zero (though perhaps still smaller than the one we observe) and also suggests useful ways to reduce both the dropout and transfer rates.

We know that both switching schools and switching majors has increased in recent decades, and we know that students from backgrounds likely to imply less information about where to go and what to study do more switching as well,[7] though some (or most or all) of that may result from financial rather than informational issues. Beyond that, we do not know very much. For example, we do not know how much of the increasing time to degree documented by Sarah Turner elsewhere in this volume results from increases over time in the extent of college and program shopping. Nor do we know how either the earlier lower levels of switching or the current higher levels of switching correspond to the optimal level of switching. Nor do we know how policy choices at the university, system, state, and federal levels regarding admissions, tuition, loans, grants, program requirements, and other issues affect the amount of switching and its value (or lack thereof) to the student and to society.

Optimal Institutional Mix

Up to this point in the paper I have treated the existing set of colleges, and their sizes and characteristics, as fixed. But, of course, in the longer run government policymakers, along with administrators, alumni, and other funders of private colleges (as well as the firms that operate for-profit colleges) can affect the available

---

7. Goldrick-Rab, op. cit.

mix. Thinking about this wider problem in the context of trying to find the best matches of heterogeneous students to heterogeneous colleges and programs raises some interesting questions indeed. The fact of government provision (combined with indirect government funding via research grants and student loans and grants at private universities) complicates the picture even further. Some existing research examines ability sorting,[8] but, in the main, we know very little.

I consider two questions here. First, do we have the right amount of heterogeneity among colleges? Casual empiricism suggests that, with a few exceptions such as Evergreen State College in Washington State, with its liberal arts flavor, or engineering schools such as Cal Tech, the public sector provides a relatively homogeneous product on several important dimensions. Certainly, public colleges do differ in important ways on certain dimensions, such as selectivity, expenditures per student, local environments, research quality, and so on, but in other ways they all seem quite similar: secular, large, and impersonal, with little monitoring of students and no central vision or theme (other than, in some cases, success at football or basketball).

Perhaps this large and (on some dimensions) rather homogeneous public sector keeps us away from a lot of potential gains that would arise from a more heterogeneous system costing the same amount of money but doing a better job of matching the specific needs of diverse students. To what extent does the subsidized tuition available at public universities deter students from attending their best match? Would a system that subsidized only students and not schools change the mix of colleges and the sorting we observe a little or a lot? Theorizing about and estimating the private and social benefits of additional college diversity and the additional sorting it would imply represents a tough research challenge; it represents an interesting and important one as well.

Another (not unrelated) question concerns the effects of tuition differentials at state universities between in-state and out-of-state residents. Do these differentials steer students away from the colleges that would yield the highest value-added? It seems likely that they deter some matching on ability that would otherwise occur, as some high-ability students in states with relatively weak flagship schools stay in their home state because of the price difference. It seems possible to use variation among states in the amount of available choice and in tuition levels and differences to pin this down. Canada, which (largely) lacks these differentials, also provides scope for a comparative analysis.

---

8. E.g., Dennis Epple, Richard Romano, and Holger Sieg, "Admission, Tuition, and Financial Aid Policies in the Market for Higher Education," *Econometrica, 74* (2006): 885–928; James Sallee, Alexandra Resch, and Paul Courant, "On the Optimal Allocation of Students and Resources in a System of Higher Education," University of Michigan (2006).

The Effects of Policy Reforms

Much of the discussion of policy reforms in higher education focuses on average effects of various sorts. For example, discussions of policies designed to increase access to higher education often focus on the simple "return to schooling" studied by economists, which (under certain rather implausible assumptions) gives the average percentage increase in earnings for an additional year of schooling.[9] Policies that affect individuals close to the margin on a particular choice often get analyzed with evidence that applies to everyone making a particular choice, as when large earnings effects for current computer science majors get cited to justify an increase in the number of computer science majors. More generally, mean effects nearly always get treated (often implicitly) as common effects, which is to say that it is assumed that every individual experiences the mean effect, rather than that the mean provides a crude summary of a wide variety of positive and negative effects.

Most policy reforms aim to move individuals not presently going to college to some sort of college or else they aim to change the college or program choices, or the rates of college completion, of very specific subgroups of students. The diversity of students, colleges, and programs emphasized in this paper suggests that the effects on outcomes of policies that affect the choices only of particular subgroups of individuals in specific ways may differ quite substantially from the average effect over all students.

To make things concrete, consider a particular policy reform, namely, a program providing modest scholarships to poor kids presently on the margin of college attendance. What would happen in response to this reform depends on whether or not the marginal students have avoided college in the past due to an inability to borrow to cover tuition (what economists call "credit constraints"), or because of a lack of information about the college process,[10] or because they perceive the costs to exceed the benefits in the absence of the scholarship (where it matters whether those perceptions were, on average, correct or incorrect). In the first case, we might expect the students receiving the scholarships to experience larger labor market effects of college than other students, as this group may include students for whom college represents a very good investment but who

---

9. Jessica Goldberg and Jeffrey Smith, "The Effect of Education on Labor Market Outcomes," in *Handbook of Education Finance and Policy*, Edward Fiske and Helen Ladd, Eds. (Laurence Erlbaum, 2007); James Heckman, Lance Lochner and Petra Todd, "Earnings Functions, Rates of Return and Treatment Effects, the Mincer Equation and Beyond," in *Handbook of the Economics of Education, 1*, Eric Hanushek and Finis Welch, Eds. (Amsterdam: Elsevier, 2006).

10. Paul Courant, Michael McPherson and Alexandra Resch, "The Public Role in Higher Education," *National Tax Journal, 59* (2006): 291–318.

were previously unable to secure financing for that investment.[11] In contrast, if the issue consists solely of information, we might expect the affected group to have labor market effects of college attendance similar to those of the broader population of students, while if the issue consists of the affected students correctly (on average) estimating a low value-added to attending college, then we would expect relatively small impacts on their labor market outcomes (of course, if the students were mistaken in their beliefs regarding the value of college attendance, we would expect larger effects).

In each case, the reality of a modest scholarship, combined with the similarly modest test scores typically associated with being on the margin of college attendance, suggest that those affected would differentially attend community colleges or public non-selective four-year schools near enough to allow them to live at home. This in turn suggests that they may not end up optimally matched to a college or program, which suggests lower than average labor market effects from college attendance. The broader literature on college quality suggests a similar pattern.[12] Moreover, we would expect to observe the scholarship recipients differentially sorting into programs with relatively low requirements in terms of technical preparation in high school (i.e., sociology and not engineering) as well as into programs more common in two-year colleges, such as law enforcement.

The general point is that the extensive diversity of students, colleges, and programs combined with a complicated relationship linking them to labor market outcomes means that the effects of particular reforms that affect certain, nonrandom groups of students in certain colleges and certain majors require both better evidence and more careful reasoning than they receive in policy discussions. The reasoning in this section also suggests the value of more carefully targeted, and thus more easily evaluated, policy reforms at all levels: school, state, and federal.

Conclusions and Recommendations

I begin this section with a quotation from a speech by former Princeton University and Mellon Foundation President William Bowen, given recently at the University of North Carolina:

---

11. See David Card, "The Causal Effect of Education on Earnings," in *Handbook of Labor Economics, 3*, Orley Ashenfelter and David Card, Eds. (Amsterdam: North-Holland, 1999), and Pedro Carneiro and James Heckman, "The Evidence on Credit Constraints in Post-Secondary Schooling" *Economic Journal, 112* (2002): 705–734, for two entries in the lively literature debating the empirical importance of credit constraints.
12. See, e.g., Dan Black, Kermit Daniel, and Jeffrey Smith, op. cit.

"I think (hope) we can agree that accountability is key in connection with essentially everything we have been discussing: admissions policies, financial aid structures, pedagogy, graduation rates, and so on. Fortunately, there seems to be much more willingness today than in times gone by to look with a cold eye at the actual evidence concerning outcomes, and to be willing to make adjustments, or even to shift directions entirely, if something is not working. It will not do simply to assume that what appears to be a good idea is in fact a good idea."

I am not so sure that I see the time trend that Bowen sees (though I have a shorter time series of personal observations to work with), but I certainly agree with his call for more systematic evaluation of all aspects of what universities do. Those of us at universities preach about the value of research, the accumulation of knowledge and its use in policymaking, and openness about research findings to our students, our governments, and our society at large, and yet often universities themselves practice none of these when managing their own affairs.

In the course of this paper, I have suggested a number of valuable and often relatively untouched research agendas related to higher education. The central argument of this paper suggests that research in higher education will have complications that the study of some other institutions may not, due to the wide heterogeneity of students, institutions, and programs. This heterogeneity in turn has implications for the design of research initiatives, as we are likely to learn the most from highly targeted initiatives that affect one or just a few margins of choice, rather than from broad policy reforms that change every aspect of the sorting of students among universities and programs.

I can add a few other items to the many research ideas already scattered throughout the text. Systematic ethnographic and survey-based studies of college choice remain too scarce. Thoughtful comparative research on alternative systems in other jurisdictions for matching students, colleges, and programs would also add real value. The economics literature offers many examples of studies of specific assignment mechanisms[13] but little in the higher education context. Such research would include both centralized application systems, as in Ontario, centralized allocation systems and systems in which students apply not just to a college, but to a specific program within a college, as at the graduate level in the United States. Indeed, a consideration of why we organize this process differently

---

13. See, e.g., Alvin Roth, "The Evolution of the Labor Market for Medical Interns and Residents: A Case Study in Game Theory," *Journal of Political Economy*, 92 (1984): 991–1016.

at the graduate and undergraduate levels in the U.S. would not be amiss. In short, as this list suggests, the opportunities for valuable research on higher education motivated by thinking in terms of heterogeneity and its implications seem nearly endless.

Creating the evidence on which to base evidence-based policymaking in higher education requires data—more of it than we currently have available. Indeed, I would argue that lack of good data represents one of the main reasons that research in higher education lags behind that in primary and secondary education in both quality and quantity. Thus, I end with some thoughts on how we can improve the data available.

First, it would be a great boon to have reliable data on the characteristics of all colleges, two-year and four-year, public and private, good and bad. The existing Integrated Postsecondary Education Data System (IPEDS) represents a good start but it has three key problems: it suffers from a lot of item nonresponse; that is, many schools do not report all of the requested variables; it has very poor coverage for two-year colleges; and it lacks a number of variables that would aid in analysis, such as more detailed information about the size and admission requirements for particular programs.

Second, and more important, colleges could also contribute by making their data readily available to serious researchers studying reasonable topics. Several states, including Texas and North Carolina, have made detailed individual-level data on all public school students in certain grades available to the research community (with appropriate safeguards for student confidentiality). The research undertaken with these data has added quite a lot to our understanding of public primary and secondary schools and their effects. I have little doubt that a similar bounty of knowledge about higher education will follow upon the availability of complete individual-level data from one or more state university systems. The many fine papers and books that have relied on the "College and Beyond" data hint at the possibilities. Broader data, that included the large segments of the college world missed by the "College and Beyond" data, and perhaps allowed researchers to capture almost all of one or more entering classes in a state where most students stay in-state, would allow researchers to paint a more complete picture.

Section III:

College Success—
A Presidential Perspective

Institutional Perspectives on Student Success

David W. Breneman

Assessment of student success is a contested area, with views of faculty and administrators often differing from those of accrediting officials, state and federal policymakers, and members of the business community. The Macalester Conference, *Succeeding in College: What It Means and How to Make It Happen*, held June 11–13, 2007, in Evanston, Illinois, explored numerous approaches to the measurement and evaluation of success in college. The conference topic reflects the growing understanding that ensuring access to college is a necessary but not sufficient measure of good public policy. Instead, what happens to students once enrolled is equally—if not more—important. When significant numbers of students fail to complete academic programs, or if they graduate but fail to learn useful skills for the workplace and for civic life, serious questions are raised about the value of the collegiate experience. As the cost of college to students, families, and the public soars, ineffectiveness of teaching and learning cannot be tolerated. While all parties would likely accept that proposition, agreement on how to assess the quality of teaching and learning is far from settled, rendering this topic controversial and contested.

To understand better the view from the academy on these issues, four college presidents, representing very different institutions, were asked to discuss how they determine successful outcomes in their own settings. The four were: Henry Bienen of Northwestern University, Wilson Bradshaw of Metropolitan State University, Richard Miller of Franklin W. Olin College of Engineering, and Ann Wynia of North Hennepin Community College. Their views will be described subsequently, together with a brief summary of the discussion prompted by their remarks. Before turning to their presentations, however, a few remarks will help to set the context for this chapter.

Why Is Learning Assessment Contested Within the Academy?

One of the leading scholars in the field of assessment, Peter Ewell, has written in a report published by the Association of Governing Boards of Universities and Colleges, that board members need to focus on the following questions about their institutions:

1. How good is our product?

2. How good are we at producing our product?

3. Are our customers satisfied?

4. Do we have the right "mix" of products?

5. Do we make the grade?[1]

While acknowledging that these questions are borrowed from the business world, Ewell argues that leaders of colleges and universities have an obligation to students and those who support them to provide answers to these basic questions of purpose and quality. Such language, however, typically has not been applied to the academic world, and many faculty members do not view students as customers or higher education as a product. Hence, when stakeholders and critics outside the academy apply this business framework to college work, the result within the academy is often irritation, rejection, and dismissal.

How might faculty members or college leaders respond to critics who argue that colleges fail to assess teaching and learning? First, they could note that the typical undergraduate takes, on average, 32 to 40 courses in earning a bachelor's degree, and receives a grade in each course. Each of these grades is a shorthand way of evaluating the quality of the student's learning, and the GPA overall tells the student, the family, and prospective employers or graduate schools how well the student did in college. Thus, faculty might argue that students are regularly and thoroughly assessed in the normal course of undergraduate studies, with the official college transcript providing all necessary detail on courses and distribution of grades.

With regard to what is taught, faculty and administrators can point to the college curriculum, which sets forth the vision of an educated person upheld by the institution. Breadth of coverage is typically determined by the first two years of general education and distribution requirements, indicating that knowledge of mathematics, physical science, social science, humanities, foreign language, and the like are expected of those who seek the college's degree. Depth in an area is determined by the requirements of each major field of study, described in detail in the course catalog. In this sense, faculty can argue that they both prescribe what students should learn in both breadth and depth, and evaluate their work in each course, and overall. Hence all the talk about the need to measure learning outcomes tends to fall on deaf ears with many faculty members.

Graduation rates are also routinely collected and widely reported by most institutions, and as such are not controversial. Where disagreement may arise, however, is in the interpretation of these data. For example, critics often point to the lengthening time to degree, with relatively few students finishing degree

---

1. Peter T. Ewell, *Making the Grade: How Boards Can Ensure Academic Quality* (Washington, DC: Association of Governing Boards, 2006), pp. viii–ix.

work in four years. Administrators point to numerous reasons for the stretch-out, including the need many students have to work nearly full-time to support themselves and pay college expenses, decisions to change majors, poor academic planning, uncertainty of focus, stopout behavior, and so forth. Some community college leaders argue that many students are not motivated by degree completion but rather by skill acquisition, and when they have learned what they need to acquire a job or to advance beyond a current position, they withdraw, whether a degree is finished or not. College officials also place blame on inadequate financing of both student expenses and college budgets, such that students must work more and colleges often cannot offer enough sections of required courses to meet the need.

College leaders also argue that the requirements of both regional and specialized accrediting bodies provide external scrutiny of quality and performance, as does the competition for enrollments, the responses of employers, even the rankings published annually by *U.S. News & World Report*, not to mention the numerous guidebooks to colleges available at any bookstore. There is also concern that the emphasis on testing found at the K–12 level in the No Child Left Behind Act will unwittingly and naively work its way into higher education. In sum, many faculty and college leaders believe that their work is sufficiently scrutinized already, and are thus not sympathetic to the growing chorus of voices from outside the academy seeking better measures of learning outcomes. Even if greater interest in such measures did exist, considerable skepticism remains that something as complex and differentiated as college learning could be realistically and responsibly assessed beyond the level currently undertaken through courses and grades. There is also concern that such efforts would ignore the significant differences among institutions, and try to force a "one-size-fits-all" method onto very different colleges and universities.

What Do the Critics Want?

Critics are motivated by numerous concerns, including a desire for greater institutional accountability, a desire to measure analytically and comparatively skills developed by college work, worry about international competitiveness, concern over the rising costs of college education, and by a loss of faith in the effectiveness of quality assurance mechanisms such as accreditation and faculty grading.[2] Higher education in the United States has become an enormously

2. A recent national report by the Spellings Commission on Higher Education provides ample evidence of the types of concerns motivating thoughtful people, both inside and outside higher education. The report can be downloaded from the Web at: http://www. ed.gov/about/bdscomm/list/hiedfuture/reports/final-report.pdf.

important economic enterprise, absorbing roughly 3 percent of the nation's GDP, and it is not unreasonable for policymakers and other stakeholders to seek objective measures of performance. Those outside the academy are increasingly unwilling to trust on faith alone that money is well spent, and that students are learning what they need to function effectively as workers and citizens in the global economy of the twenty-first century.

Comments by College Presidents

Northwestern University's President, Henry Bienen, began by noting that as a highly selective private university, graduation rates are not defining for the institution. All Northwestern students, whether athletes, performers, or minorities, have high rates of graduation, so good results on that outcome measure is assumed. He spoke at length about alumni success after college as more meaningful, although not defined exclusively by newsworthy achievement. He indicated that if many graduates lead quiet lives, lives well lived, he would take equal pride in that outcome. Northwestern does what it can to encourage achievement through an emphasis on undergraduate research and through organizing charitable and community service work. The university identifies undergraduates who appear early on to be likely candidates for the most competitive awards, such as Rhodes, Marshall, and Truman Scholarships, and they have a small office that coaches candidates on how to compete effectively for such awards. Pedagogically, Bienen believes that having more seminars, immersion experiences, and study and research abroad opportunities increase the likelihood that students will flourish, both while enrolled and after graduation.

The main source of data that Bienen mentioned as particularly useful to Northwestern is that compiled by the Consortium on Financing Higher Education (COFHE), a self-selected group of 31 highly selective private colleges and universities, with offices at MIT.[3] As a condition of membership, institutions must agree to participate in the numerous surveys conducted by staff for the use only of the member institutions. The organization's Web page lists the following types of studies and activities:

- Collecting from and reporting to the member institutions historical data relating to admission, financial aid, and costs.
- Conducting periodic and special studies, as desired, to investigate aspects of institutional policy and administrative practices.
- Convening meetings of the membership for general policy and research discussions of broad interest and import.

---

3. For information on COFHE, see: http://web.mit.edu/cofhe/.

- Monitoring developments within the federal government and the private sector as these developments relate to the financing of higher education, with specific emphasis on financial aid and student loan programs.
- Cooperating and coordinating with other organizations concerned with higher education.

Bienen noted that in response to various of these surveys the University has altered its student financial aid policies, and in response to a question after the four presentations, noted that Northwestern has worked hard to increase a sense of community on campus, as concerns were noted on that issue in various student surveys.

In subsequent discussion with conference participants Bienen also noted one of the most difficult assessment issues confronting all institutions, but particularly those that are highly selective, namely how to determine the value-added by the institution. The students at Northwestern are not a random selection of college students, but have been carefully evaluated and admitted based on promise. That such students go on to rewarding and productive careers is not surprising, but how much credit Northwestern can take is less clear. Because problems of selectivity bias are rampant in the area of college choice and outcomes, Bienen expressed concern at the notion that the federal government might try to wade into this area with blunt instruments that produce nonsense. Perhaps the key challenge of this line of investigation is to honor and make sense of the diversity of institutional types and purposes, evaluating each institution in light of its own mission and identity.

Wilson Bradshaw, president of Metropolitan State University in St. Paul, Minnesota, spoke eloquently about the complexities of finding suitable measurements for an institution such as his, a four-year comprehensive public university, offering a range of bachelor's and master's degrees to a largely commuting and part-time student body. Statistics taken from the University's Web page highlight the challenge:

Enrollment

8,868	total students served (unduplicated head count 2005–2006)
4,479	full-year equivalent (2005–2006)
91.6%	undergraduate students
64.4%	part-time students

Student diversity

60.6%	female students
39.4%	male students
26.0%	students of color
2.3%	out-of-state students
2.6%	international students
32	average age of students
16–72	age range of students

Bradshaw emphasized his concern that in the rush to measure outcomes by traditional measures of time to degree and completion, the goals and aspirations of students are being ignored. He noted that community college leaders have long stressed that older, part-time students enter postsecondary education with a wide range of personal goals, only some of which relate to degree completion. His university has sought to work with each student to determine what he or she seeks, focusing on "goal attainment" as the policy.

He also observed that his type of institution is often penalized by data systems that cannot track students who transfer and continue academic work at another college or university. Such students are treated by the data systems as dropouts, when in fact they are simply transferring to another campus, a common pattern in large urban areas. One response to this problem has been advocacy for a "student-unit record system," that would track each student through an identifying number as that student moves from campus to campus, perhaps eventually earning a degree, and perhaps not. Without such student-unit records, however, universities such as Metropolitan State will always be at a disadvantage in measuring graduation rates. Unfortunately, this idea has been caught in legitimate, if exaggerated, debates about student privacy, and is opposed by many college presidents, particularly those in the private, nonprofit sector.

Two other ideas that Bradshaw mentioned favorably were a proposal by King Alexander, president of California State University at Long Beach, to design a three-part measure of institutional effectiveness: In addition to the traditional graduation-rate measure would be added the raw number of graduates plus the proportion of students enrolled who are eligible to receive Pell Grants, the federal grant program for low-income students. In Bradshaw's view, this augmented set of measures would reduce the incentive institutions might otherwise have to enroll only well-prepared students, basing outcomes largely on the strength of student inputs. The other idea he mentioned was a proposal put forward by the Joint Commission on Accountability Reporting in 1996 that several measures be taken: The "Catalog Award Time," being those who earn a four-year degree in four years, the "Extended Award Time," those who earn a four-year degree within six years, and an "Eventual Award Time," the point at which 95 percent of an entering cohort has graduated.

Clearly, nonselective institutions such as Metropolitan State struggle with success measures for the types of students enrolled. It would be the height of folly, however, if an obsession with graduation rates were to drive universities such as this one to abandon older part-time students who are at risk of not adding luster to the institution's success rate. Any measurable item carries within it a clear incentive for administrative behavior, and the trick in this era of accountability is to identify measures that produce beneficial incentives rather than perverse ones.

The third president, Richard Miller, represents a brand-new institution, the Franklin W. Olin College of Engineering, founded in 1997 to be an independent undergraduate college of engineering. The assets of the Franklin W. Olin Foundation, now valued at approximately $460 million, were transferred to create this new institution. Located in Needham, Massachusetts, Olin College enrolls 300 students and awards Bachelor of Science degrees in Electrical and Computer Engineering, Mechanical Engineering, and Engineering with concentrations in BioEngineering, Computing, Materials Science, and Systems Engineering. The sizable endowment allows a 9 to 1 student/faculty ratio, and admitted students are charged no tuition. There are no academic departments, and faculty members do not receive academic tenure. In many ways, Olin College represents a new and unique type of institution, and is dedicated to continuous improvement in its academic program.

Given that the education offered is of high quality, and students pay no tuition, one is not surprised to learn that Olin College attracts very able students. Fully 40 percent are National Merit Scholars, and the median SAT scores are in the range of 1440 to 1540. The 300 students come from 44 states, and 46 percent are women. Indeed, one of the distinctive emphases of Olin College is its effort to attract more women to the field of engineering.

President Miller observed that engineers are generally good at mathematics, science, and problem solving, but poor at communication, teamwork, social interaction, creativity, and entrepreneurship. Olin College seeks to change that situation, and hopes to "prepare future leaders through an innovative engineering education that bridges science and technology, enterprise, and society. Skilled in independent learning and the art of design, our graduates will see opportunities and take initiative to make a positive difference in the world."[4]

---

4. Taken from the mission statement of Olin College.

It is a bit early to evaluate the success of Olin College, as the first graduates were awarded degrees in 2006. Thus far, the College boasts a 90 percent four-year graduation rate, with 94 percent of graduates enrolled in graduate school or employed within six months of graduation. Thus far, the College has a 100 percent alumni-giving rate, and 13 percent of graduates list themselves as entrepreneurs. But there remain a number of open questions, noted by President Miller, for such a young and experimental institution:

1. Is Olin College attracting the right people to the study of engineering?

2. What are appropriate expectations for student achievement and engagement in the educational process?

3. What can be done to enhance creativity and innovation?

4. How can the study of engineering be made more fun and less tedious while retaining rigor?

5. What is needed to attract more women to the study of engineering?

6. What can be done to enhance students' motivation and ability to learn independently, and continuously throughout their careers?

7. How can students best be taught entrepreneurial thinking?

8. How can engineers be prepared better to stand and deliver and field questions in a professional environment?

Olin College is clearly one of the most interesting new institutions in U.S. higher education, and one can only wish them the best as they explore these significant questions. It is too early, however, to reach any sort of definitive conclusion regarding the success of the college in achieving its ambitious goals.

Ann Wynia, president of North Hennepin Community College in Brooklyn Park, Minnesota, made the final presentation in this panel of presidents. She gave some basic statistics about her community college:

1. Enrollment of roughly 9,000 students

2. Average age of students is 27

3. Sixty percent are female

4. Twenty-five percent are minorities

5. Eleven percent are not U.S. citizens

6. Fifty percent are first-generation college enrollees

7. Eighty-five percent work 20 hours or more per week

She stressed that NHCC is reasonably typical of community colleges in the United States, with demographics that are similar to that of Metropolitan State University.

When President Wynia thinks about student success in her setting, she divides her students into three categories. The first she calls the "Ready-to-Go," making up about 45 percent of total enrollment. These are students at various ages and stages of life, but who have definite goals and objectives that explain their presence at NHCC. Some are students who have B.A. degrees but are seeking more specific career skills; some are high school students enrolled as part of a Minnesota program that allows dual enrollment and the ability to earn college credit while still in high school; some are adult business owners seeking specific accounting or marketing skills; and some are working adults seeking to complete degrees.

The next category, which she calls the "At-Risk-Unsure," also constitutes about 45 percent of student enrollments. The identifying mark of these students is that they are not sure about why they are at NHCC or what to expect in college. These students include recent high school graduates who require remedial work. Others, a bit older, have spent time in the workforce and now want a better paying job. Some did not graduate from high school; a few previously attended college. All now face significant barriers—family complications, emotional or learning disabilities, lack of academic readiness, or work schedules. Also in this category are recent immigrants, who often face language barriers and are academically unprepared for college-level work.

Her third category, making up only about 10 percent of students, she calls the "University-Ready," students who are of more traditional college age, are well prepared academically, could be enrolled in a university or four-year college, but have chosen to start their work in the local community college. Many of these students are first-generation, and thus are not as skilled at making college decisions, and many are from low-income families, and are enrolled at NHCC to reduce their college expenses. A small number are Muslim students, with families who will send sons to the university but wish to keep daughters closer to home.

President Wynia then discussed the issues that get in the way of academic success for all of the students in these three groupings:

1. Poor time management

2. Working too much; studying too little

3. Not understanding what college requires

4. Lack of academic preparation

5. Personal health issues—physical and mental

6. Family crises—sick child, abusive boyfriend, job loss or change of hours, kicked out of home, car breaks down

She discussed various strategies that the college employs with each group to increase success, including differential times and places of instruction, Web-based work, partnerships with other local institutions, emphasis on the first-year experience and effective advising, peer tutors and mentors, 24/7 tutoring online, and math and writing centers. She concluded her remarks by arguing that success in college is much more than completing a two-year degree in two years or a four-year degree in four years. She clearly embraces a more differentiated and nuanced form of evaluation, tailored to the specific needs and interests of individual students. In that respect, her conclusions and those of President Bradshaw were similar.

Observations and Concluding Thoughts

We heard in this panel how four experienced presidents think about success for their students, and how different the measures are depending on the nature and type of students enrolled. Their remarks were intelligent, thoughtful, and clearly reflected the detail and granularity of their experiences at four very different types of institutions.

What was most interesting, however, was the absence in their comments of any reference to the efforts being undertaken by a variety of scholars and policymakers to focus on learning outcomes specifically. Going back to the report by Peter Ewell mentioned early in this chapter, one found no reference to the following surveys and instruments highlighted by Ewell as being valuable and relevant to the assessment of learning:

1. The Freshman Survey offered by the Cooperative Institutional Research Program (CIRP) at UCLA;
2. The National Survey of Student Engagement (NSSE);
3. The College Student Experience Questionnaire (CESQ);
4. The Noel-Levitz Student Satisfaction Inventory;
5. The Evaluation Survey Services (ESS) offered by ACT;
6. Your First College Year, offered through UCLA[5]

---

5. Ewell, *Making the Grade*, op. cit, pp. 34–35.

One might also mention the Collegiate Learning Assessment (CLA) developed by the RAND Corporation and the Council for Aid to Education; WorkKeys, a skill assessment program from ACT; the various licensing tests available in professional fields; and tests such as the GRE and related professional school exams developed by ETS for use by admissions committees. In a report prepared for the National Center for Public Policy and Higher Education, Peter Ewell and Margaret Miller discuss in detail the types of assessment of college-level learning that are available to states and institutions that seek to understand more fully what students have learned.[6]

None of this apparatus was mentioned by any of the four presidents, which poses an interesting question for the field of higher education. External parties are pressing higher education to be more transparent regarding processes and outcomes, but as noted at the beginning of this chapter, the academy generally has not embraced the various efforts being made to define and measure student learning. As a former college president, I have much sympathy with the stance taken by the four presidents on this panel, and I can understand why the academic community is dubious at best, hostile at worst, to these efforts to impose measures on academic work. On the other hand, one of the most poignant remarks at the conference came from the president of a distinguished Midwestern liberal arts college who stated that he spends day after day talking to parents and supporters of the College, making claims which he believes are true but for which he has not a shred of hard evidence. Resolving this dilemma in a way that does no harm to the academy but helps to improve the information available to potential students and supporters would appear to be one of the key challenges facing higher education in years ahead.

---

6. Margaret A. Miller and Peter T. Ewell, *Measuring Up on College-Level Learning* (San Jose, CA: National Center for Public Policy and Higher Education, Report #05-8, October 2005).

College Success in the Long Arc of Life

Diana Chapman Walsh

We are privileged to have the opportunity to publish the text of Diana Chapman Walsh's keynote address at the conference on college success that gave rise to this volume. President Walsh spoke to us at an extraordinary moment in her career: just as her successful 14-year run as president of Wellesley College was coming to a close. Fittingly, she spoke in a personal vein and managed to convey much both about the experiences that shaped her own conception of educational success, and the judgments and convictions that have shaped her leadership for Wellesley and for liberal education generally. Rather than trying to render her text into the more impersonal style usually found in volumes of the present kind, we have preserved the immediacy and sense of occasion that lend the following remarks such strength.

I come to you at the end of a full and emotional two months, wrapping up a 14-year presidency. Commencement, my final meeting with the board of trustees, and a culminating (and quite magical) farewell party were all packed into one day, June first. I went down to the Cape on June third to begin reflecting on what I might say to you. Reunion came the following weekend (last weekend) and involved saying good-by to some 2,000 of the alumnae faithful …every single one of them, so it seemed.

The moving vans arrive June 20. I turn in the keys on June 30 and then return to the Cape to begin a new life that I have not even begun to contemplate, much less define or plan. I made a deliberate decision, 14 months ago, when I announced my intention to leave, that I would protect at least a year after completing the presidency before making major commitments about the future.

I had two reasons. First, I wanted to leave Wellesley as I had led Wellesley—fully engaged, mind and heart, right up to the end, and not to be distracted by thoughts of the future. The 2015 Commission work described in the report I sent you is part of that commitment. Second, I wanted to carve out some time, after walking out the door, to clear my head and explore who it is that I've become, and who it is I want to be, before I sit down to write the next chapter of my life. So I join you in a strange amalgam of frenzy (associated with the move) and free fall (associated with the absence of any plan), if such a combination is even conceivable.

I knew when I received the invitation to speak tonight that it would be rash—bordering on insane—to accept it. I also knew that I didn't want to say no to Mike—as foolish as I knew it would be to think I could fit this in. And there was a selfish element. I didn't want to pass up the opportunity to be with this interesting group, discussing a topic I care about, because it seemed to me that it might afford an early glimpse of one direction in which I might want to invest some energy next. Or, at least I used that possibility as my rationale for saying yes to my friend Mike.

As the time drew closer, not surprisingly, the insanity part was outweighing the rationalization part, and that tipping of the scales left me with less time than I would have liked to prepare a tidy talk for you. So we'll be vectoring off toward the insanity end of the continuum, but not too far I hope (as I'm sure you do too).

Fortunately, you have some terrific resource people to provide grist for your topic, including my friend, Dick Light, who has written the book (literally) on succeeding in college. Derek Bok has written the other one and you have access to him, and my friend and neighbor, Rick Miller, has invented the institution, Olin College, that is experimenting with many of the answers to your question, in my view. So you have many creative thinkers on this topic that is suddenly everywhere in the air in higher education councils.

With that in mind, what I decided I would do in the time I have with you for this after-dinner talk is to speak more personally than I normally might—to trace my story as it has been evolving—the intellectual odyssey that (for now) has just culminated in the celebration of what, by most accounts, was a successful college presidency.

We can imagine, then, that I'm offering a different slant on "succeeding in college"—from a longer time horizon (45 years, to be exact, the elapsed time since I, myself, arrived at Wellesley as a freshman). What I hope is that we can use my story (and your own stories as they may come to you while you're following along with mine) as a frame for thinking about our more specific subject, namely what "succeeding in college" might look like, and what we might do to foster it.

My point in doing this is to reinforce something we all know—that the real test of success in college is the success of college, that is, the imprint a great educational institution can have on its graduates through the long arc of their lives. This is not a success we can easily measure, to be sure, but it is a reality we must not allow an obsession with accountability and outcomes to gainsay.

I was in my first week of college—at Wellesley, in 1962—when I decided to become an English major. We all took freshman English then and my professor was new that year. He sat cross-legged on the desk at the front of the classroom and told us why he loved the study of literature, why it was his life's passion. Literature opened, he said, the best doorway he had ever found to the mysteries of the human condition. I was hooked. This was what college was supposed to be.

I devoured and loved the great literary works, took a lot of philosophy and political science too. In many ways those encounters showed me who I would be: a dweller and a digger in the garden of words and ideas for the rest of my life. I loved that place and that pursuit; love it, and always will. And my life has been greatly enriched by it, of that I am certain. I'm equally certain that it has been among the most consistent and crucial elements of any success I've had.

But I didn't feel in college that I was a particularly successful student, and wasn't— not unsuccessful, but not distinguished. I didn't feel especially smart at Wellesley then, and I shaped my student identity around a belief that I had been admitted (Early Decision) on the strength of mysterious qualities of character, or "good citizenship," for which I'd won prizes throughout secondary school, certainly not for the brilliance I was observing in some of my college friends. In short, I was writing myself a self-limiting script that it took me some years to transcend.

 I did absorb a beginning appreciation of the various interpretive modes and angles of vision characterizing different disciplines, and the ways in which they see from distinctive vantage points. I developed a protean sense of the principle of perspective, and hence of a multiplicity of perspectives, but knew I was far from being able to integrate it all. And I developed a respect for the academy as a place dedicated to preserving time-honored traditions and making innumerable connections, while searching for the highest values by which we can live.

Still, these were mostly fragmentary and subliminal impressions, not at all well integrated at that point, despite the (terrifying) general examination we all took in our major at the end of our senior year. That test of general knowledge at Wellesley was dropped in the late sixties, never to return, much to the relief of current students. But the absence of a capstone experience is a loss, in my view.

I loved the learning in college, though, and was shaped by it. But something was missing for me. The world was at arm's length. I graduated and went to work in the student activities office at Barnard College while my new husband pursued his Ph.D. in the life sciences at Rockefeller University.

And through him I have witnessed for the past four decades—from the sidelines, but in a front row seat—the unfolding of the modern biological revolution. I've seen firsthand the connected community scientists have, the dedication and passion that animates their questions, and the satisfaction of unlocking, piece by piece, the mysteries of life and the universe. There are elements as transcendent there in the world of empirical reductionism as in any pursuit I know.

Across the street from Barnard, the antiwar movement was gaining momentum at Columbia, which was under siege. Students, occupying buildings, were leaning out the windows, wearing red armbands and brandishing megaphones. I'll never forget the day the police moved in on horseback, thrashing through the crowd with heavy wooden clubs.

The genteel intellectual world from which I had just graduated felt like a distant vestige of an era that would never return. The academy was ground zero, held hostage and put at risk; alumnae from those years of tumult still often describe to me how their educational experience was diminished by the disruptions that roiled their college years.

War and resistance, justice and the abuse of power, inequality, racism, sexism, poverty, and the arrogance of large institutions—all of these questions were swirling in the air. The humanities were no longer pointing to answers, at least not to my satisfaction. I earned a master's in journalism—thinking I might put my words to work for the betterment of the world—but found no traction in a profession that was still relegating the occasional woman to the "style" section.

So (as a young mother) I returned to school for my Ph.D., drawn to the social sciences, and Peter Berger's vision of a humanistic sociology that would attend closely to rules of evidence (and teach me those)—but also to elegance of expression—and would capture profound essences of communal life by collecting and interpreting data, inventing memorable concepts, and producing rich narratives of the layered meanings of social reality.

In my graduate courses as a university scholar at Boston University, I encountered for the first time a style of pedagogy that was more open, experimental and collaborative (looser and less bedeviled by a fearful perfectionism) than I had experienced in college nearly a decade earlier. A willingness to fail, it turned out, was the secret of success. I found that liberating. It helped me begin to deconstruct my own learning process and recognize the particular kind of synthesizing intelligence I did have.

Without knowing it, I think I was beginning finally to develop what Pat Hutchins has called "pedagogical intelligence," an awareness and a skill set, she argues (and I agree), we owe all our students so that they can become lifelong learners. This was a breakthrough for me, as it enabled me to put to rest, gradually, the conviction I had long harbored that I wasn't terribly smart, that I had other gifts I should be developing.

I want to pause here and observe that this is a story I don't often tell. And I did ask myself why I would want to tell it to you tonight—not for confessional purposes, surely, but because reflecting on this experience convinces me of how much better a job the Wellesley of today (and higher education more generally) is doing than it did in the sixties (and before)—a better job of meeting individual students where they are, and pushing them to learn about (and push) themselves as self-aware learners. At least I hope that's true. But do we know, and how?

Back to the saga. After this liberating course work, I wrote a doctoral dissertation based in qualitative research, worrying all the while that I lacked an adequate answer (for myself first of all) to the question of how well (and how) I really knew that what I was seeing and writing was actually true. I'm not sure it was, despite the awards it won.

That led me deeper into more systematic research. I led a 10-year quantitative study—a randomized controlled trial—of alternative treatments for alcohol abuse. We collected highly structured data, and analyzed them using advanced biostatistical techniques. We bored deeper and deeper into our sharply framed question, as good science inevitably must, at least for a time.

The modern world has been shaped by the methods of natural science (as we know)—the breaking of complex problems into elements; building them up again to discover how they work—an iterative process of reduction and synthesis. The objectivism, reductionism, and fragmentation that advance modern science are the cost of its enormous power to explain and unify. This was my chance to understand that process, in its elegance and its limitations.

For a wider context while I was doing the alcohol study, I had another lens as a professor of public health, a discipline with a systems perspective on populations and a progressive impulse that defines the field. Here was academic work I felt was worth all I could bring to it—applying careful research to prevent needless suffering and premature death.

But then I won a Kellogg National Fellowship to study leadership and social change for three years, hone my leadership skills, travel the globe—and quite unexpectedly—to venture (at first hesitantly and with great unease and vigilance) on an interior journey far more discomfiting than any of the travels we took in those years to remote countries.

I'd been a regular runner all my adult life, a practice that aligned mind and body for me, stabilized my emotions, and released my imagination, but now I added a meditation practice and went on stealth retreats with a "spirituality group," a slippery word I couldn't define and found embarrassing.

As a junior at Wellesley I had met the great novelist, Eudora Welty, when she visited campus, and I was discovering a quarter-century later the wisdom in her observation that "all serious daring starts from within."

As surely as I came to appreciate that this inward journey was where I belonged, I had no way to reconcile it at the time with my academic work, no thought of even trying to force such a fit. I considered it private work I needed to be doing on my own to address what I saw as personal deficiencies that were mine to solve.

In short, what had been a lifelong struggle to find better ways to integrate bits of knowledge was still largely confined to the cognitive realm. In the department I chaired at the Harvard School of Public Health, one of the ambitions we had for our program in "society and health" was to try to move through levels of organization (from the micro-biological to the macro-social) and find specific causal connections that linked different levels of organization so as gradually to build an integrative model.

Years later, reading E.O. Wilson's magisterial 1998 work, Consilience, I was reminded of both the excitement of this premature dream of ours, and its enormous complexity, bordering on hubris. Our nascent project was far grander than we, in our innocence, had envisaged at the time.

So perhaps it was providential when, in 1992, my alma mater came to call with the proposition that I consider taking on the presidency, an all-consuming role that is impossible to imagine without simply wading in and hoping for the best. If ever there was a leap of faith, this was it for me.

And now as I look back on the third-longest presidency in the history of the college, I'm conscious of the multiplicity of story lines we lived while I was there. We did accomplish many things, as people have been saying to me in this final flurry of farewells, and I'm proud of what we were able to do.

Parenthetically, I want to interject (in the spirit of this conference) that among the work I'm proudest of is the effort a senior and seasoned team of my Wellesley colleagues has been leading for several years to study and address systematically the gaps in "achievement" (we looked at GPA; controlled for SAT® scores). These gaps are a complicated reflection of the disparities in educational experience and social capital students bring to college (Doug Massey's work, among others), interacting with aspects of the college's culture (Claude Steele's work, among others). We've been working intensively on this challenge (as Mike McPherson and Dick Light know) because they've been helping us.

And, as Tony Broh knows from COFHE data, the leading women's colleges have for many years been (of necessity) more socioeconomically diverse than their coeducational counterparts. There is a success story here that could be mined for some interesting clues, if it were to be studied carefully. But that's another story, for another day.

Back to my story....We did do a lot over those 14 years, but as I get ready to leave I'm also mindful that we could have done more—more (as I wrote in the 2015 Commission Report) to evolve subtler conceptions of successful outcomes for an excellent liberal education, with the quality of our students' educational experiences at the heart of it, their engagement with it, the "alivenesss" of it for them, the authenticity, depth, and power of the learning we offer them.

We could have done more to pursue those themes without fearing we would jeopardize the perception or the reality of challenge and excellence. We could have been more creative in finding ways to encompass rigor, structure, and coherence, combined with freedom and joy, in a broader curricular and pedagogic vision uniquely our own. (That's why watching Olin College emerge has been so fascinating to me; they are crafting their own unique vision.) We could have done more to prepare our students well for citizenship, and for life, in the twenty-first century, with all they will have to confront.

And so, in sum, I offer four general lessons about success from this story I've just told you. First and foremost, I acquired as a student, and have carried through my adult life, a commitment to intellectual integrity that has been both salvation and curse. And I ardently hope that our students today are internalizing—on their own terms and for their own times—an equally ferocious appreciation that a great education confers a lifelong obligation to be not only consumers of knowledge but also vigilant and vocal preservers and protectors of critical thinking, whatever else they do. If they are not learning this, we are failing them, and we are jeopardizing our future. But how do we know whether they are, or aren't?

Second, as I moved out into the world and encountered much that was new, equipped with a natural receptivity that I have come to know as both strength and weakness, I began to struggle with the varieties of worldviews that seemed to set up redoubts in my mind and wage wars there. I was learning that academic disciplines—and other competing systems of thought—are worlds unto themselves, worlds composed of words.

Some are inquiring systems with rules of procedure and standards of validity and truth, but also—and most fundamentally—they are language games. These self-contained language games evolve their own internal logic and internal consistency, as well as fetishes and blinders, pitfalls and traps.

They have checks and balances that are available to those who approach them from a critical stance, but they can be highly seductive to those who would surrender their independent judgment. How do we know our students are equipped to resist seductions?

Third, to make my life even more confusing—but probably in search of peace—I found myself at midlife falling into a foreign world of heart, soul, and spirit that seemed utterly at odds with the neat cognitive scaffolding I had been struggling to construct. Now I was wrestling with demons, and writing poetry, coming to terms with suffering, and discovering new possibilities for beauty, hope, and joy.

I came to understand that my efforts to map and repair the world had been a subtle device to hold its shadow at bay. I began to see complementarities in the paths of science and spirit, and to appreciate that critical thinking emanates from the mind and heart, and needs a community to be true to itself. What if we saw our tasks, in part, as opening students' hearts?

Fourth, when I assumed a positional leadership role, I had no choice but to deploy myself—all that I had to bring—as an instrument in the service of the work I wanted to do. Everyone was watching my every move, and imagining what I was thinking and feeling. They were hyperreactive to me and I had to learn to hold my reactions and to understand that everything I said or did—whether intended or not—was an intervention into the system.

It became clear that the rigor in this new role would grow out of the interactions between ideas and experiences and across realms of knowledge and experience. The president is the only person in a college or university who inhabits all its worlds, traversing the boundaries while translating the language games. A trustworthy translator brings curiosity, receptivity, and respect for the dignity of those who are other, alien or consigned to the margins. A trustworthy translator starts in humility and yet never fails to ask how we know what we know.

The new resources and reserves I needed to manage the complexities of this demanding role required a new alignment of separate spheres of knowing—physical, emotional, intellectual, spiritual. As I look back now, what is increasingly clear is that the integration I had been wishing for our Wellesley students from the early days of my presidency (an echo of my earlier disappointments as a student) slowly came to me as I led my college.

I thought I was seeking for myself—and wanting for my students—a unity of knowledge that would make the world more whole. Instead, I've found a state I'll call a unity of self, knowing—an alignment across domains of knowledge and experience, all held to provisional and emerging tests of consistency and plausibility—rigorously, relentlessly, and, yet, humbly and lightly.

It has taken me a lifetime to assemble all these tools, and I find very heartening the possibility we're contemplating here that we might help our students develop their full capacities as human beings without having to wander in the wilderness quite so long. But before we'll be able to provide students the more integrated learning that my story suggests they will need for their long-term success, faculty and staff will have to do a better job of modeling the serious engagement of their own differences that integrative thinking requires and that organizational change necessitates.

I'm convinced that students need their educational institutions to model the "trustworthy leadership" I've been writing and thinking about, including in the writings you have. But this evening I've ventured a step farther and wondered whether we're thinking deeply enough about trustworthy knowledge. I am worried (as Derek Bok and Vartan Gregorian and others are as well) that we are allowing this "Whatever ..." generation to graduate from college perfectly content to accept that all belief systems are equally valid and true—arriving, Derek wrote, as "naive relativists" at matriculation, and departing no less so at commencement.

We will pay a high price if we leave the next generation unable to know their own minds and hearts. They will stand helpless in a market economy hawking selfish materialism, and hopeless in a world of fundamentalisms—dangerous shortcuts to the coherence and meaning that all humans crave.

So, for me, success comes down, in the end, to a deep-enough knowledge of self around which to organize a life of engaged compassion for others, concern for the common good, and right action in the world. And these qualities of heart and mind grow, gradually, out of a lifelong passion for learning—no matter what else happens—a passion that is the greatest gift a great education can give. That, to me, is the essence of "succeeding in college"—learning to love to learn.

How do we make that happen? By resisting—or co-opting—the forces that would reduce what is an ineffable process—an unfolding life—into something simple, when it is anything but. I don't mean by this to suggest that we should stonewall the calls for greater accountability—far from it. I believe that's not a choice. But we shouldn't allow those pressures to deflect us from the essence of our work as educators, first and foremost.

I want to conclude my remarks with a few reflections on this question of learning outcomes and assessment you are here to discuss. In a former life (when I was a public health professor), I was an evaluation researcher. A colleague at Wellesley once said to me: sometimes you're a poet, sometimes a social scientist; we prefer the poet. But you are social scientists asking empirical questions and I owe you a shot at a response.

Last summer, when I was writing the 2015 Commission Report I sent you, I was focusing on the external pressures on my college and what the future might hold. All through the hot month of July, the federal government was hurling accusations and threats at higher education, floating drafts of the Spellings Commission Report laced through with shrill demands for accountability, measurement, transparency, value-added results. The tone of the report was softened in later drafts but the angry voices we heard in July were touching something real in the geist of the times.

In the face of such an assault—harsh and simplistic rhetoric denigrating and threatening core values of the academy—the impulse to circle the wagons is especially strong. The risk is that an understandably defensive posture could blind us to vulnerabilities and opportunities we ought not miss.

We do have to communicate better the good we are doing, and we have to do some things better. Derek Bok, Bill Massey, and others writing from within the academy (as distinct from the politically-tinctured criticism from outside) tell us that we may be good, but could be a lot better; they use words like "underachievement," an "erosion of trust," the "end of an era." These are strong words and we should heed them.

I wrote in the 2015 Commission Report that Wellesley needs to "make clearer choices." That's a special challenge in a wealthy institution with diffuse (shared) governance. And I argued, further, that one clear choice we ought to be making more explicitly is that student learning is our top priority. That sounds benign or banal, until you think about implications of using it as a filter for all significant decisions.

As I was writing this up, I asked our office for institutional research to think through what we actually know about what our students are learning. They wrote a thoughtful reflection on where we stand with respect to our ability to assess learning outcomes, and ended with these "parting thoughts":

> "It is clear from this exposition that we don't really have good, direct measures of any of the general or specific skills and knowledge that a good liberal arts education should nurture. We do, however, have a number of indirect measures that can indicate where our efforts are successful. The primary purpose of learning assessment should be to provide feedback to the college so it can continually improve the education it offers. Imperfect and indirect measures can do this even if they do not convert into clear indices that can be ranked by outside groups."

There is wisdom in this coda. Peter Senge, who writes thoughtfully on measurement in organizations, emphasizes that the task of assessing outcomes should be in the hands of the people doing the work. All living systems need feedback to survive, he says, and that is different from assessment from above to evaluate and judge. We need more of the former and less of the latter if people are to be motivated and mobilized to do their best work.

You may have seen a recent issue of Carnegie Perspectives, distributed through the "Tomorrow's Professor" e-mail series. In it, Alex McCormick expands this point, arguing that if the government appropriates the promising assessment tools (like the NSSE and the CLA) in the service of a mandatory "accountability regime," the result will be to compromise the candor necessary for reliable measurement. If institutions are required to go public with their scores, the emphasis "shifts" quickly from diagnosis to damage control: and the development of the assessment tools will be derailed. So let's think for a minute or two about learning assessment for continuous improvement, and then I'll let you go.

In my 14 years at Wellesley, I have watched something of a "new agenda" move to and through the highly selective sector of higher education, a response, I believe, to major forces in the larger society (access, quality, costs).

We have seen a number of policy and programmatic innovations addressing these concerns. Many of them are exciting and important. I certainly believe we have improved a Wellesley education through innovations in global education, experiential learning, interdisciplinary learning and teaching, instructional technology, and so on.

At the same time, we have tried to be careful not to be so enamored of the program-level innovation that we lose sight of questions of coherence, meaning, and overarching purpose—questions we too seldom pause to ask. How does it all add up? How does it integrate? That was the point of the personal story I've just inflicted on you.

For example, take instructional technology. The revolution in communication technology is going to bring such fundamental change in the way we live our lives—all of us—that it will infiltrate all of academic instruction, in different ways for different levels and styles of teaching and for different subject matter, in ways we can hardly imagine now. It will happen fast and those who fail to keep up will be left behind. Just look at the way the average 13-year-old (who wasn't born when I started at Wellesley) is spending her time.

We need to pay attention to technology for sure. But so often we ask how we can bring technology into the classroom as quickly as possible, or how we can measure the impact of multimedia on learning outcomes—and these questions divert our attention from less measurable questions of greater import.

How can technology improve intellectual engagement in the classroom? What effect do new instructional technologies have on the quality of the interaction between faculty and students, on moments of inspiration, insight, and awe in the learning encounter? Will students be permanently inspired by a virtuoso multimedia performance? Maybe; maybe not. We don't know and should be asking.

Or experiential learning....When students venture off campus to engage in real-world encounters, we should have explicit learning contracts, sure, and clearly-defined objectives. But in addition—and of greater importance—we need to be asking how this work affects students' quality of mind, their love of ideas, their power of argument.

Will it turn them into the people we need for a challenging future: people skilled in the use of language and analysis, who can put together a sound argument and dismantle a specious one, who can tolerate ambiguity, integrate disparate observations and ideas, draw lessons from the past, and call on human experience as revealed by writers, artists, and other creators? Will they be creators?

And will we remember these aspirations if we turn our energies to the single-minded pursuit of narrowly measured learning outcomes? If we want to assess a chemistry class, for example, using readily defined and quantifiable outcomes, will we also find ways to gauge the levels of intellectual energy in that classroom, and attend to when and how that chemistry professor is catalyzing active and questioning minds?

The point is that technology, experiential learning, global education, multiculturalism—these innovations on the new agenda—need to be understood as secondary, not primary. They are valuable not as ends in themselves, but as pathways to a larger end—developing students who are lifelong critical thinkers and learners.

These new initiatives may help us achieve this larger goal of carving out spaces for inspired and inspiring encounters between faculty and students, but we need to articulate how, and under what conditions, and we need to be alert to ways in which rigid notions about what constitutes good teaching may actually get in our way.

In closing, then, I join Lee Shulman and Alex McCormick in invoking the medical dictum, *primum non nocere*, first do no harm. As frustrating as it is to work for change in the academy, there is much we should work not to change. The academy remains one of the few remaining places in our modern culture that offers a refuge for the freedom to live our questions; to follow our causal chains wherever they may lead; to seek insight through confirmation rather than thoughtless surrender to authority; to speak truth to power; and to discipline and amplify the domains of human knowledge and thus expand outward the humanity we imperfect humans owe a wounded world. So one kind of success in college would be to preserve and enhance this vanishing habitat. I leave you with the impossible question of how we might know how well we are accomplishing that.

Note: This talk was, in substantial part, an adaptation of a closing keynote I gave in San Francisco on February 25, 2007, at a conference entitled "Uncovering the Heart of Higher Education" that was sponsored by the Fetzer Institute with a number of "partnering institutions."

Section IV:
College Success— Student and Faculty Perspectives

Ask the Students:
A Good Way to Enhance Their Success

Richard J. Light

I want to tell you about five low-cost, student-centered ways of enhancing success for large numbers of students—while each of these students is in college. First, what exactly do we mean by "student success" at college? Second, what are some concrete ways that gathering some relatively simple data from students can help faculty members and college leaders to work so that even more students "succeed?" And third, what are a handful of concrete examples of something that has actually changed on a campus, and I will use my own campus to illustrate, as a result of gathering these simple data from undergraduates.

What Do We Mean by 'Helping Students to Succeed in College'?

When at the suggestion of then president of Harvard, Derek Bok, I invited more than 30 colleagues from my campus, plus deans and senior faculty members from 24 other colleges and universities, our first task was to define what we mean by "helping students to succeed." This may seem simple, yet it turned out to be a bit more complicated for our group of campus leaders. Our group of 65 colleagues from 25 campuses came up with three definitions of "student success."

1. **Determining "how much our students know now."** That was for many campus leaders the most obvious first step. An illustration from my own campus is that just two years ago, we asked a random sample of 100 graduating seniors a series of short, specific questions. *Example*: "Talk for two minutes about the Human Genome Project." The entire question was that one sentence. Notice that there is no specific, simple answer. Nor is this a multiple-choice question. The goal was to simply see what proportion of all graduating seniors from Harvard College could say a few thoughtful, well-informed sentences about the Human Genome Project. What is it? Why do it?

2. **How much do students gain, or grow, or improve a certain skill while at college?** This second definition of "student success" is quite different. For example, suppose a group of students arrives at a relatively nonselective college, and on average they don't write very well. The simple fact is that in high school they never really learned to write well.

And at graduation from college, suppose an objective rater finds that on the average, the students' writing has improved dramatically, and to a statistically significant degree. In this situation, I would argue that the college has served these students well. While the graduating seniors at this college might still not write as well, on average, as graduating seniors from Princeton, or Amherst, or Stanford, it could well be that the "value added" of their college experience for improving their writing was, by any standard, an impressive success.

3. **What can students do, and what can faculty and campus leaders do, to encourage students to prosper, to learn, and to think critically and rigorously?** Put another way, how can we organize the college experience to best engage students with their academic work, so that they learn habits of thought and analysis that will serve them well and help them to grow for the rest of their lives?

This third definition of "helping students to succeed" is a bit more vague than simply asking a student to "tell about the human genome" or to measure, "how much has writing improved?" Yet, I can report that our group at Harvard, after many evenings of vigorous debate, decided to emphasize this third approach to "helping students succeed."

Ways to Help Students Succeed

Let me now move to a brief summary of some findings that my colleagues and students and I have developed over the last 15 years. Working with undergraduate interviewers, each one carefully trained, we have now completed well over 2,000 one-to-one, in-depth interviews with undergraduates. In addition, I have visited more than 140 campuses to see whether the findings are generalizable across many different kinds of campuses. Large versus small; private versus public; highly selective versus hardly selective. The findings are those which are applicable at just about *every* kind of campus to help students succeed.

I. Interactive Relationships Organized Around Academic Work

There is a common wisdom at many colleges that the best advice for students, in addition to just attending classes and doing homework, is: get involved. Get involved in activities of all sorts: Writing; Singing; Drama; Politics; Public Service; Athletics. This is excellent advice. I continue to share it with my own advisees. But there is a different kind of involvement, a more subtle kind, and the students who are both happiest and academically the most successful stress its importance.

Nearly without exception, these students have at least one, and often more than one, intense relationship *built around academic work with other people on campus*. Some have it with a professor. Some have it with an adviser. Some build it with a group of fellow students outside of the classroom. The critical point is that this relationship is not merely social. It is organized to accomplish some work. It is a substantive exploration that students describe, in their interviews, as "stretching them." And nearly without exception, students who feel they have not yet "found themselves," nor fully hit their stride, report that they have not developed such relationships at college. Any college can take several concrete and low-cost steps to help students work more collegially.

One suggestion is for professors who teach large courses. Students understand it is unrealistic for colleges, and especially for larger universities, to offer introductory courses to popular fields, such as biology or economics or chemistry or history, in very small classes. Such courses have large enrollments nearly everywhere. But in these large courses, a professor can encourage student study groups to *work together outside of classes*.

In fact, some professors deal with this challenge directly. They don't just urge students to study regularly in small groups outside of class—they actually create the groups. It is easy for a professor with 100 or more students to divide them into groups of five or six. Each group then must find its own time and place to meet, but at least the first step—creating the group—is in place for everyone. Even for those who normally would be hesitant or shy about participating. Students report that in some introductory classes the professor even goes one step further. This is especially true at strong, smaller colleges. He or she meets with each of the small study groups, at least once early in the semester, to help it get started. This demonstrates in a compelling way to students that studying in such small groups outside of the classroom is in fact an integral "part of this class experience."

One by-product of establishing early study relationships is that they can reduce uncertainty and volatility in students' choices of a major field of study. As recently as 10 years ago, about half of all our entering freshmen, if asked their during first week on campus, "What do you hope and plan to major in?" about half responded by naming a science, or math, or computer science, or engineering. So my campus had a large number of new, entering students who planned to focus on science, math, or technology.

Yet if we went back to these same students four years later, just before graduation, and asked, "So what did you actually major in?" Only 48 percent actually ended up in a science or math. In other words, my campus had half of these students "switching" majors, to a social science or to the humanities, during college. And the traffic among student changes in major was heavily one way.

As a response, my campus implemented the idea of encouraging students to form small study groups outside of classes, on a widespread basis, in all science courses. So, we might ask, has this led to any measurable change in science majors? And the answer is yes. Last year, more than 63 percent of students intending to study science stayed with their intended science. This is a dramatic and measurable change over just a few years.

II. Class Discussion of Students' Written Assignments

A second idea for enhancing student engagement at college, and ultimately students' success, comes again from many interviews. And this second suggestion is for professors who teach small classes. It applies especially to any class that has several writing assignments over a term, and where the professor leads class discussion. The suggestion is to ask several students, each week, to prepare their papers a few days early. Then photocopy those papers, one copy for each member of the class, and leave the collection of copies in a place where everyone else in the class can pick them up and read them as part of the routine "homework" before the next session. Class discussion can then be built, at least in part, around the students' papers that all the other, fellow students have now read.

This sounds simple. The logistics are easily manageable.

Several professors teaching modest-sized classes do it now. Students from these classes rave about the benefits. This remarkably simple idea illustrates how for a low cost, faculty members can help students become more engaged with their work. What is so special about this remarkably simple, low-cost, and low-tech idea?

First, those who are writing "this week's papers" work day and night to do a good job. After all, their work won't just be seen by one person, the professor, who will give it a grade. *It will be read by everyone in the class.* Second, the student writers gain from writing for an audience of their peers. Traditionally, in most classes, students write papers for a professor and the only person who sees each student's work is his or her professor.

Therefore, students tend to write a certain way. They assume they are writing for an expert on the topic. Therefore they may not bother to spell out all assumptions, or to explain every argument in detail. Writing for one's fellow students changes the author's voice. Several students report that the first time they were asked to do this, on my campus, they struggled for days thinking about how to change their presentation. Writing for a real audience of peers is very different from writing only for a professor to get a grade.

Still other benefits flow from this simple, low-tech idea. Class members make reading their fellow students' work before class a high priority. In other words, they come to class extraordinarily well prepared each time. They know their own turn will soon come, and that others will be reading and discussing their work. Therefore, since all members of the class actually DO the readings, and do them seriously, class discussion is enriched enormously.

In our interviews, several seniors bring up one final benefit of sharing papers in advance in classes. They say that seeing fellow students' work opens their eyes to new possibilities. They report feeling empowered in their own work as they see for themselves how different ways of presenting an argument, while responding to the same question from a professor, can work well. Many add that in addition to seeing different styles of presentation, they become able to distinguish different levels of excellence.

As an aside, notice how this format capitalizes on the principle of students' engaging with faculty, or with one another, around substantive ideas and academic work. When students' papers are read by the entire class, an overview of different styles and arguments that heretofore have been available only to the professor now becomes available to each student. Most love it. Most would give this as an example of helping students to succeed at college.

III. The Importance of Working in College to Improve Writing

There is one academic goal that is so widely shared by students, when they define their own academic "success," that it swamps all others. They want to improve their writing. They know they will be asked to write an enormous amount at college. Most expect this to continue after they graduate.

Faculty members share this goal. When asked at our seminar meetings, across 25 campuses, what aspect of student growth they would like to explore in depth, a large number chose writing. What we learned, from our questions to, and interviews with, students, reflects just what most faculty members suspect: writing plays a landmark role in the academic lives—and the academic success— of most students on most campuses.

We chose a random sample of 365 undergraduates and asked each to simply list the classes he or she is currently taking. Each was then asked to describe each course. Three items in particular are revealing: "In relation to your other courses, what is your level of total time commitment to this class? What level of intellectual challenge does this course pose to you? What is your level of academic engagement in this course?"

Students' responses to these questions varied widely. Our student data analysts then posed one, final and simple question. They asked how much writing is required for each course. A critic might observe that five pages in an economics course is not exactly equivalent to five pages in a creative writing course. True. But aggregating over dozens of classes gives a general picture of how students deal with different writing demands.

The results are stunning. The relationship between the amount of writing for a course and students' level of engagement—whether engagement is measured by time spent on the course, or the challenge it presents, or students' self-reported level of interest in it—is stronger than any relationship we found between student "success" in courses and any other course characteristic.

It is stronger than the relation between student engagement and class size. It is far stronger than the relationship between level of engagement and why a student chooses a course (required versus elective; major field versus not in the major field). The simple correlation between the amount of writing required in a course and students' overall commitment to it tells us a lot about the importance of writing for enhancing students' success at college.

IV. When a Course Requires Much Writing, Does It Matter How Assignments Are Structured?

This next finding is related to the one just above, yet the emphasis is quite different, and the implications for "helping students to succeed at college" are quite different.

Many classes on many campuses already routinely ask students to write a certain amount—say 20 to 30 pages of final draft over one semester. Faculty members in the humanities across more than a dozen different campuses wanted to explore a more detailed question. For teachers who plan to require, say, 20 pages of written work in an economics course, will noticeable differences turn up in students' engagement, and in their success at college, if the professor assigns five, 4-page essays, rather than one 20-pager that is due at the end of the course?

It turns out that the answer to this question is that yes, we find dramatic differences in student engagement. And the students quickly and quite comfortably tell us why. First, students report they learn *much* more from many shorter papers, rather than having one long research paper to hand in at the end of a class.

Why might that be? The key reason is that faculty members can give each student feedback. And then, any student who does *not* "succeed" and do well on, say, the first paper, has several more opportunities to make a "midcourse correction" and to improve on the several upcoming assignments. In other words, that student can actually learn, and see himself or herself improving in "real time."

My favorite example of this is how a history major who entered college less well prepared than many of his fellow students, handled his freshman year history seminar. He chose this class because his adviser, keeping in mind the point about opportunities to make midcourse corrections, urged him to take a class with many short papers. This turned out to be a critical ingredient for the student's later success at college.

The student tells how his history class had eight assigned papers over the entire semester, each of just three pages. When he handed in his first paper, he thought it would receive an "A." In fact, when the instructor returned his paper, his grade on the cover said, "C minus; I am convinced that you read the book just as I asked everyone to do. Yet your paper simply summarized the material from the homework reading. My assignment, in contrast, was for you to analyze the quality of the argument made by the author. You did a great job summarizing what you read, yet you didn't give your analysis at all."

One can quickly guess the end of this story. Now the student could make his midcourse correction. For each of the next seven assignments, he now knew what was expected of him as a college student instead of what he had done in high school. And as a result, after doing a far better job on his next seven short papers in this same course, his final grade was an A minus in the course. It was well earned with hard work.

Just think what would have happened if this student, as a freshman, had chosen to take a history course where the one main assignment was a single 25-page final paper. He would have never gotten the professor's clarification, and therefore he might well have received the C minus as his grade on his one and only, long, final course paper. Yet by the time this happened, the course would be over. No chance to improve. No chance to learn. No chance to make any midcourse correction.

My takeaway from this fourth finding is utterly straightforward. Students at any college, and especially first-year students, should be encouraged to choose classes where they have multiple opportunities to grow, to make changes, and to learn. A single, final paper may be a wonderful assignment for seniors at a college, yet may be a disaster for that exact same student three years earlier, when he or she is just getting started. For just about any student, receiving a C-minus at the end of a course, when it is too late to change anything, or to make changes in that course, is not a recipe for success at college.

V. Feedback and Revision

Undergraduates at most campuses are very clear about which of their courses they respect most, where they learn most, and which classes are most critical for their success, and why. I would like to share the main points of what students report, in the spirit of searching for shared features of courses that students consider most effective. Three strong results emerge.

The big point—it comes up over and over as crucial—is the importance of quick and detailed feedback. Whether they have 2 tests or 20 in a semester course, students overwhelmingly report that the single most important ingredient for making a class effective is getting rapid response on assignments and quizzes. This makes each assignment a genuine learning experience (as the history student's story illustrates), rather than simply an obligation to complete toward a final course grade.

Several students offer the specific suggestion that in certain courses it should be possible to get *immediate feedback* on homework, quizzes, and even in-class exams. These courses especially include math, sciences, and languages. Students suggest that at the end of a class, as they hand in their quiz or exam or homework assignment, the professor should hand out an example of an excellent answer. This answer can easily be prepared in advance, and it catches students just at the moment when they are concentrating on those same ideas and topics.

Students are utterly convinced that immediate feedback has the best effect on learning. And, on ultimately, student success at college. Receiving the exact information three weeks later simply doesn't help as much. Many students stress that this observation should not be interpreted as a gripe—many professors already do give fast feedback.

Students' second point about the way they learn best, focuses on revisions to papers they write. An overwhelming majority are convinced they learn most, and succeed at college in the best sense, when they have a chance to submit an early version of their work, get detailed feedback and criticism, and then hand in a final revised version for a grade. This comment is clearly more appropriate for courses requiring papers and essays, rather than courses with short, concrete problem sets, such as math, the sciences, or basic languages. Students understand that for faculty members, this process of giving feedback is time consuming. But they find their most successful learning spurt occurs when they get comments on an early draft of a paper and then work to improve it, sometimes making major revisions before handing it in for a final time. A surprising fraction of students mention spontaneously that such revisions are "fun," and observe that their most memorable learning opportunities came from courses where such feedback is routine policy.

In the spirit of including one feature here that cuts in a different direction, students are less sure about how these frequent opportunities for feedback and revision and midcourse corrections affect their attitudes toward a course, in contrast to their learning. About 45 percent of our student interviewees admit that they sometimes find frequent quizzes and papers an irritant. Yet two-thirds of these students, and nearly all of the other 55 percent, assert that these exercises have a clear, positive effect on their attitudes toward any class, as well as enhancing their success in that class.

Takeaway Messages

I have now presented five findings about enhancing student success. What are the takeaway points that emerge from the entire collection? I believe there are several.

First, every one of these five findings emerged from my colleagues, my students, or my asking undergraduates a series of utterly straightforward questions. So my first message that I invite everyone to consider is, why aren't more campuses doing this as a routine matter? We can learn so much from students' experiences, and what they tell us works for them and doesn't work for them. Yet I find, as I visit many campuses, that while just about every campus leader has good intentions, it is a rare college that systematically collects these kinds of data.

Second, there seems to me a wonderful philosophical point that underlies all of the work I have just described. Many of us who work on college campuses talk about the importance of respect. How important it is for students to respect one another, and how important it is for us, as faculty, to respect our students just as we expect they will respect us. So let me pose the question, what better way to truly respect our students than to ask them questions such as those I have described, and to then act on what they say in response to our questions about "what works to maximize your success at college?" I can think of no better way to honor our students, on every one of our different campuses, than to ask them a series of questions and then take what they say seriously.

Third, and finally, is doing this sort of work—asking students what makes for a successful college experience, and then implementing some new ideas—a highly expensive proposition? It is not. Just about any campus can do it; even a campus where dollars are scarce. Not a single one of the five findings and suggestions involve buying millions of dollars of new technology. Not one involves hiring lots of new people. Not one involves initiating expensive, new classes. The common theme from all of these findings is how easy and inexpensive they are to carry out on any campus. I hope you find these suggestions helpful. They can make an enormous difference for student success on just about any campus.

What Is Good College Teaching?

Susan L. Engel

It always surprises me that conferences about higher education often give little direct attention to issues of teaching and learning, focusing instead on matters of finance, admissions policy, governance and the like. I value the opportunity to learn about such matters, but have little to contribute. I am a psychologist, not an economist or scholar of public policy. Instead of talking about models, and outcomes, I am going to describe something about the processes of learning and teaching—which I consider to be at the very heart of the educational enterprise, essential to student success at college.

I'm going to discuss three dilemmas that many college teachers struggle with whether they realize it or not. But before I do so, I need to talk a little about my own educational values. Nothing shapes a teacher like the teachers she has had—so let me communicate my values with a brief story about one of my own undergraduate teachers.

When I was a senior I finally gained admission into one of my college's legendary seminars, a course on twentieth-century literature, taught by a famously intense, brilliant, neurotic middle-aged man, Daniel Kaiser. Each Tuesday and Thursday, we students would wait for him in the hallway just outside the small seminar room. He'd always arrive about a minute before class time, rushing past us, looking slightly hunched and furtive as if he was hoping to avoid making contact with any of us. There were about 15 of us in the class, and as far as I can recall, we were a fairly serious and intense bunch, eager to discuss the book at hand. I remember once saying something that turned out to be interesting to him, and as I spoke, though he continued to stare down at the seminar table, he began pulling strands of his hair straight up, and then smashing them back on the top of his head, so that it looked as if he were hitting himself on his balding scalp. I was thrown, but he was also nodding vociferously, making it clear that I should continue developing my thought, that it was a good one.

But the single most powerful memory I have of that course, the one I have thought of often in my 20-something years of college teaching, is the day I began to argue with his claim that James Joyce did not believe in the possibility of a narrative world. I kept insisting, pointing out that no one could write as potently and warmly as Joyce did of Molly Bloom, if they didn't have some deep seated belief in real readers getting to know real characters. Though I began the argument with more feeling than knowledge, as I dug in deeper and deeper I was forced to draw on information and analysis. Finally, Danny Kaiser snorted one of his weird snorts, glancing at me only fleetingly, before looking away, out of the window. He raised his hands, snorted again, and said, "OK, OK. You've convinced me. The way you put it, I have to agree. I think you may be right. I hadn't thought of Joyce that way."

I am not telling this story because I think good teachers have to be eccentric passionate geniuses. I tell it because of the immense and easily overlooked impact a teacher can have by genuinely engaging with a student. That day I had the truly transforming experience of changing the mind of someone smarter and more knowledgeable than I. In his talk about teaching at Harvard, Richard Light spoke about the importance of getting college freshmen to change their minds. I would argue that such open-mindedness begins with faculty who change their minds in the company of their students. When Danny Kaiser gave in to my argument, I felt the power of real exchange, and realized that dialogue was worth something—that the ideas developed between people were different, and often better, than the ones developed alone. Because it wasn't easy to change Kaiser's mind; I had to use good argument, and I had to believe in what I was saying. I had to know the book well enough to combat his thorough familiarity with every page. As he threw up his hands to acquiesce, I also learned that knowledgeable people are open-minded. Most importantly, I felt the pleasure of serious intellectual debate. I had no expectation that it was going to lead to a better grade—we did not receive grades. But the give and take of points of view was deeply satisfying.

In his comments, Light also mentioned the mission statements of several colleges and implied that there is a wide distance between those lofty and somewhat general commitments and what really goes on in college classrooms. But what good is a mission statement if it doesn't inform practice? In Jerome Bruner's still relevant and potent book, *The Process of Education*,[1] he asks, "What shall we teach, and to what end?" Bruner makes it clear that the topics and assignments our students encounter must be linked to our educational purposes. As Diana Chapman Walsh pointed out in her account of liberal arts education, if a college really believes, for instance, in educating students to contribute to society, the college ought to do something to make sure that happens.[2]

As with the education of children and teenagers, it is impossible to talk about good college teaching without articulating a clear and *constraining* educational goal (you can't do everything, and some goals are mutually exclusive, given the

---

1. Jerome Bruner, *The Process of Education* (Cambridge, MA: Harvard University Press, 1960).
2. Diana Chapman Walsh, Keynote Address, Spencer/Macalester Conference, Evanston, IL, June 12, 2007.

typical time constraints of a college course). We probably don't all have the same goals. But nobody can reflect or improve on their college teaching, if they don't know what their goals are. Light's comments suggest that it is not enough for a college to have a mission statement tucked away in the first page of the brochure. Each professor must know what his or her goals are, and continually hold his or her practices up against those goals. So let me say a word about mine.

A few years ago I ran an interdisciplinary faculty seminar at Williams, on teaching. I asked each of my colleagues to say what they hoped their students would know or be able to do at the end of the class, and in five years, as a result of having taken their course. Few of them had ever thought about their teaching in this way before. Their first thought was to identify all the specific things they wanted their students to know (how bacteria are carried within the body, the geometry of bubbles, or what *The Sorrows of Young Werther* is really about). By the end of the semester, all nine members of the seminar had come to realize that they didn't really care if their students "knew" (e.g., remembered) those things. Instead they wanted their students to develop a lifelong interest in their disciplines, and ways of asking and answering questions. They hoped their students had learned how to "pay attention," though the ways in which one pays attention in chemistry may be slightly different from the ways one pays attention in German Literature. I would put it this way for my own teaching: I don't want my students to get through my course unscathed. By that I mean I want them to be transformed by the experience, and to emerge that much closer to becoming socially engaged intellectuals. I want all of my students (not just the bright ones, or the ones destined for a career in academia) to be those things. Second, I want them to fall in love with my own particular topics: psychology and/or education. I want the undergraduates who take my courses to become addicted to thinking in a certain way, to discover the pleasure and profit of being intellectually uncomfortable, and of pushing themselves to make decisions about information.

These outcomes are more measurable than many economists and educators may think. So far, in considering the topic of this conference, success at college, my colleagues here have described the results of studies that have measured the characteristics that *could* be measured, sometimes bypassing the characteristics scholars most value. But if we value qualities such as open-mindedness or the ability to pay attention, we probably can find a way, albeit imperfectly, to measure them.

So, now that I've articulated my teaching goals let me describe the three dilemmas that plague me most and, I believe, plague much of contemporary college and university teaching:

Dilemma #1: To cover or not to cover

Any time two or more faculty members begin chatting, especially right in the middle of the semester, they fret about how they are possibly going to *cover all the material*. Each time I hear that phrase, I feel my mental brakes go on. What do we mean when we say "cover the material"? The phrase always sparks an image in my mind of the professor solemnly walking into class in front of an attentive room full of students, and carefully, thoroughly draping a blanket over all the books and notes which comprise "the material." It's possible that to fully cover the material the professor might have to drape the blanket over himself and his students, as well.

Don't get me wrong. I fully embrace the notion that one cannot think well, or deeply, without real information about which to think. A class cannot be valuable, or a teacher effective, if there is no substance to the course. We discovered in the 60's that one could not learn to learn, without learning *something*.[3] And like most undergraduate professors, I am eager to share what I know about my discipline, eager for my students to learn all the wonderful studies, methods, and ideas that psychologists and educators have constructed. However, the urge to cover the material rests on a mistaken assumption: that what we cover is what they learn.

A few years ago my psychology colleagues and I were debating the benefits and drawbacks of our requirement that all psychology students take a course in statistics. We were agreeing that even having taken the course, the students seemed not to know much statistics when they took our upper-level seminars. One earnest young colleague said, in exasperated mystification, "I don't understand why they never seem to know that procedure. I teach the statistics course, so I know they learned it, because I taught it to them!" But to quote Red Auerbach, famed coach of the Boston Celtics, "It's not what you say that matters, it's what they hear."

Covering the material assumes, implicitly, that the students are empty vessels and that whatever we cover is what gets poured into those empty vessels. But 80 years of research in developmental psychology has shown that even young children have all kinds of ideas, knowledge and perspectives to which they assimilate the new experiences and information they encounter. As Piaget showed in the first half of the twentieth-century, knowledge is not accrued like coins in a piggy bank.[4] Higher intellectual functioning (for example, problem solving within a domain, finding connections between bodies of information,

---

3. Ann L. Brown, "Transforming Schools Into Communities of Thinking and Learning About Serious Matters," *American Psychologist, 52* (April 1997): 399–314.

4. Jean Piaget, *The Origins of Intelligence in Children* (London: Routledge and Kegan Paul, 1936).

and using skilled intuition) is never simply a matter of memorization. Such thinking involves, instead, the active construction of knowledge.[5] Those familiar with the history of developmental psychology will recall that this debate, first waged between John Watson and Jean Piaget, was settled long ago with regard to children. But if five-year-olds come to each learning situation armed with knowledge, expectations, and assumptions, imagine how much more complex and dense are the schemas to which a 20-year-old assimilates new input. Our only mistake has been our failure to apply what we know about the construction of knowledge to college students.

We are mistaken to imagine that the perfectly organized information, clearly conveyed, will simply be transported, directly into our students' heads, and that what we have covered is what they have learned.

Many of us feel that if only we cover material in a lively enough way (good PowerPoints, charismatic delivery, and great stories) that will do the trick—we will use a fancy lovely wrapping, and then the material will be well covered. The students will "get it" if we offer it to them in a good package that makes it appealing. It is true that the charismatic lecturer, the good storyteller, and the lively presentation all make a lecture more memorable. But even the best "coverage" of the material involves telling students what you know, rather than helping them develop their own knowledge. And this, it seems to me, neglects a basic premise of great liberal arts teaching—the importance of uncovering the material. Uncovering requires the professor to illuminate inconsistencies, guide students toward discovering new connections, and most challenging of all, lead them toward raising difficult questions about the relationship between the "facts" of your discipline and the application of those facts to everyday life.

Acquiring facts is important, but fairly useless without a sense of what those facts mean in the context of the larger world. I am not talking here about the supposed distance between the ivory tower and the real world. I am talking about the importance of helping students to evaluate ideas in terms of their manifestation in everyday life, and to experience everyday life under the illumination of good ideas. Once again, the origins of this notion lie in work about education for children, which has been woefully ignored by college educators: the work of John Dewey.

Just about a century ago, Dewey began arguing for the importance of connecting academic topics taught in schools to the real concerns of children's

---

5. Piaget, *The Origins of Intelligence in Children*; Ulric Neisser, *Cognition and Reality* (New York: W.H. Freeman, 1976); Jerome Bruner, *Beyond the Information Given: Studies in the Psychology of Knowing* (New York: Norton, 1973); George A. Miller, Eugene Galanter, and Karl H. Pribram, *Plans and the Structure of Behavior* (New York: Henry Holt, 1986).

lives.[6] He did not mean simply that everything must have a practical application, but that learners are social creatures, embedded in communities, and that they would learn best when what they learned in school had some meaning beyond school. His argument, which emerged from the school of Pragmatism he helped author, implied that the interplay between abstract ideas and their concrete realization must be kept alive for the learner. Naturally this means something different for college students than it does for elementary school students. College students must examine the meaning of what they are learning, so that they can take the ideas and concepts with them, outside of the classroom. In his remarks, Richard Light told us that Harvard now offers noncredit seminars on life. I would like to suggest that teaching about life and teaching about our disciplines cannot and should not be separated. If I teach about research and theories in developmental psychology without relating them to broader issues, my students ultimately will have little use for any technical expertise they may gain in my course. But teaching in such a way involves uncovering the material rather than covering it. And that brings me to my second dilemma.

Dilemma #2: The disorganized discussion or the coherent lecture?

I have a colleague who regularly argues with me about the relative virtues of lecture versus discussion. When I extol the virtues of a seminar discussion she says, "If running it like a seminar means they are going to have a meandering mush fest, I'd rather lecture and at least know that they learned something." Clearly there are some cases where one must lecture (a room of more than 50 people), though I know of at least one professor who runs even a class of 200 like a discussion. However, many of us feel torn between using a lecture format and leading a seminar discussion, even when there are as few as 12 students in the room. Yet legions of studies have shown that students learn more when they act upon the material to be learned—whether it is a skill, a collection of information, or a complex idea.[7] The more students sit passively at their desks, simply copying what you say as an aid to their memory, while you devote yourself to the lively lecture, the less likely they are to act upon it and thus learn it, in any lasting way. What does it mean for a college student to act on the material? It might mean using a scientific concept to design and carry out a laboratory experiment. But

---

6. John Dewey, *The Child and the Curriculum* (Chicago: University of Chicago Press, 1902).

7. Peter A. Ornstein, *Memory Development in Children* (New York: W. H. Freeman, 1990); Fergus I. M. Craik and Endel Tulving, "Depth of Processing and the Retention of Words in Episodic Memory," *Journal of Experimental Psychology, 104* (1975): 268–294; Ann L. Brown, "Learning, Remembering, and Understanding," in P. H. Mussen, Ed., *Handbook of Child Psychology, Vol. 3: Cognitive Development* (New York: John Wiley, 1983); Brown, "Transforming Schools."

just as often it involves applying a theoretical proposition to a real scenario, or thinking through what kinds of evidence would disprove an idea. In a lecture it is all too easy for the majority of students to sit back in their seats and let someone else do the intellectual work.

Research has also shown that experts make far better use of large amounts of detailed information than novices do.[8] For example, when a surgeon attends a lecture on a particular procedure, she is likely to know a great deal about anatomy, previous treatments, and many of the basic mechanics of surgery, which frees her to absorb the details and the new information she hears. In other words, as an expert, the surgeon has a well-developed schema in which to fit the new information. College students on the other hand, who are novices in almost all of the disciplines we teach at college, have little on which to hang copious amounts of information. In other words, lively entertaining lectures may draw freshmen into a discipline but they may not provide much education. Sophisticated, informed, serious lectures probably are best saved for students who already have some expertise in the field.

The choice between a clear informative lecture and a mushy meandering discussion is a false one. The third, often better option, is an effective and powerful seminar discussion. But what makes a discussion effective and powerful? Clearly it's not enough to see that the students are interested. Nor is it satisfactory if they simply talk a lot but say little. Students need to be engaged, but they also must articulate substantive ideas and information—they need to speak to one another so that their comments, taken together, build on an idea, or an analysis. Professor and students need to think across speakers.

The notion that seminar discussions can be evaluated this way comes from the world of language research—specifically, studies on the development of conversational skills.[9] The basic idea is to look at a conversation (with two or more participants) as a collaborative construction, and read across the speakers' dialogic turns. If a professor, using this approach, can see an idea building, with new information or analysis emerging as the conversation develops, the conversation is probably valuable for all participants. Each participant, in other

---

8. Michelene T. H. Chi, "Knowledge Structures and Memory Development," in *Children's Thinking: What Develops?* R. Siegler, Ed. (Hillsdale, NJ: Lawrence Erlbaum Associates, 1978): 73–96; James J. Gibson, *The Ecological Approach to Visual Perception* (Hillsdale, NJ, Lawrence Elrbaum Associates, 1986).

9. William Labov and Joshua Waletzky, "Narrative Analysis: Oral Versions of Personal Experience," in *Essays on the Verbal and Visual Arts*, J. Helms, Ed. (Seattle, WA: University of Washington Press, 1967); Ronald Scollon, "A Real Early Stage: An Unzippered Condensation of a Dissertation on Child Language" in *Developmental Pragmatics*, E. Ochs and B. Scheifflin, Eds. (New York: Academic Press, 1979); Catherine E. Snow and Charles A. Ferguson, Eds., *Talking to Children* (Cambridge, UK: Cambridge University Press, 1977).

words, benefits from everything that is said, not just what he or she has said, and not just what she has heard from the professor. In addition, each speaker profits from the ways in which other speakers spur him or her to clarify, defend, or expand on what he or she says. But this view of classroom discussion hinges on the belief that peers have as much to teach one another as the teacher does. Plenty of research supports this premise.

The soviet psychologist Lev Vygotsky first showed that children's mental development is spurred and shaped by the input of others.[10] Research has also shown that people benefit from making explicit what is implicit.[11] Thus less able or knowledgeable students learn from their wiser peers, and the brightest students in the class learn from explaining their ideas to others. In other words, everyone's mind is improved by the exchange.

At many good colleges, including Williams, students have been trained for 16 years to believe that their job is to internalize information from their smart knowledgeable teachers. They chose and gained admission to our colleges partly because they were so good at doing just that. So it's not easy to convince them that a discussion where they spend as much time talking as much as their professor does is worthwhile. It can be daunting, trying to convince a student that a discussion might be more valuable than a PowerPoint for which they already have the handout. In his wonderful book, *Our Underachieving Colleges*, Derek Bok, former president of Harvard University, identifies the student culture as a sometimes formidable obstacle in changing the way we do things.[12] In fact, in the last five years at Williams, I have found students more resistant than they were 10 or 15 years ago, to the seminar discussion. My sense however, is that the answer is not to back away from discussion, but to make sure, as a teacher, that I lead it well.

But, how do you start a good seminar conversation? You need to ask questions that force the students to combine what they've learned with what they think. You cannot ask questions that simply elicit a demonstration of their knowledge. In my case, if I have assigned a section of Piaget's work on mental development, I do not ask "What were Piaget's four stages of development?" Nor do I ask "What did you think of Piaget?" I might show them a short video of a local classroom and ask, "Would Piaget admire this classroom? If so why? What would he criticize?" I try to ask questions whose answers might surprise me.

---

10. Lev S. Vygotsky, *Mind in Society: The Development of Higher Psychological Processes* (Cambridge MA: Harvard University Press, 1978).

11. Brown, Transforming Schools.

12. Derek Bok, *Our Underachieving Colleges: A Candid Look at How Much Students Learn and Why They Should Be Learning More* (Princeton, NJ: Princeton University Press, 2005).

Sometimes I begin with a question whose answer I am pretty sure will surprise them—for instance, I ask them on the first day of my education class to describe the most well-educated person they know. Then I list the qualities exhibited in the people they have described, and we discuss which of these qualities are taught in school. They are usually taken aback by how few of the qualities have anything to do with traditional schooling. I do this to make them, in the words of my seminar colleagues, "pay attention," or as novelists say, to make the familiar strange. I want them to be uncomfortable, and to like where such discomfort leads them.

Having started a good conversation, how does one lead it? I do several different things: I rephrase what students say to make it just a little better. When parents do this with their young children, it is known as scaffolding.[13] A toddler using her limited linguistic skills says a word (for instance, "Soup"). The parent responds by expanding what the child has said into a full sentence ("You want soup?"), or asks a question that requires the child to try something just a little more linguistically complicated (the parent says, "Soup? What about it?" and the child says, "Drink soup."

Studies have shown that all kinds of experts, in a wide range of cultures, scaffold skills so that junior members of their community (novices) can become experts. It is often referred to as the apprenticeship model of learning.[14] In a college class, I try to scaffold the building of ideas. When a student says something, I try to expand and strengthen the idea implicit in what they have said. Often in doing that I extend their statement, so that someone else in the class will want to add their own idea. Here an example might help illustrate the point. If a student says "I think Piaget would have liked the block corner because he argued that children think with their bodies." I might rephrase and extend by saying, "So you think Piaget would argue that the blocks provide children with a chance to develop more complex schemas about the physical world; by stacking them in different configurations the child might come to discover the principle, for instance, of conservation of number? Does that kind of play need to be guided?" I have embellished the student's idea, and at the same time taken it one step further, hoping someone else will want to jump in and answer the question. When my classes discussed the work of Bruner, I might ask "If Bruner is right that informed intuition is a powerful component of thinking, can it be taught, and if so, how?"

If a student offers an idea that is based on faulty reasoning or information, I ask if anyone has a response. I am hoping they will challenge one another to

---

13. Jerome Bruner, "The Ontogenesis of Speech Acts," *Journal of Child Language, 2* (1975), 1–21; Jerome Bruner, *Child's Talk: Learning to Use Language* (New York: Norton, 1983).
14. Barbara Rogoff, *The Cultural Nature of Human Development* (Oxford, UK: Oxford University Press, 2003).

be more rigorous and informed. But I also want the final "transcript" of the discussion to contain accurate information and compelling ideas.

When the students really get going and begin to talk with one another, I shift my role a bit. I begin trying to make sure they are offering informed opinions, building on one another's comments. I discourage them from saying things only to show me what they know. I encourage them to challenge one another respectfully. Periodically I take a turn and offer a point of view on what they have been discussing, using this as an opportunity to provide whatever important ideas or information I feel have gotten lost, and I also use such a turn to move the discussion in a new direction if need be. Sometimes, when they are all agreeing with one another, I state a strong point of view and beg them to convince me otherwise. When this works, it's superb. In trying to convince me of a point of view they need to marshal their forces, be articulate, and stick to their guns. They end up engaging in the kind of reasoned debate and collective idea building that is at the heart of a rational society.

In my experience a good discussion requires four things of a teacher:

1. Asking genuine questions to which the answers are complicated, interesting, and not predetermined.
2. Asking questions about things that matter beyond the academic context in which they are discussed.
3. Being comfortable tracking and shaping an unpredictable conversation.
4. Constructing an integrative summary, something I am not particularly skilled at. One of my college teachers, Margery B. Franklin, was able, at the end of a two-hour seminar discussion, to review the different ideas and information that had been contributed. Her summary demonstrated how the different ideas fit together, and provided us with a framework for understanding the development of our conversation as well as offering a coherent rendering of the work we had done. Often, as she summarized, she drew a diagram of the discussion on the board. This kind of summary cannot simply be a list of main ideas or a PowerPoint which presents conclusions. It must adequately convey the arc as well as substance of the discussion, thus offering students not only a sense of clarity and conclusion, but a demonstration of how they, too, can record, crystallize, and reflect on a dynamic intellectual exchange.

Needless to say, there is a time and a place for a great lecture, and some settings demand it. But that's another discussion.

Dilemma #3 Who is your audience?

Laced through all my daily successes and failures as a college teacher is a question about which I cannot agree with myself much less my colleagues. To whom are we pitching our classes?

At Williams I teach highly able bright, motivated students. But many of them are not going on in my fields—they are not going to be teachers, or research psychologists. Do I teach differently for those who are going to become lawyers, or sculptors, or editors? Would I teach differently if my students were going to be carpenters, or factory workers?

Do I plan my courses for the serious and enthusiastic student or the bright students who stay on the sidelines, the future graduate student, the generalist (the liberal arts student), the brightest student or the academically weak student? Here is where I invoke, again, the apprenticeship model as a way of learning, I teach everyone as if they were my apprentices, bit by bit taking on the knowledge and activities that would qualify them as expert practitioners. I teach this way for those who really will become psychologists and teachers, and for the vast majority who will not.

I assume that the kinds of thinking and work students will do in my class will be as good for the nonspecialist as they will for the future specialist. I am not interested in making college just like graduate school, but I am equally uninterested in teaching students who remain at nervous arm's length to the work of scholarship. This is premised on the idea that in order to learn about something you must do it. As the educator John Holt once said, you cannot learn to play the cello by studying about other people. You must play the cello. This is no less true about academic disciplines.[15]

My most recent experience with the apprenticeship model was also my most exciting. Last January, a newspaper columnist and I team taught a one month intensive called "Great Teaching Great Writing."

We taught the class as if all of our students would be writers and teachers. Each week the students taught the rest of us a "mini class" on a topic. They also submitted a column on that same topic. We critiqued their class and their column. We didn't talk about teaching or writing. We just taught and wrote, and tried to get better at both.

Not all disciplines lend themselves so easily to such a lively use of a practitioner model. But it can work more often than people think. In order for it to work, one has to accept that you cannot cover the material, and that you will not be giving too many lectures. But, by and large, when students engage in the work itself

---

15. John Holt, *How Children Learn* (New York: Perseus Publishing, 1995).

rather than learning about the work (whether that work be the identification of a new formula, a new analysis of an event in history, or a close reading of James Joyce's *Ulysses*) they are apt to be transformed by the experience.

When Ishmael said, "A whale-ship was my Yale College and my Harvard," he was offering good advice, even for those of us who read Melville rather than hunt whales.

Let me end with a fourth dilemma which faces those of us who are interested not only in teaching good classes but in shaping institutions of higher education. Good teaching is essential to good colleges. And while our colleges and universities vary greatly in how much they value teaching, even the ones who care about it most do little to make sure it happens. Individual teachers must articulate, and constantly reconsider and reconfirm their educational goals, using those goals as a guide to evaluating their teaching, day in and day out. As Atul Gawande says in his book, *Better: A Surgeon's Notes on Performance*, improvement requires vigilance and perseverance.[16] But it is up to those who shape and lead colleges to figure out how to insist that professors teach well, and to help fine scholars become effective teachers. We need fresh ideas about that, and leaders who put those ideas into action.

---

16. Atul Gawande, *Better: A Surgeon's Notes on Performance* (New York: Metropolitan Books, 2007).

Section V:
Looking Beyond
Material Success

Assessing the College
Contribution to Civic Engagement

Thomas S. Dee

Introduction

The notion that the social benefits of investments in education extend beyond the narrow economic gains that accrue to individual students has a wide and enduring currency. In particular, a frequent and fundamental motivation for policies that expand access to education is that they will promote and improve civic engagement later in life. For example, on the occasion of signing the Higher Education Act of 1965, landmark legislation that expanded access to college, President Lyndon B. Johnson remarked "We will reap the rewards of their wiser citizenship and their greater productivity for decades to come."

In this chapter, I discuss and assess the evidence for this widely held view. More specifically, I examine the empirical evidence for the claim that college access and attendance leads to increases in the diverse forms of adult civic engagement. Then, I turn my attention to what is known about the effectiveness of campus-based initiatives to promote civic engagement, which appear to have proliferated in recent years. I also present new evidence on whether college volunteering increases civic participation in adulthood. A pervasive challenge in this work is determining whether going to college or participating in a civic education program actually changes student behavior, or whether it merely shows that those who go to college or to join civic education programs were more inclined to be civically active in the first place. I examine the influence of this "selection bias" on these estimates by relying on a new bounding technique,[1] which uses the observed determinants of civic participation in college and adulthood as a guide to the bias generated by the unobserved determinants that bring students into these activities. The concluding section summarizes these results and suggests some future directions for this literature.

Are There Civic Returns to College?

Investments in education are often portrayed as a fundamental input to a stable, functioning democracy because schooling is thought to improve both the quality and the quantity of civic participation. In particular, proponents of

---

1. Joseph G. Altonji, Todd E. Elder, and Christopher R. Taber, "Selection on Observed and Unobserved Variables: Assessing the Effectiveness of Catholic Schools," *Journal of Political Economy 113* (1) (2005): 151–184.

social investments in education argue that schooling allows citizens to make more informed evaluations of complex social, political and technological issues. However, the contemporary literature among political scientists has also put a particular stress on the positive effects that schooling may have on the likelihood of civic participation (e.g., voting and volunteering). Levels of schooling could influence civic participation through at least two broad channels. One is that schooling may lower the effective costs of civic participation by promoting cognitive skills, which facilitate decision making and make it easier to negotiate the various bureaucratic and technological impediments to participation. However, a second and particularly important mechanism is that effective schooling is thought to promote an individual sense of responsibility and enthusiasm for civic participation. Similarly, investments in schooling are also thought to enhance civic engagement by inculcating students with fundamental democratic and pluralistic.values.

Interestingly, there are also a number of plausible ways in which increased schooling could reduce civic participation. For example, by raising the opportunity cost of an individual's time, increased schooling could reduce the amount of time and attention allocated to civic activity. This could be particularly relevant for volunteering, which, unlike voting, can involve a substantial commitment of time. Furthermore, schooling could also reduce voter turnout by promoting an awareness of voting as an essentially expressive act with an infinitesimally small probability of influencing actual policy (i.e., the "paradox of voting").[2]

Much of the available empirical evidence seems to provide an emphatic confirmation of the conventional view that education does indeed promote civic engagement. Numerous studies over the last 50 years have demonstrated that higher levels of individual schooling are strongly associated with civic behaviors and knowledge. For example, in a widely repeated interpretation of this empirical evidence, Converse (1972) refers to educational attainment as the "universal solvent" of political participation.[3] Similarly, Putnam (2001) notes that "education is by far the strongest correlate that I have discovered of civic engagement in all its forms."[4] Also, in their earlier study of voting participation, Wolfinger and Rosenstone (1980) suggest that their core finding is the "transcendent importance of education."[5]

---

2. Dennis C. Mueller, *Public Choice II* (New York: Cambridge University Press, 1989).

3. Philip E. Converse, "Change in the American Electorate," in *The Human Meaning of Social Change*, Angus Campbell and Philip E. Converse, Eds. (New York: Russell Sage, 1972).

4. Robert D. Putnam, "Community-Based Social Capital and Educational Performance," in *Making Good Citizens: Education and Civil Society*, Diane Ravitch and Joseph P. Viteritti, Eds. (New Haven: Yale University Press, 2001).

5. Raymond E. Wolfinger and Steven J. Rosenstone, *Who Votes?* (New Haven: Yale University Press, 1980).

National Education Longitudinal Study of 1988 (NELS:88)

In this section, I present new evidence on the effects of schooling on adult civic engagement with a particular emphasis on more contemporary data and on the apparent effects of schooling for those who were on the margin of attending college. The first evidence is drawn from the National Education Longitudinal Study of 1988 (NELS:88). NELS:88 is a nationally representative, longitudinal study, which was sponsored by the U.S. Department of Education and began in 1988 with a sample of 24,599 eighth-grade students from 1,052 public and private schools (Curtin et al., 2002).[6] NELS:88 was based on a two-stage sampling design. In the first stage, schools, which were the primary sampling unit, were selected with probabilities proportional to their eighth-grade enrollment. Approximately 26 students were then randomly chosen and surveyed within each participating school. Follow-up interviews of the NELS:88 participants occurred in 1990, 1992, 1994, and in 2000. During the 2000 follow-up interview, 11,559 of the original eighth-grade cohort were interviewed. And the survey instrument asked several questions about civic participation.

Three separate questions asked the respondents whether they had participated in specific types of volunteering within the past year: in a youth organization, in a civic or community organization, and in a political campaign. While over 20 percent reported that they had participated in youth or civics-related volunteering, less than 4 percent had volunteered in a political campaign. Three other questions focused on voter participation. More specifically, they asked whether the respondent was registered to vote, whether they had voted in the 1996 presidential election and whether they had voted anytime in the last 24 months.[7]

Table 1 reports the estimated effect of having ever attended a postsecondary institution on each of these six measures of civic participation. The baseline specification controls only for the observed demographic traits of the student: gender, race/ethnicity (i.e., black, Hispanic, other), age (i.e., born before 1974), and language-minority status. The subsequent specifications examine the robustness of these baseline results to the introduction of a variety of additional control variables. One of the prominent features of NELS:88 is that it provides unusually detailed and well-measured controls for each student's parents, family, and school. In part, this is because NELS:88 solicited information directly from parents rather than relying on student self-reports. The family-level controls based on the parents'

---

6. T. R. Curtin, S. J. Ingels, S. Wu, and R. Heuer, *National Education Longitudinal Study of 1988: Base-Year to Fourth Follow-up Data File User's Manual* (NCES 2002-323) (Washington, DC: U.S. Department of Education, National Center for Education Statistics, 2002).

7. See Table 1.

survey consist of measures unique to each available category of family composition (6), family size (9), parental education (7), and family income (15).

The clustered sampling design of NELS:88 also makes it possible to control effectively for all the unobservable traits unique to each student's school and community. More specifically, because NELS:88 sampled multiple students *within* each of the more than 1,000 participating schools, it is possible to study factors affecting behavior within schools while eliminating the effects of differences across schools. The results of this specification effectively compare the adult civic participation of college matriculants and nonmatriculants among students who attended the same school for eighth grade.

The key regression results for the six outcome variables and three specifications are reported in Table 1. The results indicate that those who have attended college are substantially more likely than those who have not to engage in all six forms of civic participation. For example, the third specification indicates that college matriculants are 8.8 percentage points more likely to engage in civic volunteering as adults relative to nonmatriculants. This shift implies a 40 percent increase in the mean probability of civic volunteering (i.e., 22 percent). For the remaining outcome measures, college matriculation implies a 16 to 38 percent increase in the mean probability of civic participation. These point estimates are all statistically significant at the 0.01 level. And this basic finding is basically robust to the introduction of the family controls and school fixed effects. Nonetheless, it should be noted that these point estimates tend to fall in magnitude as additional controls are introduced and that a large portion of the variation in each outcome variable remains unexplained (i.e., no model explains more than 20 percent of the variation in an outcome variable).

1972–2004 General Social Surveys (GSS)[8]

One prominent shortcoming of the results in Table 1 is that they focus on only one general dimension of civic engagement; namely, participation. However, the putative civic returns to higher education also include gains in citizen knowledge of politics and current events as well as support for fundamental democratic values. In other words, investments in education are thought to promote not only citizen involvement but also the quality of that involvement. To examine the apparent effects of college attendance on these particular aspects of adult

---

8. James A. Davis, Tom W. Smith, and Peter V. Marsden, "General Social Surveys, 1972–2004," [Cumulative File] [Computer file] ICPSR04295-v2 (Chicago, IL: National Opinion Research Center [producer], 2005) (Storrs, CT: Roper Center for Public Opinion Research, University of Connecticut/Ann Arbor, MI: Interuniversity Consortium for Political and Social Research [distributors], 2006-04-05).

civic engagement, I examined pooled data from the General Social Surveys (GSS) fielded between 1972 and 2004.

The GSS is a personal-interview survey conducted every one to two years since 1972 and designed to track a broad range of social attitudes and behaviors over time.[9] These surveys were based on multistage probability samples of English-speaking persons aged 18 and over living in noninstitutional settings. The structure of the sampling design was broadly consistent over time. The primary sampling units were generally Standard Metropolitan Statistical Areas (SMSA), counties and independent cities. In the second stage, block groups and enumeration districts were chosen. In block groups and enumeration districts with large numbers of dwellings, a third stage was sometimes carried out to select dwellings within a block. One interview was conducted at each selected house. The 1972–2004 cumulative data file consists of 46,510 respondents. However, limiting the analytical sample to those aged 26 to 65 lowers the number of respondents to 32,749.

The GSS included a variety of questions related to civic engagement. For example, in each survey, these respondents were asked whether they voted in the last presidential election. On average, 71 percent of the GSS respondents in the analytical sample claimed to have voted in the most recent presidential election. In most, but not all, survey years, GSS respondents were also asked about how often they read the newspaper, about their group memberships (e.g., fraternal and community-service groups, political clubs, school-service and youth groups, church-service groups, etc.) and about their attitudes toward free speech for particular groups. The GSS respondents report an average of 1.9 group memberships. The frequency of newspaper readership is based on five possible responses (never, less than once a week, once a week, a few times a week, and every day) coded here as varying from 0 to 4 (mean=3.8). This measure of newspaper readership is meant to indicate whether voters stay informed about current affairs.

However, it is possible that newspaper readership is a poor proxy for civic awareness. Fortunately, two other survey questions address the issue of civic awareness more directly. In the 1987 survey, respondents were asked to name their governor and their U.S. representative. Nearly 79 percent of respondents could correctly name their governor while only about 37 percent could correctly name their congressional representative. Interestingly, among the small sample of 1987 respondents, newspaper readership is strongly correlated with being able to identify correctly one's political representatives. Specifically, conditional on all the covariates discussed below, a one-unit increase in the measure of newspaper

9. *Ibid.*

readership implies a 21 percent increase in the mean probability of correctly identifying one's congressional representative. This suggests that the frequency of newspaper readership is a reasonable proxy for the degree of civic awareness.

In most years, the GSS also fielded questions that identified individual attitudes toward free speech. More specifically, a series of separate questions asked respondents whether they would allow particular types of people to speak in their community. These types include someone against churches and religion (an antireligionist), an admitted Communist, an admitted homosexual, someone who advocates outlawing elections and letting the military run the country (a militarist), and someone who believes blacks are inferior (a racist). Support for allowing free speech among the respondents in this sample ranges from 64 percent for the militarist to 77 percent for the homosexual.

The GSS also provides a variety of background information on each respondent. The baseline specification reported here conditions on the year of the survey, the birth decade of the respondent (8 categories), and each of the nine possible census divisions of residence. The baseline specification also conditions on individual demographic traits such as age and age squared as well as gender, race (3 categories), and religious preference (5 categories). The second specification adds to the first a variety of effects based on how each respondent described their family and community environment at age 16. For example, the GSS respondents described their family income at age 16 related to average income (6 categories), their family's structure at age 16 (6 categories), and their parent's highest educational degree (5 categories). This specification also includes the census division in which the respondent resided at age 16 (10 categories including those who resided abroad) and the urbanicity of their residence at age 16 (7 categories). The third and final specification adds controls for the place and time of the GSS interview as well as the place and time of each respondent's upbringing. More specifically, this is done by introducing indicators of the current census division that are specific to each survey year and the census division at age 16 that are specific to each decade of birth.

Table 2 reports the key results of regressions, based on the GSS data, which examine the effect of college matriculation on the measures of civic participation and knowledge. These results suggest that college attendance increased adult voter participation by at least 18.6 percentage points, an estimate quite similar to that based on the NELS:88 data.[10] Furthermore, college entrants are members of approximately 1.2 more groups than those who did not attend college, an increase of roughly 64 percent relative to the mean. Those who attended college also rated significantly higher on measures of civic knowledge. For example, the index of

10. See Table 1.

newspaper readership is nearly 6 percent higher among college entrants than nonentrants. Furthermore, data from the 1987 GSS indicate that college entrants are roughly 10 to 14 percentage points more likely to name their governor and congressional representative correctly (i.e., changes of 13 to 39 percent relative to the respective means).

Table 3 presents the corresponding results for the survey questions related to free speech. The results indicate that college entrants are significantly more likely than those who have not attended college to sanction free speech for the given parties. The sizes of these differences range from 11 to 18 percentage points (i.e., 15 to 27 percent relative to the respective means). The point estimates reported in Tables 2 and 3 are statistically significant at the 0.01 level with the exception of some of the results based only on the 1987 survey, which are statistically significant at the 0.05 level.[11] The apparent gains in civic engagement associated with college attendance are robust to the introduction of the various control variables.[12] However, the introduction of additional controls generally reduces the suggested impact of college attendance.

Correlation or causality?

The evidence in Tables 1, 2, and 3 is consistent with an extensive body of empirical research documenting a strong correlation between measures of educational attainment and forms of adult civic engagement. Most of the extant literature interprets this sort of evidence—and its robustness to controlling for other observed traits—as indicating that investments in schooling have a causal effect on later civic outcomes. For example, in the most recent contribution to this literature, Nie and Hillygus (2001) note that this orthodox view is "largely uncontested."[13]

However, the basic approach of introducing controls for observed traits does not convincingly resolve the question of whether the strong correlations between education and civic outcomes actually reflect the true causal effects. In particular, this is because so many of the shared determinants of civic behavior and educational attainment are inherently difficult for researchers both to identify and measure well. For example, children who were raised in families that stressed civic responsibility are, in all likelihood, more likely to attend college. This could occur simply because civic-minded families were more likely

---

11. See Table 2.

12. See Tables 2 and 3.

13. Norman Nie and D. Sunshine Hillygus. "Education and Democratic Citizenship," in *Making Good Citizens: Education and Civil Society*, Diane Ravitch and Jospeh P. Viteritti, Eds. (New Haven: Yale University Press, 2001).

to impart values to their children that encourage college attendance. Similarly, students with a taste for altruistic and civic-minded behavior may have lower discount rates that also encourage them to make schooling investments. It should be noted that similar sources of "omitted variables bias" could occur at the school and community level. For example, communities that do more to ensure that their children attend well-funded, high-quality schools that promote college access may also be more effective at promoting adult civic engagement. However, the robustness of the relationship between college attendance and civic participation in specifications that condition on school attended suggests that differences across students and families *within* schools are a more likely source of potentially confounding variables.[14]

The quite plausible existence of unobserved traits that simultaneously influence both college attendance and adult civic engagement suggests that correlations like those documented in Tables 1, 2, and 3 should be viewed with considerable caution. Furthermore, the recent schooling and civic-engagement trends in the United States—increases in college attendance not matched by increases in voter turnout or political knowledge—suggest that the association between education and civic engagement could be specious.[15] It should also be noted that at least two prior studies in the political science literature provide more formal evidence that such concerns about omitted variable biases may be empirically relevant. Both Luskin (1990) and Cassel and Lo (1997) present evidence that the apparent influence of education on civic outcomes (political literacy and sophistication) may reflect the spurious influence of other individual traits (e.g., intelligence and parents' socioeconomic status).[16]

Several recent studies have revisited the issue of whether educational attainment improves adult civic engagement with an explicit focus on the problems of distinguishing correlations from causality. In particular, these studies have adopted the research designs historically used by labor economists to separate the true wage effects of additional schooling from the potentially spurious influences of unobserved ability and measurement error. For example, one approach used by labor economists to isolate the effects of schooling from the effects of unobserved family and individual traits has been to make comparisons within monozygotic twin pairs. Gibson (2001), using data from 85 twin pairs from New Zealand, used this approach to examine the effects of years of schooling

---

14. See Table 1.

15. William A. Galston, "Political Knowledge, Political Engagement and Civic Education," *Annual Review of Political Science, 4* (2001): 217–234.

16. Robert C Luskin, "Explaining Political Sophistication," *Political Behavior, 1* (1990): 331–362; Carol Cassel and Celia C. Lo, "Theories of Political Literacy," *Political Behavior, 19(4)* (1997): 317–335.

on volunteering behavior.[17] The results of that study suggested that additional schooling actually appears to reduce the probability of volunteering as well as the time spent volunteering, results consistent with the effect of additional schooling on the opportunity cost of time.

Two other recent studies, using nationally representative data from the United States, have taken a quasi-experimental approach to identifying the effects of schooling on adult civic engagement.[18] More specifically, the research designs used in these studies have exploited the more plausibly exogenous variation in levels of secondary schooling generated by changes in child labor and compulsory schooling laws. The results of those studies suggest that the increases in secondary schooling generated by these laws did lead to statistically significant increases in various types of adult civic engagement.

However, only the study by Dee (2004) also focused explicitly on the postsecondary margin. More specifically, Dee examined data from a major longitudinal study, *High School and Beyond (HS&B)*, and relied on the geographic proximity of two-year colleges as a quasi-experiment that significantly influenced the likelihood of attending college.[19] The results of that study indicated that college attendance appears to have had positive causal effects on adult voter participation (though the effects on adult volunteering are smaller and imprecisely estimated).

However, it should be noted that the validity of these inferences turns on important assumptions. In particular, a valid quasi-experiment needs to influence both the treatment of interest (in this case, college attendance) and to be otherwise unrelated to the outcomes of interest (i.e., adult civic engagement). Dee presented evidence both that the geographic proximity of two-year colleges appeared to influence college attendance and that these college-access measures were otherwise unrelated to the unobserved determinants of adult civic outcomes. For example, Dee found that the effects of the geographic proximity of two-year colleges on the likelihood of attending college were concentrated among students whose parents were more poorly educated. Dee found that the geographic proximity of two-year colleges was not significantly related to predictors of adult civic engagement when measured before college attendance (e.g., scores on a high school civics exam). That evidence is consistent with the maintained assumption

17. John Gibson, "Unobservable Family Effects and the Apparent External Benefits of Education," *Economics of Education Review, 20(3)* (June 2001): 225–233.

18. Thomas S. Dee, "Are There Civic Returns to Education?" *Journal of Public Economics 88(9)* (August 2004): 1697–1720; Kevin Milligan, Enrico Moretti, and Philip Oreopolous, "Does Education Improve Citizenship? Evidence from the United States and the United Kingdom," *Journal of Public Economics, 88* (2004): 1667–1695.

19. Daniel Zahs, Steven Pedlow, Marjorie Morrissey, Patricia Marnell, and Bronwyn Nichols, *High School and Beyond Fourth Follow-Up Methodology Report* (NCES 95426), National Center for Education Statistics (January 1995).

that the quasi-experiment is not polluted by unobserved traits that also influence adult civic outcomes.

In sum, the available evidence is broadly consistent with the claims made by President Johnson when he signed the Higher Education Act of 1965. College attendance appears to be strongly and robustly correlated with multiple and diverse measures of adult civic engagement. Furthermore, there is direct evidence that some of these correlations (e.g., with respect to voter turnout) reflect the causal effects of schooling and college access as measured by the availability of two-year colleges. The lack of more complete evidence on this point does imply that some agnosticism is warranted. However, it should also be noted that the absence of more complete evidence (e.g., focusing on alternative measures of college access and more diverse measures of adult civic engagement) is simply due to the limited overlap of powerful and credible quasi-experiments and rich, longitudinal data on adult civic outcomes.

Campus Initiatives

While the results discussed in the previous section provide evidence that college attendance contributes to different aspects of adult civic engagement, the exact mechanisms underlying these important relationships are not clear. For example, access to college may contribute to adult civic engagement both through the development of key cognitive skills as well as through socialization to pluralistic, democratic norms through peers and classroom environments. Furthermore, it is often noted that the college experience can provide unparalleled opportunities for civic engagement (e.g., political activism and volunteering), which might be vital, formative experiences for later adulthood.

Interestingly, some limited evidence suggests that colleges and universities are increasingly embracing their civic and community missions through the introduction of diverse initiatives explicitly designed to promote and sustain civic engagement among students. One prominent example is Campus Compact, a coalition of higher-education institutions, which began in 1985 and provides its members with training and resources designed to support institutional commitments to civic engagement. Between 2000 and 2006, the institutional membership in Campus Compact grew 52 percent (i.e., from 689 to 1045). Another similar and recent innovation is the American Democracy Project, an initiative organized by the American Association of State Colleges and Universities (AASCU), in conjunction with the New York Times, to foster institutional commitments to civic engagement among its 219 member institutions. Project Pericles, a nonprofit corporation which began in 2000 and currently has 22 member institutions, is another related and recent innovation. Membership in Project Pericles requires an explicit institutional commitment (i.e., by board resolution) to embrace the promotion of citizenship in a manner that is integrated with students' academic and cocurricular experiences.

Another distinctive and relatively recent initiative is the Bonner Scholars Program. This program grants four-year community service scholarships to selected students at 27 participating schools. Among other things, these students are required to serve an average of ten hours a week of community service during the school year and to complete at least one full-time, summer-service internship. It should be noted that not all of the recent activity to promote civic education on college campuses has occurred through the "grass-roots" activity of institutions and coalitions. Most obviously, the Corporation for National and Community Service has provided financial support to institutions and participants engaged in civic activity through programs like AmeriCorps and Learn and Serve America. Interestingly, during this period of policy and institutional ferment, the share of college students who spend time volunteering appears to have increased.[20] For example, Dote et al. (2006), using data from supplements to the Current Population Survey (CPS), finds that since September 2001, the percent of college students who volunteer has increased from 27.1 percent to 30.2 percent.[21]

Prior evidence

What is known about the efficacy of the diverse initiatives recently introduced at postsecondary institutions to promote good citizenship? In general, the available empirical evidence suggests that these programs have been highly effective at promoting civic engagement among participating students (e.g., see Eyler et al., 2001).[22] While this literature is too voluminous to review exhaustively in this short space, a few prominent examples can provide a sense of the key features of the research designs that form the basis for these inferences.

The approach adopted to assess some targeted initiatives (e.g., the Political Engagement Project) has been to field baseline and follow-up surveys of

20. Corporation for National and Community Service, Office of Research and Policy Development, "Serving Country and Community: A Longitudinal Study of Service in AmeriCorps" (Washington, DC: Corporation for National and Community Service, 2004).

21. Lillian Dote, Kevin Cramer, Nathan Dietz, and Robert Grimm, Jr., "College Students Helping America," Corporation for National and Community Service (October 2006).

22. Janet S. Eyler, Dwight E. Giles, Jr., Christine M. Stenson, and Charlene J. Gray, *At a glance: What we know about the effects of service-learning on college students, faculty, institutions and communities, 1993–2000*, Third Edition (Scotts Valley: Learn and Serve America National Service Learning Clearinghouse, 2001).

program participants soon after their participation has ended. Then, the pre-post differences in measures of civic engagement are, after controlling for observable traits, interpreted as measures of program efficacy. However, some of the most relevant analyses have been based on data collected by the Cooperative Institutional Research Program (CIRP) at UCLA's Higher Education Research Institute (HERI). Two features distinguish the analyses based on CIRP data.[23] One is that they are based on large samples of students from multiple institutions. Second, they are also based on data from longitudinal follow-up interviews, which make it possible to track how college activities related to civic engagement relate to adult outcomes.

More specifically, the baseline data for these studies is CIRP's widely used Freshman Survey, which collects information on the background traits, attitudes, and achievements of incoming cohorts of college students. This annual survey is completed by more than 300,000 first-year students at roughly 600 colleges and universities.[24] However, the analytical samples for these studies are based on the more than 200 institutions that fielded follow-up surveys 4, and 9 to 10 years after the Freshman Survey. The studies by Astin et al. (1999) and Sax (2004) are based on the 1985 Freshman Survey and follow-up interviews that occurred in 1989 and 1994 while the study by Misa et al. (2005) is based on 1994 freshmen who were interviewed in 1998 and 2004.[25]

The more recent study by Misa et al. (2005) examined the effect of performing community/volunteer service in college on the long-term civic engagement of 1994 freshmen. These regression analyses controlled for a variety of observable traits including race, gender, SAT scores, socioeconomic status, and volunteer service in high school. Their two outcome measures are factors drawn from the 2004 follow-up survey and reflect working with communities and political activism. They find that volunteering in college is a "strong and consistent predictor of civic and political engagement." The earlier studies by Astin et al. (1999) and Sax (2004) report similar long-term effects of volunteering during college.[26]

Does the existing empirical evidence provide strong support to the claim that the recent institutional efforts to promote civic engagement among

23. Alexander W. Astin, Linda J. Sax, and Juan Avalos, "Long-term effects of volunteerism during the undergraduate years," *Review of Higher Education 22(2)* (1999): 187–202; [Reference Needed for "Sax, 2004"]; Kim Misa, Jodi Anderson, and Erica Yamamura, "The Lasting Impact of College on Young Adults' Civic and Political Engagement," presented at the 2005 Association for the Study of Higher Education Annual Conference, Philadelphia, PA (2005).

24. Linda J. Sax, "Citizenship Development and the American College Student," *New Directions for Institutional Research 122* (Summer 2004): 65–80.

25. Astin et al., 1999; Sax, 2004; Misa et al., 2005.

26. Astin et al., 1999; Sax, 2004.

students are likely to have been effective? Unfortunately, the answer to that question appears to be no. One problem with the available evidence is the types of recently introduced innovations are simply too diverse (e.g., forms of service learning and volunteer initiatives) to be assessed by a small number of studies. However, the fundamental problem with the extant evidence is a methodological one. More specifically, virtually all of the available empirical evidence cannot credibly separate the true treatment effect of participation in such programs from the bias introduced by nonrandom self-selection. It should be stressed that this is not to say that these innovations have been ineffective but rather that the question should remain largely unanswered until there is more definitive evidence that can credibly identify treatment effects.

For example, consider the general question of whether volunteering in college promotes civic engagement in later adulthood. Volunteering and other forms of civic engagement, both while in college and in later adulthood, will be influenced by a variety of individual, family, school, and community traits that are inherently difficult to measure accurately and, therefore, unobservable to researchers. This implies that the partial correlations between volunteering in college and civic engagement in adulthood could simply be a specious reflection of these unobserved, but correlated, traits. Similar criticisms apply to smaller-scale assessments that rely on pre-post comparisons of program participants and find evidence of growth in civic engagement. For example, a very different interpretation of such evidence is that the individuals who self-select into such programs are poised for growth in civic engagement, regardless of their program participation.

A preferable approach to assessing these initiatives would be to adopt a research design that exploits plausibly *exogenous* variation in whether subjects volunteer. Unfortunately, the evidence based on such credibly experimental variation appears to be much more limited and contradictory. For example, Helms (2006) examined the effect of Maryland's statewide service requirement for high school graduation and found that the introduction of this policy shifted the timing but not the overall level of volunteer activity.[27] However, another notable study, which focused on students at the postsecondary level and utilized random assignment, found that community-service requirements increased levels of civic engagement. The study by Markus et al. (1993) was based on 89 University of Michigan undergraduates in a large political science course.[28] Students in this course

27. Sara E. Helms, "Involuntary Volunteering: The Impact of Mandated Service in Public Schools," (unpublished paper, January 2007).
28. G. B. Markus, J. P. F. Howard, and D. C. King, "Integrating community service and classroom instruction enhances learning: results from an experiment," *Education Evaluation and Policy Analysis, 15* (1993): 410419.

registered for one of eight discussion sections, two of which were subsequently randomly designated as "community service" sections. They found that students in the treatment sections had greater awareness of social problems and higher academic achievement at the end of the course. One potential criticism of this study is that the existence of only two treatment sections and six control sections suggests the possibility of some spurious imbalance across the treatment and control conditions (e.g., if the treatment sections attracted less apathetic students because they were scheduled earlier in the day). However, Markus et al. (1993) fielded a baseline survey of student values and attitudes and found that these measures (as well as other student observables) were similar across the treatment and control conditions. [29]

Evidence from NELS:88

In this section, I present new empirical evidence on whether the recent college initiatives designed to promote adult civic engagement are likely to be effective. More specifically, I examine the effect of participating in community volunteering during college on the prevalence of civic participation in later adulthood. This analysis is based on the NELS:88 data introduced in the previous section. The sample for this analysis consists of the roughly 6,600 base-year participants who attended a postsecondary institution and participated in the final follow-up interview that occurred in 2000.

The evidence from these data makes two contributions to the existing literature. One is that these data are based on a nationally representative sample of students rather than on data from one or more self-selected college campuses. Second, as noted earlier, NELS:88 has unusually comprehensive and well-measured data on each student's background traits. In part, this is due to the fact that *parents* were surveyed about their family characteristics (e.g., income, family composition, and parental education). However, another key feature of NELS:88 is that its clustered sampling design makes it possible to condition on roughly 1,000 specific characteristics unique to each participating eighth-grade school. The use of these items effectively controls for all the unobserved traits unique to a particular school and community and constructs comparisons among students who attended the same school.

During the 1994 survey (i.e., the third follow-up), NELS:88 participants who had attended a postsecondary institution were asked whether they had participated in "volunteer services to community groups" while attending that institution. Roughly 31 percent of the sample reported that they did engage

---

29. *Ibid.*

in community volunteering. Table 4 presents regression results that examine how volunteering in college appears to have influenced the six types of civic participation as reported in the 2000 interview.

The first specification (i.e., column (1)) controls only for the demographic traits of the respondents (i.e., gender, race/ethnicity, age, and language-minority status). The second specification introduces the controls for observed family and parental traits. The third specification introduces a binary indicator for whether the respondent performed community services more than "rarely or never" at the time of the first follow-up interview (i.e., 1990) when most respondents were in tenth grade. This variable was set to zero for the roughly 5 percent of the sample who did not respond to this question. A separate binary indicator, which is also included as a control in this specification, identifies these nonresponders. The fourth and final specification introduces fixed effects unique to each of the roughly 1,000 participating base-year schools.

The results of these different specifications uniformly suggest that community volunteering during college has quite large and statistically significant effects on the probability of civic participation in adulthood. For example, those who had volunteered during college were 12.6 percentage points more likely than those who had not to participate in youth-oriented volunteering as an adult.[30] This constitutes a 54 percent increase in volunteering relative to the mean probability. The estimated increases in civic and campaign volunteering due to volunteering during college are similarly large (i.e., increases of 48 and 42 percent relative to their respective means). The estimates in Table 4 also suggest that college volunteering increased the measures of adult voter participation by 12.4 to 18.3 percentage points (i.e., increases of 4 percent to 20 percent relative to the respective means).

Bounding treatment effects using selection on observables

The evidence presented in Table 4 is entirely consistent with prior observational studies. Students who volunteered in college are significantly more likely to engage in civic participation in adulthood. Furthermore, these results appear to be quite robust as we compare the results of the four specifications. And, interestingly, these four specifications exhibit dramatic increases in explanatory power. More specifically, as we move from the first to the fourth specifications in Table 4, the percent of the variation in the outcome variables that is explained by these models increases by factors of 6 to 46. However, the estimated effect of college volunteering appears reasonably robust. This kind

---

30. See Table 4.

of ad-hoc approach to examining the robustness of results from regressions is quite common in instances where credible experiments or quasi-experiments are unavailable.

A recent study by Altonji, Elder, and Taber (2005) offers a formalized means of taking advantage of the intuitive notion that the sensitivity of results to introduced observed control variables provides evidence about the likely impact of introducing unobserved control variables (if only we could).[31] The Appendix describes the application of this new bounding technique to the analysis reported here. Overall, the results in the Appendix suggest that we should interpret the robust correlation between college volunteering and adult civic participation cautiously. With respect to most of the volunteering and voting measures (i.e., four out of six), the observed pattern of selection does not allow us to exclude the possibility that college volunteering actually has no effect or, even, negative effects. Again, it is important to stress that this evidence does not imply that college volunteering has no (or negative) effects on adult civic participation. Instead, this evidence suggests the limitations of what can be credibly inferred from conventional analyses of observational data and the use of student observables as controls for the unobserved traits that influence both participation in civic-engagement initiatives and subsequent civics-related outcomes.

Concluding Thoughts

What do we know about the contribution of the college experience to adult civic engagement? The results presented here and in numerous other studies indicate that those who have attended college have significantly higher levels of civic engagement in its many forms than those who have not attended college. Similarly, the available evidence indicates that college students who participate in the growing number of campus initiatives designed to cultivate civic engagement (e.g., community volunteering) do subsequently have higher levels of civic engagement.

However, despite this empirical evidence, more than a little agnosticism is warranted. Relatively few studies have addressed the fundamental problem of disentangling the true treatment effects of attending college (or specific college programs) from the corresponding selection biases. However, in the case of college attendance, at least one quasi-experimental study finds that plausibly exogenous increases in college access and college attendance lead to improvements in adult civic engagement.[32] But it should be noted that, because of data restrictions, this evidence focuses on only one measure of college access (i.e., geographic

---

31. Altonji et al., 2005.
32. Dee, 2004.

proximity to two-year colleges) and only on the participatory dimensions of civic engagement.

The available evidence on the efficacy of campus-based initiatives to promote civic engagement is subject to rather more ambiguity. While participation in such programs is generally correlated with higher levels of civic engagement, the only available experimental evidence of program efficacy appears to be from one small-scale study.[33] In this chapter, I presented new evidence on this issue by examining the robustness of the link between college volunteering and forms of civic participation in adulthood. More specifically, I presented evidence on the extent to which this relationship could reflect selection bias by implementing a recently developed bounding technique that uses the degree of selection on observables as a guide to the degree of selection on unobservables.[34] The results provide, at best, mixed evidence that we can form reliable statistical inferences about the causal effects of college volunteering on adult civic participation from conventional, observational data.

The limitations of the currently available assessment evidence should not in any way be viewed as a criticism of recent campus initiatives. The descriptive nature of most program assessments can still be useful to institutions that have introduced such initiatives in that they provide focal points for critical reflection and improvement. Furthermore, many of the civic-engagement programs being introduced on campuses are relatively young. And it is not uncommon for programmatic innovations such as these to proliferate in advance of a robust research base. In fact, this chronological sequencing may even be desirable from a program-evaluation perspective because it allows for the assessment of programs that have been refined through experience. A relevant aphorism attributed to Donald Campbell is "evaluate no program until it is proud."

However, the current enthusiasm for these campus initiatives, their considerable diversity, and the limitations of the available assessment evidence all suggest that there is a propitious opportunity for high-quality research to promote and shape the future development of civic education in colleges and universities. Other important areas in education policy (e.g., class size and early-childhood education) provide motivating examples of how the evidence from just a few randomized trials (e.g., Project STAR, the Perry Preschool Project, and the Carolina Abecedarian Project) can be disproportionately influential in forging a research consensus and catalyzing political and financial support. Similar opportunities exist with respect to campus initiatives designed to promote civic engagement. More convincing and comprehensive evidence of program

33. Markus et al., 1993.
34. Altonji et al., 2005.

efficacy would provide a reliable guide to effective practices that are worthy of replication. Furthermore, such evidence could also promote and sustain society's growing interest in (and support for) colleges and universities as a fundamentally important resource in the development of civic engagement.

Addendum

As noted in the text, an ad hoc assumption in some interpretations of the comparative results from multiple regressions is that the consequences of introducing *observed* control variables provides some guidance as to the likely effects of controlling for *unobserved* traits. A recent study by Altonji, Elder, and Taber (2005, hereafter AET) introduces a bounding technique that effectively formalizes this sort of ad-hoc interpretation of regression results.[35] In particular, this approach bounds estimated treatment effects by assuming that an index of observed determinants, which influences both outcomes and treatment status, provides a valid guide to the influence of unobserved determinants.

More specifically, AET define ρ as the correlation between the unobservables that influence adult outcomes, e, and the unobservables that influence treatment status, u, after controlling for observables (i.e., $\rho = corr\,(e, u \mid X)$). In conventional, observational studies (e.g., Table 4), the identifying assumption is that $corr\,(e, u \mid X) = 0$. In other words, researchers typically hope that the vector of control variables, X, is sufficiently detailed that the bias-inducing correlation between e and u is broken. However, confounding selection bias occurs when there is a positive correlation between e and u. This implies that one can determine the extent of this bias under various assumptions regarding the magnitude of ρ. The basic intuition of AET's approach is that bounds on ρ (i.e., "selection on unobservables") can be identified by examining the strength of the relationship between observables that influence both volunteering and adult outcomes (i.e., "selection on observables").

Equation (10) in AET (2005) provides an explicit formula for using the observables to identify bounds on ρ.[36] There are three key assumptions that underlie AET's result. First, the observable covariates, X, are chosen at random from the full set of factors that determine the outcome, y. Second, the number of observable and unobservable factors is large. And, third, the part of the outcome variable that is related to the observables has the same relationship to the endogenous variable as the part of the outcome that is related to the unobservables. While these are strong assumptions that will not be met fully in any empirical application, AET outline a compelling case that they are at least as plausible as the standard assumptions underlying regression analysis. In other words, this approach can be seen as a complement to conventional regression analyses because it provides evidence under assumptions that are not less reasonable than the usual, unstated assumption that $\rho = corr\,(e, u) = 0$.

---

35. Altonji et al., 2005.
36. *Ibid.*

Table A1 presents the key results of an AET-inspired bounding exercise for the relationship between volunteering during college and adult civic participation. The top two rows in Table A1 reiterate, for ease of reference, the point estimates from specifications (1) and (4) in Table 4. With regard to five of the six dependent variables, the introduction of the additional control variables *reduced* the estimated impact of volunteering on adult civic participation. If we take the sensitivity of these estimates to the introduction of observable control variables as a guide, it suggests that the estimated effect of volunteering during college is biased upwards by the presence of unobserved traits that positively influence both the probability of volunteering during college and the probability of civic participation as an adult.

Another row in Table A1 provides a measure of the implied degree of selection by reporting the maximum estimate of ρ based on AET's approach. It should be noted that these estimates turn on comparisons of the first and fourth specifications. In other words, though all of the models condition on the demographic traits, it is the other observed traits (i.e., family traits, volunteering in high school, and school fixed effects) that are used to estimate ρ. The maximum estimated values of ρ are positive in five of the six cases, which suggests that the estimates in Table 4 are biased upwards. However, the magnitudes of the estimated ρ are fairly small (i.e., less than 0.1 in absolute value) with respect to all of the outcomes other than civic volunteering.

However, the explanatory power in these models is also relatively weak. In Table 4, no model explains more than 22 percent of the variation in an outcome variable. The existence of a relatively large amount of unexplained variation in the outcome variable implies that a small amount of selection on unobservables could lead to a large bias in the estimated treatment effect. The final rows in Table A1 address this issue explicitly by reporting the estimated effect of college volunteering under different assumptions about ρ. More specifically, these final rows report the maximum-likelihood estimates of the effect of college volunteering in models where the degree of selection (i.e., the value of ρ) is fixed at particular values.

The results for youth-volunteering suggest that college volunteering does have long-term effects that are robust to the concerns raised here about selection bias. The "naïve" estimate from Table 4 implies that college volunteering increases youth-focused volunteering in adulthood by 12.6 percentage points. The fact that this estimate became smaller after the introduction of additional control variables implies that students with a propensity to volunteer in college also had a propensity to volunteer in adulthood (i.e., $\rho > 0$). However, the degree of selection, though positive, is relatively small (i.e., $\rho = 0.049$). When one assumes that ρ takes on its maximum value, the estimated effect of college volunteering is still quite large (i.e., 8.1 percentage points) and statistically distinguishable from zero at the 0.01 level.

The results for the "Voted in the last 24 months" variable also suggest that college volunteering leads to long-term gains in adult voter participation. The "naïve" regression estimate actually becomes larger in size after introducing the control variables. This suggests that the conventional approach understates the true effect of college volunteering (i.e., $\rho < 0$). However, the degree of selection bias is also quite small in this instance. This implies that, even if ρ takes on its maximum absolute value, the estimated effect of college volunteering is not larger than 13.2 percentage points.

For the remaining four dependent variables, the results of this bounding exercise are much less dispositive. For example, the "naïve" results for civic volunteering are relatively sensitive to the introduction of control variables, which implies a large upper bound for ρ (i.e., 0.215). That degree of selection implies that college volunteering actually has negative effects on civic volunteering in adulthood. Only more modest amounts of selection (i.e., a quarter to a half of ρ) are consistent with positive and statistically significant effects. For the remaining three dependent variables (i.e., campaign volunteering, voter registration, and voted in 1996), the estimates of ρ are much smaller. However, the "naïve" estimates of the effect of college volunteering on these outcomes are smaller as well. For these three outcomes, the bounding exercise suggests that the effects of college volunteering could be zero or slightly negative.

Table 1. Estimated effect of college attendance on adult civic participation, NELS:88

Dependent Variable	Dependent Mean	(1)	(2)	(3)	Sample Size
Volunteering—Youth	0.205	0.082 (0.009)	0.070 (0.010)	0.068 (0.011)	11,339
R^2		0.0124	0.0178	0.1161	
Volunteering—Civic	0.221	0.114 (0.009)	0.081 (0.009)	0.088 (0.010)	11,337
R^2		0.0165	0.0299	0.1292	
Volunteering—Campaign	0.037	0.021 (0.004)	0.015 (0.004)	0.014 (0.004)	11,338
R^2		0.0030	0.0081	0.1102	
Registered to Vote	0.789	0.144 (0.011)	0.124 (0.012)	0.124 (0.013)	11,262
R^2		0.0316	0.0379	0.0613	
Voted in 1996	0.574	0.246 (0.012)	0.188 (0.012)	0.183 (0.014)	11,240
R^2		0.0585	0.0755	0.1763	
Voted in last 24 months	0.425	0.162 (0.012)	0.129 (0.012)	0.132 (0.013)	11,323
R^2		0.0289	0.0372	0.1553	
Demographic controls		yes	yes	yes	
Family controls		no	yes	yes	
School fixed effects		no	no	yes	

These results are based on the 2000 follow-up interviews of NELS:88 respondents (n=11,559). Standard errors, adjusted for school-level clustering, are reported in parentheses. All point estimates are statistically significant at the 0.01 level. The demographic controls consist of fixed effects for categories of sex (1), race/ethnicity (3), birth year (1), and language-minority status (1). The family controls consist of fixed effects for categories of family composition (6), family size (9), parental education (7), and family income (15).

Table 2. Estimated effect of college attendance on adult civic participation and knowledge, GSS

Dependent Variable	Dependent Mean	(1)	(2)	(3)	Sample Size
Voted in last presidential election	0.706	0.227 (0.013)	0.185 (0.009)	0.186 (0.009)	31,579
R^2		0.1028	0.1296	0.1394	
Group memberships	1.9	1.402 (0.082)	1.221 (0.068)	1.218 (0.064)	14,468
R^2		0.1286	0.1459	0.1592	
Newspaper readership	3.8	0.263 (0.023)	0.211 (0.020)	0.211 (0.020)	32,656
R^2		0.2301	0.2413	0.2489	
Can name own governor	0.786	0.134 (0.038)	0.100* (0.039)	0.112* (0.038)	1,252
R^2		0.0930	0.1211	0.1556	
Can name own congressional representative	0.369	0.156* (0.052)	0.143* (0.056)	0.145* (0.056)	1,235
R^2		0.0982	0.1182	0.1490	
Demographic controls		yes	yes	yes	
Family controls		no	yes	yes	
Census division x survey year fixed effects		no	no	yes	
Census division at age 16 x decade of birth fixed effects		no	no	yes	

These results are based on 26- to 65-year-old respondents to the pooled 1972–2004 General Social Surveys. Standard errors, adjusted for clustering at the level of census division of residence at age 16, are reported in parentheses. All point estimates are statistically significant at the 0.01 level except for those with an asterisk, which are significant at the 0.05 level. All results condition on fixed effects for survey year and census division of residence (9). The demographic controls consist of fixed effects for categories of sex (1), race/ethnicity (3), birth decade (8), and religious preference (5). The family controls consist of fixed effects for categories of family income at age 16 (6), family structure at age 16 (6), parental education (6), urbanicity of residence at age 16, and census division of residence at age 16 (10).

Table 3. Estimated effect of college attendance on adult support for free speech, GSS

Dependent Variable	Dependent Mean	(1)	(2)	(3)	Sample Size
Allow antireligionist to speak	0.731	0.164 (0.012)	0.126 (0.008)	0.126 (0.008)	20,916
R^2		0.1172	0.1452	0.1602	
Allow Communist to speak	0.656	0.224 (0.010)	0.180 (0.007)	0.179 (0.007)	20,670
R^2		0.1282	0.1538	0.1643	
Allow homosexual to speak	0.775	0.148 (0.012)	0.113 (0.007)	0.114 (0.007)	19,496
R^2		0.1099	0.1407	0.1539	
Allow militarist to speak	0.645	0.192 (0.011)	0.156 (0.007)	0.154 (0.007)	17,576
R^2		0.1047	0.1258	0.1369	
Allow racist to speak	0.647	0.139 (0.012)	0.112 (0.009)	0.111 (0.009)	17,596
R^2		0.0587	0.0745	0.0893	
Demographic controls		yes	yes	yes	
Family controls		no	yes	yes	
Census division x survey year fixed effects		no	no	yes	
Census division at age 16 x decade of birth fixed effects		no	no	yes	

These results are based on 26- to 65-year-old respondents to the pooled 1972–2004 General Social Surveys. Standard errors, adjusted for clustering at the level of census division of residence at age 16, are reported in parentheses. All point estimates are statistically significant at the 0.01 level. All results condition on fixed effects for survey year and census division of residence (9). The demographic controls consist of fixed effects for categories of sex (1), race (3), birth decade (8), and religious preference (5). The family controls consist of fixed effects for categories of family income at age 16 (6), family structure at age 16 (6), parental education (6), urbanicity of residence at age 16, and census division of residence at age 16 (10).

Table 4. Estimated effect of college volunteering on adult civic participation NELS:88

Dependent Variable	Dependent Mean	(1)	(2)	(3)	(4)	Sample Size
Volunteering—Youth	0.234	0.134 (0.011)	0.130 (0.012)	0.120 (0.012)	0.126 (0.014)	6,579
R^2		0.0278	0.0330	0.0403	0.1985	
Volunteering—Civic	0.270	0.166 (0.012)	0.155 (0.013)	0.144 (0.013)	0.129 (0.015)	6,577
R^2		0.0365	0.0440	0.0525	0.2076	
Volunteering—Campaign	0.048	0.025 (0.006)	0.022 (0.007)	0.019 (0.007)	0.020 (0.008)	6,578
R^2		0.0038	0.0090	0.0112	0.1738	
Registered to Vote	0.838	0.039 (0.010)	0.035 (0.010)	0.031 (0.010)	0.033 (0.012)	6,543
R^2		0.0210	0.0278	0.0294	0.1874	
Voted in 1996	0.665	0.093 (0.012)	0.084 (0.012)	0.075 (0.012)	0.076 (0.014)	6,537
R^2		0.0306	0.0428	0.0470	0.2005	
Voted in last 24 months	0.486	0.089 (0.014)	0.088 (0.014)	0.076 (0.014)	0.095 (0.016)	6,573
R^2		0.021 7	0.0311	0.0371	0.2102	
Demographic controls		yes	yes	yes	yes	
Family controls		no	yes	yes	yes	
High school volunteering		no	no	yes	yes	
School fixed effects		no	no	no	yes	

These results are based on the 2000 follow-up interviews of NELS:88 respondents who attended a postsecondary institution (n = 6,669). Standard errors, adjusted for school-level clustering, are reported in parentheses. All point estimates are statistically significant at the 0.01 level. The demographic controls consist of fixed effects for categories of sex (1), race/ethnicity (3), birth year (1), and language-minority status (1). The family controls consist of fixed effects for categories of family composition (6), family size (9), parental education (7), and family income (15).

Table A1. Sensitivity of the estimated effects of college volunteering about the degree of selection on unobservables

Assumption	Volunteering—Youth	Volunteering—Civic	Volunteering—Campaign	Registered to Vote	Voted in 1996	Voted in Last 24 Months
College-volunteering estimate from specification (1)	0.134 (0.011)	0.166 (0.012)	0.025 (0.006)	0.039 (0.010)	0.093 (0.012)	0.089 (0.014)
College-volunteering estimate from specification (4)	0.126 (0.014)	0.129 (0.015)	0.020 (0.008)	0.033 (0.012)	0.076 (0.014)	0.095 (0.016)
R2 from specification (4)	0.1985	0.2076	0.1738	0.1874	0.2005	0.2102
Implied direction of bias	Upward	Upward	Upward	Upward	Upward	Downward
Estimated max(ρ)	0.049	0.215	0.061	0.040	0.099	-0.034
Estimated treatment effect assuming						
$\rho=(.25)\max(\hat{\rho})$	0.115 (0.013)	0.078 (0.014)	0.013* (0.007)	0.025** (0.011)	0.051 (0.013)	0.104 (0.015)
$\rho=(0.5)\max(\hat{\rho})$	0.103* (0.013)	0.026* (0.014)	0.006 (0.007)	0.016 (0.011)	0.026* (0.013)	0.114 (0.015)
$\rho=\max(\hat{\rho})$	0.081 (0.013)	-0.081 (0.014)	-0.009 (0.007)	0.0002 (0.011)	-0.025* (0.013)	0.132 (0.015)

These results are based on the 2000 follow-up interviews of NELS:88 respondents who attended a postsecondary institution (n = 6,669). Standard errors, adjusted for school-level clustering, are reported in parentheses. All point estimates are statistically significant at the 0.01 level except for those indicated by ** and *, which are statistically significant at the 0.05 and 0.10 levels, respectively. See Table 4 for descriptions of specifications (1) and (4) and the text for a description of ρ and how it is estimated.

Conclusion

Michael S. McPherson and Morton Owen Schapiro

"Do what you can with what you have, where you are."
—Theodore Roosevelt

That familiar quotation from Teddy Roosevelt serves as the motto of the volume on college access that is a companion to this one on college success. A major theme in that volume is that helping students get into college is "everybody's business": there are important roles for the nation's high schools, for federal and state governments, for families, and for the colleges and universities themselves. Moreover, the roles of these actors depend on their individual situations: what you can do depends on what you have and where you are. A wealthy university, for example, can encourage attendance by low-income students with generous financial aid that may not be feasible for a less well-funded place to match.

In some ways, responsibility for college success is more focused than responsibility for college access: the two main actors are the college or university the student attends and the student himself or herself. But of course that formulation is too simple: The chapters in this volume—most notably that by Melissa Roderick and Jenny Nagaoka—make clear that the roots of college success lie in successful preparation at an early age. And as James Rosenbaum and Lisbeth Goble stress in their piece, giving more realistic feedback and guidance to students at an early age about what it will take to succeed in college motivates that preparation. Further, as William Trent's chapter on the Gates Millennium Scholarship emphasizes, money, in the form of financial aid, matters to success as well as to access.

Teddy Roosevelt's maxim applies to the role that colleges themselves play in fostering student success. The circumstances of the students who arrive in different types of postsecondary institutions vary markedly, as do their educational aims. According to David Breneman's report on the college presidents' discussions, adapting effectively to differing levels of readiness and differing aspirations is a major task for college leaders, faculty, and staff. Even within an individual university or college, variations in student preparation, interests, and aptitudes are a major consideration. The amazing heterogeneity in higher education described by Jeffrey Smith is a challenging issue not only for education researchers but for professors, advisers, and students as well.

The maxim to do "what you can" with "what you have" underscores the basic truth set forth in the introduction: College success has to be understood in terms of transformative change; it is not what students bring to the college but how they are "moved forward" that ultimately matters. The fact that success is multidimensional and that goals and capacities vary among students make assessing and improving university effectiveness even more difficult. Yet despite these complications, we agree with Diana Walsh that working hard on measuring success needs to be a major commitment among colleges. Future students and their families need reliable information about colleges on which to base their application decisions. Funders of colleges, including both governments and private donors, have a legitimate interest in learning what they can about how effectively those resources are used. It is crucial to develop institution-wide measurements that are appropriately responsive to variations in mission and clientele. But the most interesting developments will most likely be seen in local efforts at measurement and improvement.

It is ironic that colleges and universities find it so difficult to behave like "learning organizations," meaning by that phrase enterprises that endeavor to measure performance, innovate, and measure the effectiveness of the innovation. Richard Light in his paper offers instructive examples of local efforts at performance measurement and systematic assessment of innovations. Embedding habits that continually improve the practices of higher education institutions is a promising road to college success.

If there is, as Susan Engel argues, a regrettable tendency to neglect the subtle and many-sided role of good teaching, there is perhaps an even greater tendency to neglect the role of the learner. Colleges need to work harder to understand their students' capacities and interests, and they need to do a better job than they often do of advising students on how to make good choices about course selection, study habits, and career goals—a task that is especially important for first-generation college students who haven't grown up with the experience of college in their backgrounds. Nevertheless, the students themselves have to set their own goals, determine where academic effort fits into their lives and priorities, and take responsibility for meeting relevant standards.

As Sarah Turner reminds us, a rising college enrollment rate isn't that impressive in the face of a declining college completion rate. The surprising decline in the percentage of a high school cohort earning bachelor's degrees not only has serious economic ramifications. Thomas Dee points to some potential social costs as well.

So controversies about how to measure college success and how to foster it shouldn't make us throw up our hands in despair. Instead, we should build on available empirical and qualitative studies, while drawing on the wisdom of faculty, students, and administrators who, even if they struggle to define exactly what they mean by college success, know it when they see it.

Acknowledgments

This book about college success is a companion volume to one we published with the College Board in 2006 entitled *College Access: Opportunity or Privilege?* Alan Heaps, Kevin Iwano, and others at the College Board have once again done a terrific job in preparing this manuscript for press. We are grateful to Gaston Caperton, president of the College Board, for his vision in supporting our efforts to bring the message of this book to the secondary and postsecondary leaders who make up the College Board.

Humphrey Doermann has been an indispensable partner in this enterprise, as he has in our past work. His remarkable care, thoughtfulness, and support throughout the effort have done much to make this volume possible. We are again indebted to Dave Breneman and to Sandy Baum for sharing with us their good ideas and advice. Doris Fischer has displayed a delightful combination of tact and diligence in coordinating arrangements, overseeing details, and keeping the various participants on the same page. Francie Streich, Jum Warritay, and Matt Smith, research associates at the Spencer Foundation, have provided much valued assistance. We have, as always, relied heavily on Bill Bowen's advice and intellectual leadership in shaping this work.

This volume grew out of papers prepared for a conference sponsored by the Spencer Foundation and Macalester College, with financial assistance from the Andrew W. Mellon Foundation, and held June 12–13, 2007, in Evanston, Illinois. We have benefited from the continuing support and encouragement of Brian Rosenberg, President of Macalester College. The conference was attended by 93 scholars, college and university leaders, and observers of U.S. postsecondary education. The conference series is supported by the Mellon Foundation and has been held either at Macalester College, Saint Paul, or under Spencer Foundation auspices in the Chicago area. The 2007 conference was the fifth in this series of biennial meetings concerning major issues in higher education.

Michael S. McPherson
Morton Owen Schapiro
September 2007

Contributing Authors

David W. Breneman is university professor and dean of the Curry School of Education at the University of Virginia in Charlottesville. Breneman is an economist and an authority on the economics of higher education. His prior appointments include visiting professor at the Harvard Graduate School of Education and president of Kalamazoo College. He is author of *Liberal Arts Colleges: Thriving, Surviving, or Endangered?* (The Brookings Institution), 2004.

Thomas S. Dee is an associate professor of economics at Swarthmore College and director of the College's public policy program. He was visiting scholar at the Stanford University's School of Education this past year. His research interests include several areas of education policy such as the determinants of teacher quality, the effects of class-size reductions, and the effects of schooling on civic engagement.

Susan L. Engel is senior lecturer in psychology and director of the Program in Teaching at Williams College. In addition to her teaching and research in developmental psychology, Engel has taught students from age three to adults. She is cofounder of the Hayground School, an experimental school on eastern Long Island . Her research interests center on the development of autobiographical memory, narrative processes in childhood, imagination and play in childhood, and the development of curiosity. Engel's most recent book is *Real Kids: Creating Meaning in Everyday Life* (Harvard University Press), 2005. She currently writes a column on teaching called "Lessons" for the *New York Times*.

Lisbeth J. Goble is a doctoral student in human development and social policy at Northwestern University. In this volume she collaborates with James E. Rosenbaum. Her current research interests include the high school to college transition and educational evaluation.

Richard J. Light is Walter H. Gale Professor of Education jointly at the Harvard Kennedy School of Government and the Graduate School of Education. He teaches statistics, program evaluation, and policy analysis, and is founder (2005) and chair of the Forum for Excellence and Innovation in Higher Education. He also chairs the multi-college Young Faculty Leaders Forum, encouraging collaboration among emerging leaders in education, business, and government. Light's most recent book is *Making the Most of College: Students Speak Their Minds* (Harvard University Press), 2001.

Michael S. McPherson is president of the Spencer Foundation in Chicago and former president of Macalester College in St. Paul, Minnesota. Much of his prior career was at Williams College, where he was a professor, chair of the Economics Department, and dean of faculty. McPherson collaborated with Morton Owen Schapiro in editing this volume, as he has in coauthoring other books and articles on college access. Their other collaborator in this volume is Francie Streich.

Jenny Nagaoka is the project director of the Consortium on Chicago School Research's Chicago Postsecondary Transition Project. The project provides the data and analysis that she and Melissa Roderick together summarize in this volume. Previously, Nagaoka was a research analyst at the Consortium on Chicago School Research, evaluating selected aspects of teaching and learning in the Chicago Public Schools.

Melissa Roderick is the Herman Dunlap Smith Professor of Social Service Administration at the University of Chicago, and a codirector at the Consortium on Chicago School Research. Her work has concentrated on the transitions to high school and college among Chicago public school students. From 2001 to 2003, she joined the administration of the Chicago Public Schools to establish a Department of Planning and Development to help develop a new education plan for the school district.

James E. Rosenbaum is professor of sociology, education, and social policy at Northwestern University. He has served as educational adviser to the Chicago Public Schools, and to the Office of the Mayor. His books include *Beyond College for All* (Russell Sage Foundation), 2001; and *After Admission: From College Access to College Success* (Russell Sage Foundation), 2006. In this volume he collaborates with Lisbeth J. Goble, a Northwestern graduate student in human development and social policy.

Morton Owen Schapiro is a professor of economics and president of Williams College. Most of his academic career has been at Williams College, except during the 1990s when he was chair of the Department of Economics at the University of Southern California and then dean of the College of Arts and Letters. He is a long-term collaborator with Michael S. McPherson on the economics of higher education. McPherson and Schapiro are coauthors of *The Student Aid Game: Meeting Need and Rewarding Talent in American Higher Education* (Princeton University Press), 1998.

Jeffrey A. Smith is a professor of economics at the University of Michigan and editor of the *Journal of Labor Economics*. He held previous economics faculty appointments at the University of Western Ontario and the University of Maryland. His current research interests include evaluation of education, social, health, and job-training programs.

Francie Streich is a research associate at the Spencer Foundation. In this volume she collaborates with Michael S. McPherson and Morton Owen Schapiro in their discussion of financial aid in public universities. Her current research interests span several areas in the field of public economics, including taxation, environmental economics, and the economics of education.

William T. Trent is professor of educational policy studies and sociology at the University of Illinois at Urbana-Champaign. His research centers on K–12 and postsecondary educational inequality. He is a member of the Research Advisory Committee for the GATES Millennium Scholarship research program and was a Spencer Resident Fellow in 2006-07.

Sarah E. Turner is associate professor of education and economics at the University of Virginia in Charlottesville and is a faculty research associate of the National Bureau of Economic Research. She has written extensively on the economics of higher education, including the behavioral effects of financial aid policy.

Diana Chapman Walsh completed a 14-year presidency of Wellesley College in June 2007 and was elected president emerita. Previously, she was named professor and department chair at the Harvard School of Public Health. At Wellesley, Walsh presided over a strengthening of the college's faculty and student body, its campus and its finances, and its curricular and cocurricular offerings (emphasizing global education, interdisciplinarity, experiential learning, and campus intellectual life).

Index